10649770

Dual
Transformation

Dual
Transformation

How to Reposition Today's Business
While Creating the Future

**Scott D. Anthony, Clark G. Gilbert,
and Mark W. Johnson**

Harvard Business Review Press
Boston, Massachusetts

The web addresses referenced in this book were live and correct at the time of the book's publication but may be subject to change.

Library of Congress Cataloging-in-Publication Data

Names: Anthony, Scott D., author. | Gilbert, Clark G., author.
    | Johnson, Mark W., author.
Title: Dual transformation : how to reposition today's business while creating the
    future / Scott D. Anthony, Clark G. Gilbert, and Mark W. Johnson.
Description: Boston, Massachusetts : Harvard Business Review Press, [2017]
Identifiers: LCCN 2016043734 | ISBN 9781633692480 (hbk)
Subjects: LCSH: Reengineering (Management) | Organizational resilience.
    | Organizational effectiveness. | Strategic planning.
Classification: LCC HD58.87 .A58 2017 | DDC 658.4/06—dc23 LC record available
    at https://lccn.loc.gov/2016043734

The paper used in this publication meets the requirements of the American National Standard for Permanence of Paper for Publications and Documents in Libraries and Archives Z39.48-1992.

Contents

1. Disruptive Shock Waves and Dual Transformation

The year is 1975.

The Boston Red Sox lose in the World Series in heartbreaking fashion, again. The disco era begins, with the Bee Gees' "Jive Talkin'" and Earth, Wind & Fire's "Shining Star" topping global charts. In the town of Rochester, New York, a young engineer named Steve Sasson creates a disruptive technology that allows a consumer to capture what we now call a digital image. The device is as big as a toaster and takes more than twenty seconds to capture an image, but the seeds of disruption are sown. Far from working for an upstart company, Sasson works for Eastman Kodak. At the time the company dominates the silver halide chemical film market, with an 80 percent share and a 70 percent gross profit margin. And now it has a prototype for a camera that uses no film.

What happens next?

You probably know the story. Kodak invests heavily in the new technology, introducing its first digital camera in 1990. By 2000 it emerges as one of the leading digital imaging producers. In 2001 it makes the bold move to purchase an emerging photo sharing site called Ofoto. Embracing its historical tag line, "Share memories, share life," Kodak rebrands Ofoto as Kodak Moments, transforming it into the leader of a new category called social networking, where people share pictures, personal updates, and links to news and information. In 2010, it attracts a young engineer from Google named Kevin Systrom, who takes the site to the next level. By 2015 Kodak Moments has hundreds of millions of users. Kodak still sells film to niche markets (and makes nice profits doing so), but the company's center of gravity has clearly shifted to social networking. The company deftly manages the transition and emerges from a potentially disruptive shock a *different*, but vibrant, organization.

Wait—that didn't happen.

Kodak did indeed invest in digital imaging and did indeed buy Ofoto, but instead of turning it into a vibrant social network Kodak focused on getting more people to print more pictures. It sold the business in 2011. It did indeed invest heavily in digital technologies; Sasson's quotable line in 2008 that management's response to his technology was, "That's cute, please don't tell anyone about it" was also cute but not particularly accurate. But seemingly Kodak was never able to fundamentally shift its business model, and as silver halide film began its inevitable decline, so too did the company. Kodak filed for Chapter 11 bankruptcy protection in 2012.

It's a sad story of lost potential. The American icon had the talent, the money, and even the foresight to make the transition. But instead it ended up the victim of the aftershocks of a disruptive change.

A Transformational Year for Media

On June 17, 1994, Americans are glued to their television sets watching O. J. Simpson, a charismatic retired football player who had appeared in movies and television commercials, riding in his white Ford Bronco while being chased by police. Simpson is accused of violently murdering his ex-wife and one of her friends, and the combination of violence and celebrity makes it catnip for viewers. This is the first time that television news producers, most notably Turner Broadcasting's Cable News Network, break from actual news to cover second-by-second minutia of something so voyeuristic. It was a seminal moment in the media industry, and its effects are still being felt.

An even more important event took place later that same year when Marc Andreessen and his team introduced a beta version of the Netscape browser. Since the late 1960s, academics and defense officials had been experimenting with using a distributed network of computer connections to communicate and collaborate. The Netscape browser—coupled with Tim Berners-Lee's invention of HyperText Markup Language (HTML) universal resource locators (URLs), along with a range of complementary innovations—allowed even the layperson to ride the so-called information superhighway. The disruptive effects of this internet-enabling technology reshaped the media business. The first to feel its effects were newspapers. Historically the scale economics of the printing press created significant barriers to entry, resulting in effective natural monopolies in many markets; most US cities had only one or two highly profitable papers. The rise of the commercial internet destroyed this business, with most newspaper companies decimated by 2000.

Well, not exactly. Certainly the newspaper companies felt some pain during the 2000–2002 US recession, but the years from 1994 through 2007 were actually quite good for most newspapers. Although the internet was stealing eyeballs, circulation remained relatively stable and advertising revenue continued to grow. The rise of classified-ad killers—such as Craigslist (which offered free listings for apartments, jobs, and other, less savory things) and eBay—were nuisances. But when two of us (coauthors Clark Gilbert and Scott Anthony) presented a talk at a Newspaper Association of America meeting in Miami in January 2005, the dominant sentiment was that the industry had taken the best punch the internet could throw and still stood tall.

As legendary investor Warren Buffett likes to say, when the tide goes out you see who is swimming naked. The next US recession, in 2007–2009, showed the industry's precarious position. From 1950 to 2005, industry advertising revenue grew from roughly $20 billion to $60 billion. By 2010, the market had fallen to $20 billion. Put another way, fifty-five years' worth of advertising growth was eviscerated in a handful of years. Companies went bankrupt, jobs were lost, with the few remaining players staggering to find a sustainable path forward.

A Transformational Year for Mobile Handsets

In 2007 the Boston Red Sox, miraculously, celebrate their second World Series championship in four years after an eighty-six-year gap between their last two. Disney's Pixar Animation Studios releases a movie about a rat who is also a chef, grossing more than $600 million worldwide, earning widespread critical acclaim and demonstrating why Disney paid Steve Jobs more than $7 billion in 2006 to acquire John Lasseter, Ed Catmull, Woody, Buzz, Nemo, Luxo Jr., and the rest of the Pixar team.

There were two darlings in the mobile handset industry. Nokia had emerged from bruising battles with Motorola and others as the clear market leader, with market share three times as big as that of the nearest competitor. In November, *Forbes* ran a cover story proclaiming, "One Billion Customers: Can Anyone Catch the Cellphone King?"

Um, yes. But not overnight. In fact, if you were an investor in Nokia, 2007 was indeed a very good year for you. Whereas the S&P was up by 5 percent that year, Nokia's stock surged by 155 percent, trumping another industry competitor heralded for its innovation prowess: Canada's technology darling Research in Motion (RIM), best known for its BlackBerry handset. RIM's stock almost doubled during 2007. In what turned out to be a prescient interview with CBC in April 2008, RIM's co-CEO, Jim Balsillie, said, "I don't look up too much or down too much. The great fun is doing what you do every day. I'm sort of a poster child for not sort of doing anything but what we do every day . . . We're a very poorly diversified portfolio. It either goes to the moon or crashes to the Earth."

And crash both Nokia and RIM did.

In January 2007 Steve Jobs announced, and in June Apple launched, the iPhone. Dubbed the "Jesus phone" by worshippers, the phone created a media firestorm and immediately started showing up in the hands of celebrities. In November, Google, along with a range of handset manufacturers, formed the Open Handset Alliance, powered by Google's Android operating system. Android's origins trace to a $50 million acquisition Google made in 2005 of a young startup that had hot technologies as well as Andy Rubin, a noted talent in the wireless space. Google's hope was that by making it easier for users to access the internet on mobile phones, it could expand its core advertising business.

In 2013, Nokia sold its handset business to Microsoft for more than $7 billion. Eighteen months later, Microsoft took a write-down of roughly $7 billion. RIM, renamed BlackBerry, saw its stock drop close to 95 percent from the 2008 Balsillie interview to 2015.

Kodak's digital disruption took almost forty years to fully play out. Newspapers had about a dozen years of life after the internet shock.

Nokia and RIM had only five years before great businesses painfully built over decades were ripped apart.

And thus the innovator's clock accelerates.

In the HBO sword-and-sorcery series *Game of Thrones*, and the books by George R. R. Martin that inspired the show, the gritty Stark family has a saying: winter is coming. It isn't winter that's coming to your boardroom. It is disruption. *Disruption is coming*. And it is coming at an unprecedented pace and scale.

The Circle of Disruption

Yet there's something oddly comforting in the industry case studies. It's the way of capitalism, after all. A disruptive change hits a market, making what used to be complicated simple, and what used to be expensive affordable. Lumbering giants move too slowly, toppling under their own weight. Innovative upstarts, run by young, charismatic entrepreneurs, embrace the newness of the technology, creating new business models and indeed new organizational forms. The disruption breaks open a historically constrained market, bringing new solutions to millions, if not billions, of people. Then enterprising upstarts become lumbering giants, destined to be felled by the next generation of entrepreneurs. Cue the montage, play Elton John's "Circle of Life" from *The Lion King*, and pass the popcorn.

Of course, if you're a top executive in one of the companies confronting this kind of challenge, it is anything but entertaining. In fact, we believe that it is the greatest challenge facing leaders today. Creating a new business from scratch is hard, but executives of incumbents have the dual challenge of creating new businesses while simultaneously staving off never-ending attacks on existing operations, which provide vital cash flow and capabilities to invest in growth. The hastening pace of disruptive change means leaders have precious little time to respond. In fact, the time when leaders need to be most prepared for a change is right at the moment when they feel they're at the very top of their game.

One metaphor that we've found helpful to frame the challenge is what's known as a *fitness landscape*, borrowed from the field of population ecology. A fitness landscape is a representation of a topological map, with the height of a given hill showing its general attractiveness. Study the map in figure 1-1. Imagine you run the company represented by the square at the top of the highest mountain. You've done it. You've left your competition (represented by the circle) in the dust. You're the top of the heap. The monarch of the mountain. From your commanding heights you can clearly see a new, disruptive upstart taking root (represented by the star). From your vantage point, you can see how small that hill is. It is inconsequential.

Consider your strategic choices. You are in fact sitting on what is called a "local maximum." Any strategy looks inferior to the one you're currently following. Put in simple terms, there is no direction to go but down.

This phenomenon paralyzes leaders who own a position atop a historic hill. Unfortunately, the landscape is not static. In fact, disruption rearranges the strategic topography. You wake up one day and the landscape looks like the image in figure 1-2. Consider your options now. The disruptor (still a star) is too big and powerful to attack head on, so your best chance is to establish a foothold on its hill (the circle). But that strategy, and any other, looks materially worse than what you're currently doing. Your square sits at the top of the hill, although it's a much smaller one. Once again, there's no direction to go but down.

This is tough stuff. And this is only about the fundamental *decision* to change strategy. Any leader who has gone through a reorganization

FIGURE 1-1

Industry topography, before disruption

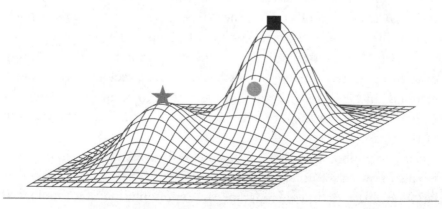

FIGURE 1-2

Industry topography, after disruption

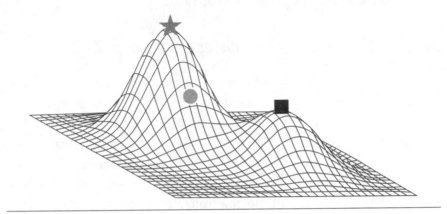

or reinvention will tell you that, as hard as it is to decide to change, it is easier than actually *making* the change.

The term often used to describe what happened to Kodak, newspaper companies, and Nokia is *creative destruction*. The phrase is generally credited to economist Joseph Schumpeter from his landmark book *Capitalism, Socialism and Demography*. In that work he vividly described the "gale of creative destruction" that tears down established institutions. Schumpeter described the destructive power of this gale, coupled with the innovative creation spurred by entrepreneurs, noting, "[T]he problem that is usually being visualized is how capitalism administers existing structures, whereas the relevant problem is how it creates and destroys them."

The emergence of a new hill creates tremendous growth for its creator. However, while we celebrate these vibrant gains, let's stop and consider the losses when the transition involves the rise of a new company and the death of an old one. Thousands of jobs, if not tens of thousands, are displaced. Communities that grew up around enterprises are torn apart. Tens of thousands of years of accumulated know-how are lost. This kind of creative destruction carries a heavy transaction tax.

What if, instead, leaders could harness the underlying forces behind these kinds of changes to power new waves of growth for their companies? More specifically, what if a company sensed the gale coming early enough and built a wall to protect its core business? Or, even better, what if it built a wind turbine to harness the energy in the gale?

This book teaches you how to do just that.

Dual Transformation and the Disruption Opportunity

There are classic examples of companies that have risen to the challenge of disruptive change. Imagine IBM in the 1990s moving from products to services, or Apple during Steve Jobs's second run as CEO moving from desktop computers to mobile devices and entertainment. There are other stories of companies that made dramatic shifts from one business to another, such as Nokia moving from rubber boots to mobile phones, or Marriott moving from a root beer stand to hotels.

We occasionally draw on these business classics, but our primary focus is on fresh, recent stories, many of which we have experienced firsthand either as advisers or as practitioners. Our experience allows us to present, for the first time, a detailed perspective of what strategic transformation looks like and, more important, what it *feels* like as you go through the journey. It's like a virtual GoPro camera recording corporate leaders as they confront the hardest challenge in business.

Our bedrock case study comes from coauthor Clark Gilbert's firsthand experience leading a transformation at Deseret Media. The *Deseret News* is one of America's oldest continually published newspapers, tracing back to 1850. Ultimately owned by the Mormon Church (which also owns the local KSL television station), the paper historically competed in Utah with *The Salt Lake Tribune* under what is known in the industry as a *joint operating agreement*, wherein the two companies share facilities and printing presses but have independent journalists, brand positions, and so forth. As the number 2 provider in its market, Deseret Media was hit particularly hard by the disruptive punch of the internet; between 2008 and 2010 the *Deseret News* lost nearly 30 percent of its print display advertising revenue and 70 percent of its print classified revenue.

In 2009, Gilbert—who had done his doctoral research at Harvard on the newspaper industry and had consulted to the industry before he became head of online learning at Brigham Young University-Idaho—was asked to launch Deseret Digital Media, a newly formed organization that contained Deseret Media's collection of websites. In May 2010,

Gilbert was also appointed to the newly created position of president of the *Deseret News*, giving him control of both the legacy business and its new growth digital ventures. Industry insiders sneered. Gilbert, after all, was an academic. Now he would learn what the real world looked like.

Five years later, however, Deseret Media had a vibrant print publication, including a national weekly that was one of the fastest growing publications in the United States. It also had built an impressive array of quickly growing digital marketplace businesses tied to its KSL classifieds products that collectively produced more than 50 percent of the organization's combined net income. These digital businesses shared brands, content, and a few other resources with the core business but largely functioned autonomously. Deseret Media had revitalized its historical core business while simultaneously pioneering the creation of a new hill on the media landscape. By the time Gilbert left in 2015 to become president of BYU-Idaho, net income at Deseret, in the midst of an industry in free fall, was up by almost 25 percent from 2010. While the specific details on figure 1-3 have been stylized to protect

FIGURE 1-3

Deseret net income

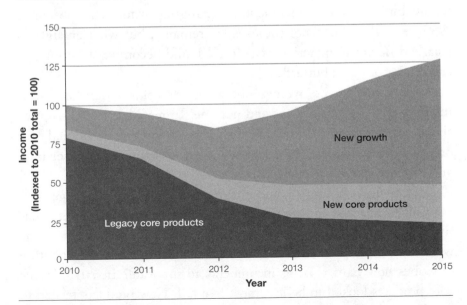

company confidential information, the picture is clear: a repositioned, stabilized core business and a quickly growing new growth business.

Rather than detailed insights about specific media business models or new revenue streams, Deseret's success, according to Gilbert, is attributed to organizing the company to adapt to two very different types of change. Rather than view change as one monolithic transformation process, Gilbert organized the company into two parallel change efforts: one to reposition the core newspaper business, and another to unlock new growth in digital markets. (Although Gilbert is an author of this book, occasionally we feature direct quotations from him to amplify key messages.)

We call this change effort *dual transformation*. Please note that our use of the term *transformation* is different from the common lexicon. Transformation often serves as shorthand for any big change, whether it's a company dramatically downsizing or a Hollywood actor gaining or losing significant weight for a role. Typically, when people use the word it is akin to what author Bill Simmons describes as "the leap" in professional basketball: a player like Stephen Curry goes from being a good player to being otherworldly, and his team, the Golden State Warriors, "transforms" into a title contender. This is a case of changing from mediocre to good, or from good to great. It is not the transformation we are describing here.

Rather, the idea of transformation in this book is materially different: businesses are fundamentally changing in form or substance. A piece of the old, if not the essence, remains, but what emerges is clearly different in material ways. It is a liquid becoming a gas. A caterpillar becoming a butterfly.

We call the process we describe a *dual* transformation because it requires two transformations and not one. In response to a disruptive shock, executives must simultaneously reposition their traditional core organization while leading a separate and focused team on a separate and distinct march up a new hill.

Look again at figure 1-3, and imagine the leadership challenges facing Gilbert and his team at Deseret. New growth businesses were relatively small in 2010. How can you convince great external talent to come work for a small piece of a languishing incumbent, when the literature describes how hard it is for incumbents to innovate? In 2012, legacy core products looked to be in almost free fall. New products related to the core were beginning to grow, but how can you convince top talent that there remains a viable future in a rapidly diminishing business?

Similarly, in that year even though the new growth engine was beginning to hum, Gilbert was three years into his tenure and hadn't turned a corner. How can you convince board members and other key stakeholders that the corner will come? And along the way, the newspaper business and the digital business are constantly in conflict, fighting for attention and assets. Which side should a leader back, and when? And at the end of the story, when the organization clearly has changed—with new growth now the dominant source of income—how do you communicate your new identity while respecting your past one?

There's no doubt that the kind of existential change required to rise to the challenge of disruption is the hardest challenge a leader will ever face. It requires looking deep into, and sometimes reimagining, the very soul of the organization. You have to make tough choices to curtail investment in yesterday's core. There will almost undoubtedly be cost cuts, some of which will be significant. In some cases, you may ultimately shut down or spin off large components of your company's legacy business. You will have to decide to place big bets on future markets in the absence of convincing data. You will have to pull recalcitrant employees, shareholders, board members, and stakeholders along, convincing them not with data but with vision and storytelling.

At the same time, *it's the greatest opportunity a leadership team will ever face.* The disruption that frequently rips an incumbent apart almost always results in net market growth. Did people stop taking pictures because Kodak went bankrupt? Of course not. The best estimates suggest that the world takes at least ten times as many pictures as a generation ago, because it is simple and affordable (those of us who live in Asia and see what Filipinos can do with selfie sticks think the number is markedly higher). Similarly, no one stopped consuming news because a local newspaper went out of business. The amount of content produced and consumed has gone up exponentially. Companies certainly haven't stopped advertising even as newspaper page counts have gone down. People didn't stop using mobile phones when the former market leader exited the business. By 2020, forecasters project that there will be more than six billion people with what used to be considered supercomputers sitting inside their pockets.

Disruption opens windows of opportunity to create massive new markets. It is the moment when the market also-ran can become the market leader. It is the moment when business legacies are created.

And getting started requires remembering nothing more than A, B, and C.

The Dual Transformation Equation: A + B + C = Δ

When you take your first algebra class, you're introduced to the Greek letter *delta*. The capital form of the fourth letter in the Greek alphabet, Δ, also serves as shorthand in math equations for change. The kind of change we're talking about here is indeed a very large *delta*. Achieving that change requires following this formula:

$$A + B + C = \Delta$$

Here's how it breaks down.

A = *transformation A*. Reposition today's business to maximize its resilience.

B = *transformation B*. Create a separate new growth engine.

C = *the capabilities link*. Fight unfairly by taking advantage of difficult-to-replicate assets without succumbing to the sucking sound of the core.

The formula's simplicity belies the complexity of its execution. None of the stories we tell in this book are perfect. Sometimes success involves avoiding a worse outcome suffered by a competitor. For example, both Barnes & Noble and Borders had to confront the fact that online retailing threatened the vitality of their historical book retailing model. Barnes & Noble sought to reposition its stores from bookstores to destinations featuring cafés, and to build new growth in electronic readers. Borders, in contrast, doubled down on running its current model more efficiently.

Barnes & Noble struggled mightily, with sales in its core sagging and its Nook reader falling behind multipurpose tablets offered by companies such as Apple, Samsung, and Amazon.com. From the launch of the Nook in June 2010 to June 2016, Barnes & Noble's stock dropped 4 percent while the S&P 500 almost doubled. Although that doesn't sound like an inspirational outcome, it is better than what happened to Borders, which went bankrupt in 2011.

We confidently predict that some of the in-process efforts described here will struggle or even stall. But we also confidently assert that, even so, these companies were very likely better off for having started the journey.

Xerox's Dual Transformation

A case example of an iconic American company that staved off disruptive threats and reinvented itself between 2000 and 2015 provides further color about each letter in our equation and also demonstrates both the opportunities and the challenges of dual transformation.

Xerox was founded in 1906 as The Haloid Photographic Company. Its modern history traces to a 1946 decision by CEO Joseph C. Wilson to commercialize a process the company had invented to print images using an electrically charged drum and dry powder toner. It branded the process *xerography*, launched its revolutionary plain paper photocopier in 1959, and changed the name of the company to Xerox in 1961. By the 1970s Xerox had become an American icon, with its name becoming a verb synonymous with photocopying.

The legendary Xerox research laboratory pioneered many of the technologies that enabled the personal computer era, including the graphical user interface, the mouse, and networking. Unfortunately, those technologies were largely commercialized by other companies, such as 3Com and, most notably, Apple, whose cofounder Steve Jobs was famously influenced by a visit to the Palo Alto Research Center (PARC) in 1979. At the turn of the century, Xerox hit the skids. Lower-cost competitors from Asia eroded the margins and share of Xerox's copiers. The rise of the internet and electronic communications raised questions about the long-term potential of paper-based copiers and printers. As the company's stock price sagged and revenues contracted, analysts began to wonder whether its heavy debt burden meant it would face the prospect of bankruptcy. Xerox stock, which tripled from 1995 to 1999, decreased more than 90 percent from June 1999 to December 2000.

Under the guidance of first Anne Mulcahy and then Ursula Burns, Xerox's fate turned. Burns ran an aggressive program to reconfigure Xerox's historic core business, simplifying product lines and outsourcing noncore functions. The resulting core was significantly smaller, but cash flow was positive and, critically, stable. This is transformation A: repositioning today's business to increase its resilience. Chapter 2 details how success with transformation A starts with determining the customer problem, or the job to be done, around which you should reposition your core and then innovating your business model to deliver against the job, measuring and tracking new metrics that reflect the new model, and burning the boats by executing rapidly.

In parallel, Xerox began to experiment with new service lines designed to optimize repeatable business processes. It built a line of businesses that produced hundreds of millions of dollars in revenue, and then in 2009 it spent more than $6 billion to buy Affiliated Computer Services (ACS), a company that specialized in business process automation. This is transformation B: creating a new growth engine. Whereas transformation A is often defensive in nature, the disruption that forces it opens opportunities to solve new (but related) problems in different (but related) ways. Put another way, the disruptive forces that threaten to rip apart today's business create conditions to build tomorrow's business.

A core threat to Xerox was commoditization in its core printer and copier business, a phenomenon driven by globalization and the rise of the internet, which dampened demand for physical solutions. Those same forces created new demand for and allowed Xerox to assemble a portfolio of service offerings under the brand Xerox Global Services (XGS). Chapter 3 describes how succeeding with transformation B requires three actions: identifying a historically constrained market that disruptive forces will open, iteratively developing a business model to win in that market, and acquiring or hiring complementary capabilities to compete successfully against new and emerging competitors.

Xerox: The Capabilities Link

Now for the C part of the equation, the capabilities link. In 1997, Innosight cofounder and Harvard Business School professor Clayton

Christensen released *The Innovator's Dilemma*, describing how well-run incumbents fail in the face of disruptive change. The capabilities link flips the dilemma. It allows a company to strike a balance where it leverages just enough capabilities to gain an advantage versus other competitors, but not so many capabilities that by definition its ability to do something new is constrained.

Xerox did not perform unrelated diversification. Rather, it combined ACS with the Xerox brand, salesforce, and R&D capability to accelerate its growth. For example, Xerox researchers applied advanced analytics software to manage the E-ZPass toll collection system in the East Coast of the United States. Xerox R&D resources developed simple cloud-based tools to make document services accessible to a wider base of customers, creating new products that, for example, enable banks to improve the mortgage approval process or law firms to increase analytical capabilities. This is the capabilities link, and chapter 4 will describe how leaders need to do three things to successfully create it: carefully select critical capabilities, strategically manage the interface between the core and the new, and actively arbitrate when disputes arise.

Xerox: The End and the Beginning

Xerox's effort to reposition its legacy business not only extended the life and profitability of the copier business but also enabled the company to invest in and ultimately take a new hill in the emerging process-outsourcing business. By 2012, Xerox had climbed back to the $21 billion revenue mark that it had achieved before the transformation process began. Most important, services outstripped technology for the first time, generating the majority of revenue for the enterprise. Xerox grew to become the world's second-largest pensions and benefits administrator. Total employment rose to almost 150,000, and its stock price increased fourfold between 2000 and 2015.

But the forces of industry change are relentless. Revenues dipped from $21 billion in 2012 to $18 billion in 2015, and Xerox's stock fell by almost 50 percent from January 2015 to January 2016. Later that year, influenced undoubtedly by pressure from activist investor Carl Icahn, Xerox announced plans to split into two companies: a business process-outsourcing company called Conduent, with 96,000 employees

FIGURE 1-4

Dual transformation

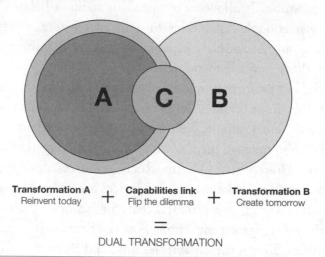

<table>
<tr><td>**Transformation A**
Reinvent today</td><td>+</td><td>**Capabilities link**
Flip the dilemma</td><td>+</td><td>**Transformation B**
Create tomorrow</td></tr>
</table>

=

DUAL TRANSFORMATION

and $7 billion in revenue; and a copier and printer business, with 39,000 employees and $7 billion in revenue. The two offshoot businesses are individually more vibrant than either would have been a decade ago but no doubt will again confront the challenge of disruptive change in their respective markets.

Figure 1-4 summarizes the core dual transformation equation. It shows how transformation B overlaps with, but is distinct from, transformation A. It also includes the conscious and thoughtful capabilities link between the two transformations. It also, with a couple of doodles, looks somewhat like a butterfly, which is a useful metaphor for dual transformation.

Dual Transformation in the Health Care Industry

An in-process example of dual transformation from the health care industry contrasts the strategies on which this book focuses with other strategies leaders can use to renew and reinvigorate organizations.

In 1961, medical giant Johnson & Johnson acquired Janssen Pharmaceuticals, a leading Belgian drug company founded by prolific drug maker Paul Janssen. Over the next five decades, Janssen served as an anchor of impressive growth for J&J. As of 2016, pharmaceutical sales contributed more than $30 billion in global revenues, close to half of the health care giant's overall revenues.

The story begins in the late 2000s, when it became clear that Janssen needed to transform. Patent expiration of major drugs had led to declining sales, and Janssen's development pipeline wasn't robust enough to close the resulting gap. More broadly, J&J's pharmaceutical sector comprised a collection of decentralized businesses, built over time through a series of acquisitions and restructurings, leading to duplicative, subscale efforts. So in the first step, the company significantly simplified and streamlined an overly complex organization by centralizing disparate operating units under the Janssen umbrella and focusing the R&D portfolio from projects in thirty-three disease areas to thirteen (it further narrowed this number to eleven over the next few years).

"It started with a change in philosophy," explained Dr. William N. Hait, Janssen's global head of R&D. "Our original philosophy was to place many small bets in small R&D organizations working semiautonomously without an overarching strategy, with the belief that what would bubble up would be great ideas leading to great products. The problem was that when we looked at what we could invest in each area compared to competitors, we realized we were spreading our investment dollars much too thin."

Then, in 2012, Janssen began to change its core drug discovery and development process. The change centered on a commitment to "transformational medical innovation": emerging science and technology that had the potential to produce radically better health outcomes. Rivals like Pfizer and Novartis were embracing the emergence of generic drugs and biosimilars (similar to off-patent biologically derived drugs), and the industry in general was focused on emerging markets as drivers of growth. Janssen's bet was that extraordinary advances in life science knowledge and technologies would lead to an acceleration of highly innovative treatments for major medical problems.

Janssen pursued a two-pronged strategy to consistently deliver against this high bar. First, it decided to develop deep expertise in what it called "disease area strongholds." The idea was to identify diseases that had significant unmet medical need, high potential for innovation, and where Janssen had—or could build—great scientific strength. The company built teams of world-class experts in selected disease areas in order to be on the cutting edge of rapidly emerging science and to accelerate the research and development of drug candidates to patients waiting for solutions.

Then Janssen amplified the disease area strongholds by making perhaps an even more fundamental shift in its R&D paradigm. Rather than focus on compounds invented by internal scientists, Janssen would become world-class at connecting with and amplifying the power of early-stage external scientists wherever those might be in the world. Janssen aspired to be the partner of choice for university researchers and early-stage startups; the idea was to identify attractive compounds early, work with inventors, and then, if it made strategic sense, license or acquire the compound and plug it in to Janssen's development and distribution machine. The company set up innovation centers in four locations around the world to be embedded in innovative ecosystems and increase access to interesting startups. It augmented those centers with no-strings-attached biotech incubators that provided fully equipped laboratory space and access to J&J expertise. Incubated startups could end up as standalone businesses, could be acquired by competitors to J&J, or J&J could acquire select startups.

"This required a shift in the culture around 'not discovered here,'" Hait commented. "We had to accept the fact that others might be ahead of us, or better than us, and we should be open to it. That culture is now deeply ingrained in Janssen. Even the most recalcitrant groups that felt that only J&J science was good have come around. It has been a huge benefit to us. Once we identify the top targets to go after, we don't care where the drug comes from. It allows us to move very quickly."

These moves significantly increased early-stage deals and enhanced Janssen's role and reputation in the innovation community. Pharmaceuticals went from a laggard to the leading sector at J&J, driving the growth of the overall corporation. Janssen became the fastest-growing large pharmaceutical company in the world's major markets, and the industry leader in R&D productivity for four years in a row between 2013 and 2016.

An example of the transformation comes from Janssen's successful development of a drug for people suffering from a variety of deadly blood cancers. Janssen's disease area stronghold experts in hemato-logical malignancies were on the lookout for molecules that inhibited an enzyme called BTK, which is implicated in the development of blood cancers. Researchers found an attractive candidate in ibrutinib, a compound being developed by biotech startup Pharmacyclics. In late 2011 Janssen made an up-front payment of $150 million for the rights to 50 percent of ibrutinib-related sales, and it drove the development process, reaching market with a drug branded Imbruvica in 2013. In 2015 AbbVie bought out Pharmacyclics, along with rights to the remaining 50 percent of Imbruvica sales, for $22 billion.

In 2015, Janssen took the next step in its journey by announcing plans to shift from treating diseases to preventing them. It put for-ward the provocative notion that it would "intercept" diseases before they manifested. The idea involves leveraging the wealth of health data increasingly available to us—from our genetics and biometrics to our family histories and the signals about our day-to-day behaviors picked up from health-tracking devices and increasingly sophisticated sensors—to stop disease-causing processes in their tracks. Imagine the human equivalent of a check engine light that appears automatically on a car dashboard, highlighting the need for some kind of preventive intervention. Further, consider receiving a regimen of customized rec-ommendations for changes in diet, lifestyle, and behavior, along with medicines or other interventions to treat your personal risk for disease, as opposed to the one-size-fits-all health and wellness recommenda-tions we get now. Hait explains:

> No one wants to be diagnosed with a disease so they can then get treated. If you're unfortunate enough to get a disease, you want it to be cured so you don't have to worry about it anymore. However, today for the most part we develop drugs that manage manifestations of disease. The disruption would be to bring medical solutions that prevent multiple myeloma, for example. With that, all of our business in selling myeloma drugs would be gone, since there would be no myeloma any longer. If that's where the disruption will come from, and that's where patients will benefit the most, let's take a look at what we'd have to do to prevent, intercept, or cure diseases, rather than wait until people are sick to then treat the manifestations of diseases.

Janssen formed an innovation group called the *disease interception accelerator* (DIA) to shape and speed the most promising research in this area. One of the DIA's ventures focuses on intercepting type 1 diabetes (T1D), which typically strikes young children and results in a lifetime of dependence on insulin. It turns out that T1D does not start when a child suddenly becomes ill with an attack of diabetic ketoacidosis and must be rushed to the hospital; rather, it is the result of a silent, multiyear, multistage autoimmune attack. Janssen scientists and their partners are working on diagnostics and interventions that target these silent early stages of the disease. The researchers' intention is to protect the pancreatic beta cells that naturally produce insulin before they're killed off and need to be artificially supplemented. Janssen's first drug candidate for this strategy entered clinical trials in 2016 in children with early-stage diabetes.

Janssen is well aware that success will require significant business model innovation. Disease interception solutions are likely to include diagnostics, consumer products, and other interventions that go beyond traditional drugs. And, in many cases, no single product will ensure interception. Rather, consumers will need to integrate a variety of products and services. Finally, it is difficult to prove the financial and societal value of disease prevention and interception, requiring deep partnership with regulators, policy makers, and payers.

To address these challenges, the DIA is working with like-minded stakeholders and exploring new business models and nontraditional partnerships. Clearly, the work to intercept diseases is still in its early stages. Nonetheless, the simultaneous pursuit of two goals—new ways to develop drugs, and a radical reframing of the fundamental problem the organization solves—positions Janssen to drive significant strategic transformation in the years to come.

The What and the How of Dual Transformation

When Janssen first confronted the challenges of commoditization and sagging performance, it had an array of strategic options. Separating the unique roles of transformation A and transformation B requires, first, a clear and consistent definition of today's business—a seemingly simple step that is easy to skip.

It is easy to describe what a company sells. In the case of Janssen that would be traditional drugs. But as Peter Drucker famously wrote in 1964, "The customer rarely buys what the company thinks it sells him." Companies think that they provide products or sell solutions, but that's not what customers perceive. They have a problem, and the company has a solution to the problem. Products and services don't define a company. Rather, *what* a company does (or the problem it solves for customers) and *how* it uniquely solves that problem—these are what define a company.

In previous publications, we've called the *what* the job to be done. The *how* involves key components of the company's business model: things, such as brands, physical assets, retail stores, patents, and so on; know-how, such as the ability to work with regulators or knowledge about managing complex networks; and *financial components*, such as how the company earns revenues, translates revenues into profits, and translates profits into free cash flow. Chapter 2 describes the concepts of jobs to be done and business models in more depth.

Historically, the *what* Janssen addressed was treating a select number of complicated medical conditions, such as schizophrenia, rheumatoid arthritis, and HIV. Its *how*, at the beginning of its transformation journey, involved investing heavily in proprietary research laboratories and drug development capabilities that produced innovative medicines to be sold by the company's skilled salesforce.

Figure 1-5 shows the set of strategic choices leaders have when they choose to fundamentally change a company. It starts in the lower-left quadrant with core optimization.

For J&J, core optimization involved the consolidation of disparate pharmaceutical businesses under the Janssen banner, while streamlining operations and the R&D portfolio. Generally, an organization should constantly be looking for ways to improve its competitive position by improving productivity, innovating to produce better products or services than competitors, or finding new paths to customers that historically have been hard to reach. This is well-covered territory and not a focus of this book. It is worth emphasizing, however, that if you can do what you're currently doing better, faster, and cheaper, that may be good, is likely necessary, and certainly helps support what follows; but it is not the kind of strategic transformation described in this book.

FIGURE 1-5

Strategic choices for leaders

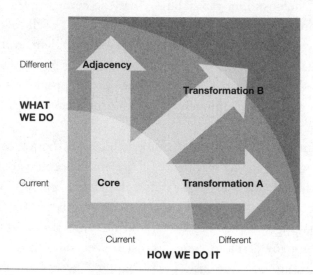

Cost cutting, in particular, might be brutally difficult, but on its own it is not what we mean by the word *transformation*. If all you are doing is playing yesterday's game better, your odds of surviving Schumpeter's gale of creative destruction are low.

Janssen's decision to focus on disease area strongholds and develop the capability to identify and ingest external innovation is transformation A, because it is a new way to solve an old problem—a move along the horizontal axis of figure 1-5. By this action, Janssen is doing the same job it historically did for the end customer—helping manage a select number of medical conditions via pharmaceutical products—but doing it in a fundamentally different way. Disease interception, on the other hand, moves toward the upper-right quadrant, because it solves a new (but related) problem in a new (but related) way. This is transformation B.

One strategy not described in Janssen's story is a popular one in the industry: growing by acquiring other large pharmaceutical companies to move into new therapeutic areas or new drug modalities (such as biologics). For example, in 2009, when Janssen began to grapple with its strategic challenges, Merck splashed out close to $50 billion to acquire Schering-Plough, and Pfizer paid almost $70 billion to buy Wyeth.

These kinds of moves, often called *adjacencies*, involve using existing capabilities to solve new problems for customers; they are represented by a vertical move toward the upper-left quadrant in figure 1-5.

A classic example of a homegrown adjacency effort is Procter & Gamble's (P&G) moves in the 1990s and 2000s into new categories like fine fragrances (which it exited in 2015), home-based teeth whitening, and quick housecleaning (through its Swiffer and Febreze brands). In each case P&G expanded to do new jobs for consumers, solving problems it never had solved before. But it was able to follow its time-tested model of distributing consumable products through mass-market retailers like Walmart and Tesco, building proprietary technologies that provided superior benefits compared with competitors', and investing heavily in advertising.

Well-structured adjacent moves can be powerful ways to grow and increase the resilience of the core business and should be a part of any company's overall growth strategy. However, because they don't require changing a company's fundamental *how*, again they tend not to change the face or nature of a company and therefore are not a focus of this book.

Leading Dual Transformation

Dual transformation shifts an organization's center of gravity. If we had to put a number on it, we would say that you have made a dual transformation when B constitutes at least one-third of the total enterprise, with a faster growth rate than A, positioning B to become tomorrow's core business. It is the hardest challenge a leader will ever face. Part II of this book details four key leadership mindsets you need to succeed.

1. *The courage to choose before the platform burns (chapter 5).* Paradoxically, the more obvious the need to transform, the harder it is to do it. Netflix founder, CEO, and chairman Reed Hastings started to change Netflix's core business years before it was necessary, an action that set his company up for a decade of successful growth. Similarly, in the face of record performance and regulatory changes that seemingly guaranteed years of growth, Aetna CEO Mark Bertolini made the historic decision to dramatically reconfigure the health insurance giant.

2. *The clarity to focus on a select few moonshots (chapter 6).* One of the greatest mistakes leaders make is to approach transformation B without a focused strategy. Just as John F. Kennedy urged the United States in 1961 to send a man to the moon and bring him back by the end of the decade, leaders need to identify a handful of high-potential opportunities. We provide a detailed view into the process a leading water utility in the Philippines followed to select two such moonshots in just ninety days.

3. *The curiosity to explore even if the probable outcome is failure (chapter 7).* Even though focus is important, leaders must recognize that the specific strategy that will power transformation B will come out of a process of trial and error, with many efforts failing along the way. For example, Singtel is an extremely disciplined telecommunications company, with a strong emphasis on financial discipline. From 2010 to 2015 it successfully branched into new markets and strengthened its culture of innovation by splicing curiosity into its corporate DNA.

4. *The conviction to persevere in the face of predictable crises (chapter 8).* There will be dark days—times when a board member doubts, when shareholders question, when even committed executives waver. Leaders must have the conviction to remain firm in the face of crises of commitment, conflict, and identity. A motivating purpose and relentless separation of the work—with leaders repeating the mantra "A does A, B does B"—helps reinforce that conviction.

Chapter 9 concludes by providing snapshots from the dual transformation journey, with insights from a diverse set of leaders reflecting on their own experiences.

The case studies in this book represent a meaningful sample of the instructive examples we have found through our research or have experienced firsthand. Historically, when disruption strikes you could place a simple bet: for the entrant, against the incumbent. Indeed, the afterword describes who's next—industries facing increasing threats over the next few years. But remember, those threats also present massive opportunities. Companies that successfully execute dual transformation can own the future instead of being disrupted by it.

Part One. Dual Transformation Framework

The next three chapters lay out the core dual transformation framework. Chapter 2 describes how Deseret Media, Adobe, and Netflix executed transformation A and repositioned their legacy core businesses by changing how they delivered value to and captured value from their customers. Chapter 3 shares how SingPost, Amazon.com, and a handful of US universities set out to drive transformation B and create tomorrow's core business by finding new ways to solve new problems. Chapter 4 homes in on coauthor Gilbert's firsthand experience at Deseret Media, detailing how thoughtfully creating a capabilities link between A and B allows established organizations to do something magical.

2. Transformation A: Repositioning the Core

In 2011, America Online (since swallowed up by Verizon) bought the Huffington Post for more than $300 million. Arianna Huffington had founded the website in 2005, and it had quickly grown to become one of the most popular destinations on the internet. "HuffPo" was one of the first companies to make itself a publishing platform. Rather than have a deep roster of full-time journalists to pump out content, HuffPo populated its site with content produced by a skeleton staff and a stable of occasional contributors. It worked. At the time of the acquisition, HuffPo had roughly the same website traffic as the venerable *New York Times*. The newcomer had fifty journalists. The *Times* employed twelve hundred.

In 1999, Marc Benioff founded Salesforce.com. He was one of the pioneers of a movement that came to be called *software as a service*, or SaaS. As internet connectivity became increasingly ubiquitous and access speeds spiked, Benioff bet on a shift in the historical means by which companies distributed computer software. Rather than require customers to go to a retail store or order shrink-wrapped software through a mail catalog, Salesforce's core customer relationship management (CRM) software, which helped companies manage their salesforce, was licensed to users, hosted and maintained by Salesforce, and delivered over the internet.

The year Benioff founded Salesforce.com, market leader Siebel Systems was on a tear, and things only improved for the next three years. The traditional software vendor's sales surged from $45 million in 1996 to $2.1 billion in 2001. As Benioff's disruptive model established itself, however, Siebel's sales reversed, declining to $1.3 billion in 2004. Oracle announced plans to acquire the company for almost $6 billion in September 2005. During the next decade Salesforce grew to almost $7 billion in revenue, and its stock rose almost 500 percent, leaving the former upstart with a $50 billion valuation in mid-2016.

These two vignettes—HuffPost and Salesforce.com—occurred in vastly different industries and contexts, but they tell the same story. In both cases, an upstart found a disruptive way to solve the customer's same fundamental problem as the incumbent. HuffPo provided news and entertainment, with many fewer full-time journalists; Salesforce.com helped businesses optimize the sales process with software delivered over the internet. As displayed in figure 2-1, the foundational problem they solved (what) did not change. The way in which they solved the problem (how), did change, upending each industry's economic models and rearranging the competitive landscape.

FIGURE 2-1

Transformation A

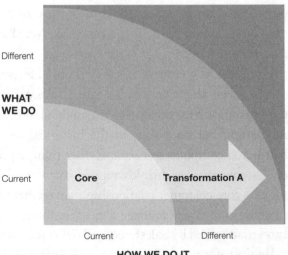

Market leaders need not be powerless victims of these kinds of changes. The stories that follow describe how Deseret Media, Adobe, and Netflix successfully repositioned the core of their existing businesses, driving what we call transformation A. After the stories we describe four steps for driving transformation A in your business.

Deseret Media: From Commodity News to a Focus on Faith and Family

When coauthor Clark Gilbert took over as president of the *Deseret News*, it was obvious that something needed to be done to create a new digital growth business. But even more pressing was addressing challenges in the core model. The team's first step was to make a detailed accounting of how much it had cost to produce each of the stories that appeared in the print and online versions of the newspaper. This kind of "story cost accounting"—multiplying hours of work and the compensation of the writers—had never been done before.

Not surprisingly, investigative journalism required substantial investment, but so did movie reviews and coverage of local sports teams. Further, journalists at the newspaper often duplicated the efforts of reporters at KSL, a sister television station that shared the same overall corporate parent. And even though some of the resulting stories were unique and generated reader interest and web traffic, much of the work was what Gilbert dubbed *commodity journalism*: content that readers could actually access through other specialized publications or websites, such as ESPN for sports news, *Rolling Stone* for album reviews, or Rotten Tomatoes for aggregated movie reviews. Making this information transparent showed the full staff how expensive it was to produce pieces that local and national competitors could easily match.

The Deseret team did three things to drive down cost per story:

1. Combined the staff of the newspaper and the television station

2. Increased the use of outsourced content providers such as The Associated Press

3. Created a network of local *stringers,* who do piecework at market rates, under the brand Deseret Connect

The cost per story of the new integrated newsroom (number 1) was about half the cost of the legacy newspaper. The cost per story of Deseret Connect (number 3) was about one-fifth that of the integrated newsroom (or one-tenth the cost of the legacy newspaper). These measures allowed Gilbert to streamline his staff. In August 2010, the *Deseret News* laid off 43 percent of its workforce, a painful but critical move to stop the newspaper from hemorrhaging money.

These moves weren't only about lowering costs. They were about freeing up capital to invest. Gilbert and his team selected six areas where they believed Deseret, despite its small size, could produce content that was as compelling as that produced by any organization in the world. These areas of editorial emphasis included strengthening the family, faith in the community, care for the needy, values in the media, excellence in education, and financial responsibility. Deseret would invest heavily—as much as five times what would be invested in a typical story—in original stories in these areas. For example, one story series described the impact of one-third of American children living without their fathers. Deseret then created a weekly print publication for a national audience interested in these topics. From 2010 to 2014, combined circulation of the daily and weekly publications surged from about 100,000 to over 200,000 subscribers, a phenomenal number in an industry where even keeping circulation flat required Herculean efforts.

As part of its core shift from providing a me-too commodity to publishing a smaller but highly differentiated paper, Deseret also diversified its core product portfolio, including special-purpose publications, custom publications, and direct mail solutions for advertisers. By the time Gilbert left in 2015 to become president of BYU-Idaho, the combination of lower costs, renewed focus, and smart expansion had fundamentally transformed Deseret's core business. Costs were radically lower, the newspaper and other print publications offered unique content, and declines in core revenues had slowed, with the new targeted products now producing more than 50 percent of the core's net income (see table 2-1). Make no mistake: the epicenter of the business shifted to Deseret Media's digital growth business (described in subsequent chapters), and the legacy print business remained at risk, but transformation A had enabled the core to remain a vital part of the overall organization.

TABLE 2-1

Transformation A at Deseret Media

Portion of company	Net income, indexed to 2010 total = 100					
	2010	2011	2012	2013	2014	2015
Old core	79	66	40	26	24	23
New core	5	8	13	21	24	25
New growth	16	21	36	47	65	80

Note: These figures have been stylized to protect company confidentiality.

Adobe: From Packaged Software to Subscriptions

Xerox's Palo Alto Research Center (PARC) was the epicenter of the modern computer world. The graphical user interface, networking, use of a mouse as an input device, and many other innovations trace to breakthroughs from Xerox scientists. Unfortunately for Xerox, most of those advances were commercialized, not by Xerox, but by companies such as Apple as well as 3Com (a spin-off) and Adobe, a software company founded in 1982 by two Xerox PARC computer scientists.

Almost everyone is familiar with Adobe's portable document format (PDF) software, which facilitates reading documents across devices. Software packages such as Photoshop and Illustrator play key roles in creative industries such as advertising; Adobe Premiere and After Effects are widely used for film and television, and Dreamweaver is and Flash Player was a backbone of the modern internet.

In December 2007, Adobe veteran Shantanu Narayen became CEO. The next year, Adobe had to contend with a global recession. The recession came at a strategic inflection point for the company. It led most of the markets in which it operated and didn't have obvious paths to drive significant growth in those markets. One of its biggest competitors, in fact, was piracy, which by some estimates cost the company almost $1 billion per year in lost revenue.

Almost a decade after Salesforce.com's founding, SaaS was now a well-established model. The recession, which led many of Adobe's corporate customers to push for more "asset-light" solutions, led Adobe leadership to assess making a bold shift from selling software to offering subscriptions to its leading products. As then CFO Mark Garrett put it, "A recession is a terrible thing to waste."

So in 2008 Adobe launched Photoshop Express as a way to test a subscription-based SaaS offering. Although the business model was jarring to a company based on selling packaged software, it had advantages. Recurring monthly revenue provides greater predictability compared with a boom-and-bust "blockbuster" model, in which sales spike after release of a new package and dwindle as the package saturates the market. Further, an online delivery model reduces the costs of producing and distributing software and allows providers to introduce updates relatively easily. A cloud-delivered offering has flexibility, creating affordable entry points for students and potential users in emerging markets. And the lack of a physical product can frustrate pirates.

Still, change never comes easily to organizations. As part of the internal change management process, Chief Technology Officer Kevin Lynch tapped forty influential managers on the shoulder and turned them into internal change advocates. "We ended up creating the gravity, where it became cool," Lynch said.

In October 2011, Adobe introduced the Creative Cloud, which offers users access-on-demand to its software. In May 2013, the company burned the boats and discontinued new creation of physical products. By 2014, the Creative Cloud constituted roughly one-third of the company's revenues, and overall profits were 20 percent above their prerecession level (see table 2-2).

Netflix: From Rentals to Subscriptions, from DVDs to Streaming

In 1998, Reed Hastings founded Netflix, a service that allowed customers to rent DVDs through the mail. When Netflix started, the dominant competitor was Blockbuster Video, which owned thousands of stores across the United States where people rented movies. Blockbuster promised customers it would always have the latest movies (blockbusters, of course) in stock. To live up to that promise, Blockbuster limited the amount of time people could keep the rented movies,

TABLE 2-2

Transformation A at Adobe

Revenue source	Revenues (US$B)				
	2011	2012	2013	2014	2015
Software	3.3	3.2	2.4	1.6	1.1
Subscriptions	0	0	0.5	1.3	2.3
Digital marketing	0.9	1.1	1.2	1.4	1.5

Note: Figures are fiscal year (December–November); subscriptions include only core digital media products.

charging substantial late fees if they missed the deadline. That allowed Blockbuster to manage its inventory shrewdly, live up to its promise, and deliver attractive returns to shareholders.

At first, Netflix looked similar to the traditional video rental store. Users would rent a single movie and would pay late fees if they kept it too long. Consumers got the convenience of home delivery and the potential to access so-called *long tail content*—videos that were too niche to appear in a retail chain—while giving up the ability to get exactly what they wanted right away.

Then in 1999 Netflix executed its first transformation A, one that ultimately led to the demise of Blockbuster and other video rental stores. Instead of renting individual DVDs, consumers paid a monthly subscription fee that allowed them unlimited rentals, as long as they held no more than a few movies at a time (the number depended on the subscription fee). As with the SaaS model, one key advantage of the model is that Netflix captured fees from customers before delivering movies and created substantial user "stickiness," as people are more likely to start a subscription than to stop one. In 2000, Netflix had discussions about selling to Blockbuster for $50 million. Blockbuster, then the market leader, passed.

Netflix set to work building sophisticated inventory management systems to help ensure that people could get the DVDs they wanted when they wanted them. The company also invested heavily to build algorithms that predicted users' desired content based on their ratings of movies they rented. The so-called recommendations engine is so critical to Netflix that in 2008 it announced a public contest wherein the team that most improved the performance of the engine would get $1 million, as long as they crossed a 10 percent improvement threshold. Two teams indeed crossed the threshold, with the winning team receiving a check from Hastings in 2009 (remarkably, that was the first time the team members met face-to-face; they had done their work virtually).

Netflix got too big for Blockbuster—which had $3 billion in revenues and a multibillion-dollar market capitalization when the story began—to ignore. Blockbuster attempted an integrated offering where people could either visit stores or access movies online. However, lacking Netflix's years of experience with the online model, Blockbuster struggled to create an offering that was either compelling to customers or financially attractive.

In 2008 Netflix began experimenting with augmenting its DVD-by-mail business with a streaming offering. From a customer's perspective, streaming had the advantage of removing the one downside to the Netflix model—the lack of instant gratification—but also limited the quality of the user experience because of existing bandwidth constraints. Everyone but the most technologically savvy had to watch on a relatively small computer versus a big, crystal-clear television set.

The *what* (discover and enjoy content) remained the same, but the *how* of streaming versus mail delivery differed significantly. Keys to succeeding with a mail-based model include effective inventory management, warehousing, and physical distribution. Keys to succeeding with a streaming business include developing and managing a complicated and ever-changing host of technologies. Netflix managed to make the transition. By 2010 Blockbuster had filed for bankruptcy protection, with its assets ultimately sold to DISH Network. By 2012 streaming constituted the majority of Netflix's revenues, and, only two years later, streaming revenues exceeded mail-based revenues by more than five times (see table 2-3).

And Netflix wasn't finished. As the sophistication of its algorithm grew, Hastings and team had a thought: "We understand our users so well, we know what content works and what doesn't so well, what if we shifted from distributing other people's content to creating our own?"

TABLE 2-3

Transformation A at Netflix

Revenue source	Revenues (US$B)					
	2010	2011	2012	2013	2014	2015
Mail	2.2	2.6	1.1	0.9	0.8	0.6
Streaming	0	0.6	2.5	3.5	4.7	6.1

Creating content is not for the faint of heart. Each year the major television networks introduce dozens of new shows, each of which has been carefully screened and tested. Only a few survive. Given these odds, most content producers naturally hedge their bets, avoiding big up-front investments in television series until there is demonstrated market interest. A noted contrast to this model is HBO, which made big bets on series like *The Sopranos* and *Game of Thrones*.

The first series Netflix commissioned was *House of Cards*, featuring critically acclaimed actor Kevin Spacey as a corrupt senator named Frank Underwood. Taking advantage of its now-robust streaming offering, Netflix introduced another twist to the world of content by releasing the entire run of *House of Cards* episodes at once rather than doling out content week by week. Consumers binge watched the show, flocking to social media to share their views.

Netflix followed with other popular shows such as *Orange Is the New Black*, *Arrested Development* (which had previously aired on FOX and generated a small but fiercely loyal audience, including one of us), and *Unbreakable Kimmy Schmidt*. The shows were well received by audiences and critics and created another reason for users to subscribe, solidifying Netflix's competitive position.

By 2015, the company had fundamentally transformed its business from sending people other people's content via the mail to web-delivering a rich mix of original and third-party content. We consider this transformation A because the core job Netflix is doing (the what) didn't materially change, but the way in which Netflix gets that job done (the how) has changed.

The legacy business can remain an important component of transformation A. When run the right way, old businesses can drive substantial cash flow and continue to create capabilities that enable new growth. As of 2015, for example, Netflix still had more than five million subscribers who received DVDs in the mail. Although that number was down 75 percent from its peak, Netflix still generated attractive profits from its mail-delivery business.

Driving Transformation A: Four Lessons

The essence of transformation A is changing the *how*—finding more effective and efficient ways to address customer needs to maximize the resilience and relevance of your historical core business. At first blush, this kind of change sounds straightforward enough. After all, you don't have to discover or demonstrate that you're targeting a real market need.

However, companies often find it painfully difficult to change how they operate. Clayton Christensen's famous book *The Innovator's Dilemma* contains numerous case examples of market leaders, in industries ranging from steel to accounting software, that struggled to respond when an entrant emerged with a disruptive way to solve an existing problem. As coauthor Mark Johnson details in his 2010 book *Seizing the White Space*, the core problem is that over time companies develop rules, norms, and metrics designed to perpetuate how they create, capture, and deliver value. Although humans are a flexible and ingenious species, these kinds of underlying systems, when organized into institutional routines, prove impervious to many types of change.

Based on the case studies we researched for this book as well as our collective field experience in leading or advising companies confronting the challenges of disruptive change, we have developed four keys to succeeding with transformation A. First, you must understand—at a detailed level—the jobs to be done that customers consider unique and meaningful. Then you innovate your business model to deliver against those jobs, measure and track new metrics that reflect the new model, and implement aggressively.

Key 1: Determine the Defensible Postdisruption Job to Be Done

The trigger point for transformation A is often the emergence of a technological or business model discontinuity that creates new possibilities for addressing an existing market. For many companies, this trigger is the continued rise of the internet and the increasing digitization of business models that served historically offline or physical products. The fundamental question for companies deciding how to rearchitect their business models is, What can we *uniquely* do for customers?

We answer that question using the idea of the *job to be done*. At its core, the idea is simple: people don't buy products or services; rather, they hire them to get jobs done in their lives. The quest for competitive advantage, then, comes from creating the key of a product or a service the opens the lock of the functional, emotional, or social progress a customer seeks in a given circumstance. Marketing scholars will note that on the surface, the concept of jobs to be done is not particularly new. Recall Peter Drucker's famous line, quoted earlier: "The customer rarely buys what the business thinks it sells him." The next two sentences are even more important: "One reason for this is, of course, that nobody pays for a 'product.' What is paid for is satisfactions."

Companies think they're selling products or providing services, but the customer doesn't think of the world that way. Consider the aphorism attributed to Harvard Business School marketing legend Ted Levitt: "People don't want quarter-inch drills—they want quarter-inch holes." That's not even quite right. People don't want quarter-inch holes; they want to hang a picture. And even that isn't quite right. People don't want to hang a picture; they want their apartment to look better so that the next time their in-laws come over, they are that much less critical.

An example of an organization grounded in a clear job to be done is Brigham Young University-Idaho (where Gilbert became president in 2015). In 2000, the school grew out of Ricks College to become a companion to its sister institution, Brigham Young University in Provo, Utah. While its core mission is spiritual, BYU-Idaho was created to address a clear job: prepare students for the real world at a reasonable price. Many universities, of course, were founded to fulfill this foundational job. Over time, however, some schools became increasingly research oriented, at higher and higher costs. Others became oriented around major athletic programs, with football coaches outearning university presidents by wide margins. Instead of building the university around research or athletics, BYU-Idaho kept a relentless focus on the foundational job of its target students. Today, BYU-Idaho provides an extremely student-focused education, with graduation and placement rates that are well above peer institutions, and it does this at a cost that is lower than that of most state schools.

To determine the job on which to base transformation A, leaders need to understand the fundamental problems facing customers, as well as the progress they're seeking to make in overcoming them. Although customers often struggle to describe what they want, they often are eloquent in explaining what they're trying to accomplish, the reasons they pick one solution over another, their frustrations with existing solutions, and so on. More specifically, you need to do one of two things. Either conduct detailed research (if you do, we highly recommend reading *Competing Against Luck*, a 2016 book by Clayton Christensen, our colleague David Duncan, Taddy Hall, and Karen Dillon) or rely on the accumulated experience of your team to provide detailed answers to these five questions.

1. Why have people historically bought from us?

2. What do we provide that they really care about?

3. What is the disruptive shift in our market?

4. What used to matter to them but doesn't really anymore?

5. What do they *wish* we could do that we don't?

It helps to have outsiders or people with a fresh perspective answer these questions, because the bias in an organization is to assume that what you're selling is what people want, and to assume that what you provided that delivered competitive advantage in the past will be critical in the future. We call this the *postdisruption job to be done* to reinforce the notion that as the world changes, what is critical to the customer also changes.

Table 2-4 provides our answers to these five questions for the case studies described in this chapter, along with Xerox and Janssen (detailed in chapter 1).

TABLE 2-4

Six postdisruption jobs to be done

Question re job to be done	Deseret Media (ca. 2010)	Adobe (ca. 2008)	Netflix (ca. 2008)	BYU-Idaho (ca. 2000)	Xerox (ca. 2004)	Janssen (ca. 2014)
Why did people historically buy from us?	Get news and information	Develop creative content	Enjoy content	Prepare for real world	Automate boring business processes	Treat diseases and chronic conditions
What do they really care about?	Unique content they can't find anywhere else	Solutions that allow them to get the job done	"Enough" choice, but on their schedule	Faculty engagement and life preparation	Simple buying process	Treatment at affordable prices
What is the disruptive shift in the market?	Online portals such as Huffington Post	Software-as-a-service model	Higher-speed internet connectivity	Lower-cost delivery models	Commoditization	Generic treatments and regulatory pressure
What used to matter but doesn't anymore?	Commodity content (movie reviews, sports scores)	Pretty packaging and detailed documentation	Concurrent scheduled TV	Faculty research, campus prestige, top-flight athletic programs	Higher performance	Brands
What do they wish we could do that we don't?	Go deep into places that no one else explores	Access upgrades more quickly	Provide instant content and self-paced consumption	Get affordable life and career coaching	Solve the problem without requiring any product	Prevent their disease

Key 2: Innovate Your Business Model

Notice that the case examples in this chapter involve many changes that aren't readily visible to the customer. Deseret Media reassigns reporters and shifts some assignments from the staff to stringers, but when customers open the paper or click on a link, all they see is a story. Adobe is providing the same software packages with the same features via its Creative Cloud, but customers pay for it in a different way. Netflix consumers are watching content, but they might access that content by clicking an app on their TV sets instead of slipping a DVD into a player, and that content might be created by Netflix rather than by a third party. The plumbing required to make these changes is largely irrelevant to the end customer, but it's of critical importance to the company, because it ensures you can deliver on the postdisruption job to be done in a way that maximizes your financial resilience.

The essence, then, of succeeding with transformation A is to redesign your core business model so that you *create* the right value for customers, *deliver* that value as efficiently as possible, and *capture* sufficient value to fund investment in future innovation. These are the three key elements of a business model. The second part of transformation A, therefore, is to innovate your business model so that it delivers against the defensible job to be done.

Seizing the White Space provides a comprehensive overview of business model components along with a range of archetypical models to consider. We recommend paying particular attention to five key business model elements:

1. *Production.* What did we do that we can now outsource? What did we used to outsource that we should do?

2. *Distribution.* Can we go direct? Use a different distribution channel?

3. *Customer support.* Can our customers support themselves?

4. *Revenue model.* Can we wrap services around our product? Products around our service? Could a "freemium" offering drive usage? Can we shift from a one-time purchase to a subscription model?

5. *Pricing model.* How frequently should we charge for our offering? How should we charge?

Not all of these elements will change, but some will. Keep the postdisruption job in mind, because your aim is to deliver customer value and not to maximize coherence with current operations. If there aren't pieces of the blueprinted business model that feel like a stretch to you, you haven't thought about it expansively enough. This was certainly true of the creation of BYU-Idaho in 2000. When Gordon B. Hinckley, president of the Church of Jesus Christ of Latter-day Saints and chairman of its Church Education System, announced the formation of the new university, he signaled the school's unambiguous student focus by declaring that teaching and advising—not research—would be the faculty's primary focus. He also announced that the school would operate on a year-round calendar and take advantage of online learning to reach more students without adding infrastructure costs. Any drivers of cost that did not enhance its clear student-focused mission would be rigorously challenged and reviewed. BYU-Idaho targeted all of its focus (and investment) at delivering against the core student job to be done.

Three final notes as you blueprint your business model. First, even though costs matter, they aren't the only thing that's important. The case studies detailed in this chapter all involved cost cuts in the historical core business. Indeed, the deeper the disruptive change affecting that core and the later you respond to them, the more likely it is that transformation A will require significant, perhaps painful, cost cuts, to the point that some companies brand transformation A a "cost transformation." It's important to note, however, that the goal isn't simply to cut costs, but to reposition the business model to increase long-term competitiveness.

Second, you need to identify, business model component by business model component, who in the world does the best, most innovative job of delivering excellence in that area. Don't constrain yourself to looking only in your category or your country. Think by analogy of what it would look like if you were to borrow that business model component and apply it to your circumstance. The resulting answer will be both robust and unique.

Finally, make sure that you think about your business model coherently. For example, don't expect a salesforce whose commissions trace to gross sales to prioritize a subscription-based offering whose revenue

TABLE 2-5

Key business model differences in six companies

Business model element	Deseret Media	Adobe	Netflix	BYU-Idaho	Xerox	Janssen
Production	Stringers and combined newsroom		Original content	Year-round calendaring	Outsourcing	External development
Distribution	National distribution of weekly paper	Web-based	Streaming	Classroom and online learning	Direct to consumer	
Support		Web-based			Outsourcing	
Revenue		Subscription				
Pricing		Per month		Tuition increases at or below inflation		

is earned over multiple years. Just as a chain is only as strong as its weakest link, a business model breaks apart if there is any incoherence.

Table 2-5 shows the key business model differences for the examples we've detailed, with blank cells indicating no significant changes to that component.

Key 3: Determine and Monitor New Metrics

As we've mentioned, transformation A is likely to involve some, and perhaps significant, cost reduction. But transformation A is distinctly different in nature from traditional cost cutting. The strategic intent of transformation A isn't to find a better way to do what you were doing before; rather, it is to map out a distinct and defensible way to provide value to the customer. If you're doing the same thing better, faster, and cheaper, that's of course a good thing, but it doesn't meaningfully change your ability to sustain your core business.

We chose the phrase "repositioning the core" to describe transformation A with great care (and after great debate). Sometimes the forces of disruption will require nothing short of reinvention. But there is often room for significant growth within the core, and the word *reinvention* sounds daunting to the point of being off-putting. Proper repositioning will reinvigorate the core, but so, too, might operational improvements and logical adjacencies. *Repositioning* for a postdisruption job to be done is a big deal that goes well beyond siphoning off 3 percent of the cost of every function.

In 2015, as we began working on this manuscript, we set up a daily Google search for the word *transformation*. Some of the case studies described in this book show up, but pop culture stories also populate our news feed. "Kylie Jenner undergoes dramatic transformation as she ditches dark hair for blonde locks," "Obese sausage dog 'Fat Vincent' stuns vets with amazing transformation," and "Jake Gyllenhaal in *Southpaw*: How actor transformed himself" are three examples. Not to dismiss any of these types of changes, but clearly they are different from the kinds of transformations described in this book.

We worry that many companies that are embarking on so-called digital transformation efforts are doing something similar. Rather than using the rise of digital technologies to fundamentally rethink operations, they are simply doing what they used to do digitally. Ripping out fax machines and installing email, ditching email for text messages, or shifting text conversations to messaging solutions like Slack—these steps may lower costs and boost customer or employee satisfaction, but the essence of the company isn't changing in a material way. In a quickly changing world, playing an old game better is insufficient.

The simplest way to understand whether you're truly transforming your core business is to ask, How have our metrics changed? Consider Netflix. A DVD-based model requires managing warehouse utilization and physical distribution costs. A streaming model requires managing website uptime and bandwidth costs. If a company is using the same metrics before and after its so-called transformation effort, it really hasn't transformed in a material way.

Key 4: Implement Aggressively

In the sixteenth century, Spanish commander Hernán Cortés set off to conquer the Aztec empire in what now constitutes central Mexico. Upon landing, he ordered the destruction of his fleet of ships, making it clear to the crew members that they would succeed in their quest or die trying.

Similarly, executing transformation A requires a burn the boats moment. Adobe stopped creating new versions of packaged software. While at Deseret, Gilbert didn't do a drip-drip-drip downsizing; he dramatically cut 40 percent of his staff on a single day. When the Mormon Church created BYU-Idaho it didn't slowly evolve out Ricks College. It turned the junior college into a four-year institution, moved to year-round operations, and eliminated the costly athletic program essentially overnight. As we discuss later, if anything, Netflix has moved *too fast* to streaming.

We have long been proponents of the value of testing and adjusting, and certainly the newer efforts that will constitute transformation B will benefit from disciplined experimentation. But remember, transformation A is a different way to deliver against a broad market need that has already been validated. Of course, you should use pilots as ways to fine-tune full-scale launch plans and to further build organizational alignment, but once you align on a clear view of transformation A, you need to execute quickly, and execute comprehensively. Any other approach creates the opportunity for compromise and backsliding.

This isn't a knee-deep execution book, but examples of organizations that have transformed their business model have some common elements. First, almost always you see heavy, hands-on involvement by top-level executives. One theme that recurs throughout *Dual Transformation* is that the sets of activities we describe are not ones that you can fully devolve to the depths of the organization. After all, in most cases the biggest obstacle is the legacy organization itself. Instead, the top executives must stand ready to arbitrate conflicts between the old and new business models and ensure that standard operating procedures don't unintentionally derail efforts. The work is emotionally taxing, especially if you're in a circumstance that requires executing deep cost cuts (chapter 8 goes into detail about the crises that leaders can expect to encounter along the journey of transformation).

Another common element is bringing in special-purpose talent. By definition, people who have progressed through an organization have developed mastery of yesterday's model. Although smart people can no doubt learn about new approaches, you can shorten the path to success by bringing in people who have already learned what is necessary to master transformation A.

Third, almost always, the kind of new business models that power transformation A require careful management of sales and distribution. The sales channel is the front end of the business spear, heavily shaping the target customer, price points, and more.

CHAPTER SUMMARY

The *Deseret News* went from providing commodity news to delivering unique content focused on faith and family. Adobe went from software sales to subscriptions. Netflix went from DVDs by mail to a streaming subscription service (with a second shift from purely distributing to also producing content). And BYU-Idaho avoided the research path to become a student-centered, teaching-focused university. In each case the organization served the same customer and delivered the same basic value. But the way in which it created, delivered, and captured the value changed.

Transformation A is all about the *how*. To succeed with transformation A, follow these steps.

1. Zero in on the defensible postdisruption job to be done.

2. Innovate your business model to deliver against the job.

3. Determine and monitor new metrics.

4. Implement aggressively.

3. Transformation B: Creating the New

There's no doubt that transformation A is difficult—so difficult that you might be tempted to stop there. But Schumpeter's gale of creative destruction is blowing, and even though the wall you built to bolster your core business will increase your resilience, transformation B creates the wind turbine to power the next wave of growth.

That is the great irony of disruption. The word itself tends to invoke fear among senior leaders. Heck, even saying it makes your mouth contort in uncomfortable ways. But history teaches us, again and again, that disruption is the greatest growth opportunity a company will ever see. The process of making the complicated simple or the expensive affordable always grows markets, even as it upends business models. Whereas transformation A is about confronting the innovator's dilemma, transformation B is about seizing the innovator's opportunity.

Consider the media industry. While traditional companies have for the most part struggled, the media industry has been a breeding ground for high-impact startups. For example, the following companies were founded after the disruptive shock of Netscape introducing its internet browser.

ALPHABET. When the company formerly known as Google was founded, it wasn't at all clear it was destined for greatness. (In 2015 the company refashioned itself into a conglomerate, formally separating its Google-branded search engine from its new growth businesses.) It wasn't the first, second, or even tenth company launched in the emerging search engine space. It was by one count the eighteenth.

Google's technology and approach were indeed compelling, but as late as 2001, analysts still wondered how the company would make money. That soon became clear. Google built a massively powerful business model based on advertising. It started by pairing advertisements with search terms, and auctioning those terms using its AdWords platform. Google then expanded its inventory by taking over the advertising of other publishers through its AdSense program. A range of innovations led the company's revenues and advertisements to soar. As of the writing of this book, Alphabet is worth almost a half-trillion dollars.

FACEBOOK. Similarly, when Mark Zuckerberg launched the first version of the social network in 2004, it looked as if he was a bit late to the party, with Myspace as the clearly established market leader. Zuckerberg started Facebook at Harvard and expanded it to the Ivy League schools and then to all schools before finally opening it to the public.

Media giant News Corp acquired Myspace for $580 million in 2005 and proceeded to bungle the acquisition, creating space for Facebook to surge past and establish a commanding lead. If Facebook were a country, it would be the world's largest, and by the end of 2016 it approached two billion users. The company deftly managed the transition from laptops to mobiles (mobile now constitutes the majority of its use and revenue). And it looks poised to continue to expand both organically and through acquisitions such as photo sharing network Instagram, messaging app WhatsApp, and virtual reality pioneer Oculus. A dozen years after its founding, Facebook stood as one of the ten most valuable companies in the world.

eBAY. eBay has one of the best origin stories of the past few decades, although, like many origin stories, the popular version isn't quite true. The story goes that founder Pierre Omidyar was looking to help his wife sell her Pez dispensers (a collectible plastic device that dishes out not particularly good candy), so he founded eBay. Although Omidyar has since admitted that the story was created largely for marketing purposes, there is no doubt that eBay's disruptive model of the online matching of buyers and sellers of all types of goods played a major role in disrupting the classifieds industry, creating a booming business that went from first-year revenues of $232,000 (everything big starts small) to $1 billion in only four years.

YAHOO. Yahoo's history often is told as a tale of opportunity lost—its core web business was eclipsed by Google before Yahoo was sold to Verizon for about $5 billion in 2016—but we should pay homage to this early, compelling search engine, which expanded to include a collection of news and information sites used by more than half a billion users. Could it have done more? Yes. But that's still an impressive accomplishment.

LINKEDIN. Whereas Facebook became the social network of choice to share personal news such as your latest baby pictures, LinkedIn dominates professional networking. In many parts of the world, instead of handing out cards people simply say, "Find me on LinkedIn." Founded by Reid Hoffman (who was part of the early team at PayPal, a disruptive online payments company), the LinkedIn network grew to more than 500 million active users by 2016. The company built a multipronged revenue model, including premium subscriptions, corporate programs to help with recruiting, and, of course, advertising. After a fierce bidding war, Microsoft bought LinkedIn for $26 billion in 2016.

TWITTER. Twitter's origin story is both interesting and true. Ev Williams and Biz Stone, both successful entrepreneurs, founded a company called Odeo, with the intent of helping people manage podcasts on their iPods. But then Apple built a feature into its software that obviated Odeo's approach, so the company needed to scrap its original plan and find something else to do. Jack Dorsey and a colleague hacked together a solution that allowed people to share short status updates, and Twitter was born. Twitter quickly became a platform for breaking news and direct perspectives from celebrities and athletes, amassing hundreds of millions of users. The company has had its ups and downs commercially, but its immediacy and rawness had transformational impact.

There are others, of course, such as InterActive Corp (worth about $6 billion as of this writing), which runs a collection of websites such

FIGURE 3-1

Transformation B

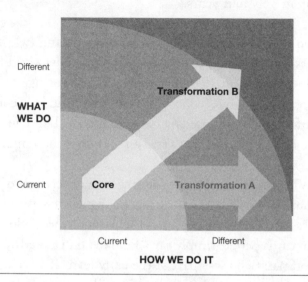

HOW WE DO IT

as Match.com, About.com, and The Daily Beast; travel recommendation site TripAdvisor (worth $10 billion); real estate platform Zillow ($1.5 billion); coupon disruptor Groupon ($3 billion); local recommendations engine Yelp ($2 billion), and listicle and algorithmic innovator BuzzFeed ($1.5 billion). As of late 2016, the dozen companies here had created almost $1 trillion in market value.

Just because newspaper publishers *didn't* create these companies doesn't mean they *couldn't* have created them. In this chapter we go through three case studies of established organizations driving transformation B, finding new ways to solve different problems (see figure 3-1). We also describe three success factors, and we end by providing unsolicited advice about what Netflix could do next.

SingPost: From Mail Delivery to Logistics Services

Although disruption can often appear in subtle ways at the fringes of markets, it doesn't take a disruptive savant to see how the forces of disruption have affected mail delivery. After all, even though we communicate more than ever before, the number of people who write and mail letters is dwindling dramatically. Additionally, companies interested in shaving costs have shifted from printing physical invoices to sending electronic copies to consumers. And companies have learned that even though direct mailing campaigns for new credit cards remains effective, hypertargeted online campaigns work even better. In the United States, mail volume dropped from 206 billion pieces in 2004 to 155 billion in 2014, a decline of about 25 percent.

In the face of this shift, the legacy postal carrier in Singapore—Singapore Post, or SingPost for short—more than doubled its business from 2004 to 2014, from roughly SGD 375 million to SGD 820 million in revenue (roughly $300 million to $700 million). How did the company achieve this boom in revenues? SingPost has transformed itself from a mail carrier to a logistics and e-commerce fulfillment service provider.

The company's history traces back more than 150 years. In 1967, it became an independent organization called the Singapore Postal Service Department and was absorbed into the Telecommunications Authority in 1982. In 1992, that authority split into a regulator (Infocomm Development Authority) and an operator (Singapore Telecommunications, or Singtel), with SingPost as its wholly owned subsidiary. In 2003, Singtel spun off SingPost as an independent business, retaining 31 percent of its shares. As of this writing, Singtel's ownership share has dwindled to 23 percent.

Beyond having to deal with general trends driving down so-called snail mail, SingPost also confronted the challenge of the 2007 expiry of its exclusive licenses for receiving, collecting, and delivering postcards, which constituted a significant portion of its business.

After its IPO, SingPost diversified its core business by introducing bill payment services at post offices (2005), building a direct mail business (2007), and offering mail room management and other business-process outsourcing solutions for small businesses (capabilities tied to its 2009 acquisition of Quantum Solutions, described below). To appeal to younger consumers, in 2010 it launched a business called KPO in the city's tourism and shopping belt, integrating a trendy pub and café that is open at night and on weekends. In 2010, then CEO Wilson Tan said, "There will be times where we must be prepared to cut off things that have been good for us in the past, but may no longer be relevant today . . . it's better to shift gears and move on."

By streamlining and strengthening its historical core business, Sing-Post was able to grow revenue from mail delivery by more than one-third between 2004 and 2013. But it was clear to management that the company had bigger growth potential and that finding new avenues to grow would be critical to ensure the enterprise's long-term viability.

Like any postal carrier SingPost had developed strong logistics and operational capabilities. After all, it processes millions of pieces of mail every day and operates more than fifty post offices across the country. Almost all letters are delivered across the island in a single day. With e-commerce growing regionally, the company decided to develop a suite of services to help merchants handle the operational challenges of doing business online, such as warehousing, storage, building and maintaining websites, and digital marketing. It created offerings such as vPost, which helps consumers obtain items purchased from global e-commerce sites without incurring backbreaking shipping charges; a remittance service helps foreign workers move money to their home countries.

The pursuit of new growth accelerated in 2009 with the acquisition of Quantum Solutions, which provided logistics and e-fulfillment services in ten countries. Two years later SingPost publicly announced a program called "ready for the future" to accelerate its strategic transformation, proclaiming a vision to become the regional leader in e-commerce logistics. As Wolfgang Baier, who became CEO in 2011 (and served until 2016), noted, "I painted out a scenario to show what would happen, with the current focus and current effort (which is already quite a lot), to our business, if we apply the prevailing market forces over a three- to five-year horizon. And it proved to be a very shocking picture . . . That was a real wake-up call—that we really need to do something. We needed to accelerate our transformation."

By mixing organic investments—including a S$182 million ($140 million) commitment to build an e-commerce logistics hub in Singapore—with targeted acquisitions, SingPost saw its new offerings constitute almost half of its business by 2014. One sign of its progress was the 2015 decision by Chinese e-commerce powerhouse Alibaba Group to invest S$312.5 million to take a 10.35 percent stake in SingPost and explore further opportunities to build a joint venture related to global e-commerce.

The ride hasn't been perfectly smooth. After winning the Best Chief Executive Officer award from Singapore Corporate Awards, Baier surprisingly announced his resignation in late 2015. In April 2016, Board Chair Lim Ho Kee stepped down after his hand-picked successor declined the job. Questions began to emerge about how SingPost was handling the goodwill from its acquisitions. Simon Israel, who had served as chair of SingPost's former owner Singtel since 2011, took over as SingPost's board chair in mid-2016. He promised to bring greater transparency while continuing SingPost's transformation, which he called "strategically sound."

Amazon: From Retailer to Cloud Computing Leader

In *Seizing the White Space*, coauthor Mark Johnson describes how Amazon.com is built to transform. The company's innovation efforts, spearheaded by founder Jeff Bezos, are relentless. In *Lead and Disrupt*, academics Charles O'Reilly III and Michael Tushman detail how Amazon's first twenty-one years of existence (from 1994 to 2015) featured twenty-five significant innovations. Many of these, such as Amazon Prime (free shipping for members) and customer reviews, fit within the rubric of transformation A, part of Amazon's continual transformation from a retailer of books to achieve its vision of the world's most customer-centered retailer. Other innovations push Amazon in new, disruptive directions.

Perhaps the company's most notable transformation B effort is the creation of Amazon Web Services (AWS), which has become the leading provider of cloud computing services. Imagine going back to 2005, when Amazon commissioned the work that ultimately spawned AWS, and predicting that a decade later the company would be the dominant market leader. People would have laughed.

AWS began as an effort led by programmer John Dalzell to accelerate internal IT projects. The idea involved breaking systems into bite-sized blocks and using open source software to build a service that made it easy for software developers to run any solution on the Amazon servers. Bezos tasked Andy Jassy, who had previously spent eighteen months as Bezos's first official "shadow" (a development role that exposes up-and-coming executives to senior leaders), with developing AWS into a commercial business. Jassy wrote a six-page memo (a standard tool Amazon uses in place of dense PowerPoint slides to describe ideas) that made the case that AWS could "enable developers and companies to use Web services to build sophisticated and scalable applications." AWS essentially allows companies to rent, rather than purchase, IT services. Initial customers were smaller companies that couldn't afford proprietary hardware, but large companies quickly found the speed and flexibility of the service appealing. The potential impact of AWS wasn't obvious to everyone. As O'Reilly and Tushman note, "When John Doerr of Kleiner Perkins, an Amazon board member, learned of this effort, he wasn't happy, seeing this as a distraction. But Bezos ignored him, believing that Amazon had a natural cost advantage in this trillion-dollar market."

Of course, Bezos turned out to be right. A report in April 2016 showed that Amazon had about 30 percent of the fragmented market for cloud infrastructure services, outpacing the combined share of Microsoft, IBM, and Alphabet. While prices for basic connectivity decreased rapidly, Amazon developed and deployed a wide range of high-margin, value-added services. In the second quarter of 2016, Amazon reported almost $3 billion in revenue for AWS, with 20 percent operating margins. AWS is beloved by entrepreneurs, because it allows them to very quickly scale up their businesses. And increasingly it plays a mission-critical role within large enterprises. Netflix, for example, uses AWS for the streaming service described in chapter 2, and the Central Intelligence Agency famously became a customer in 2014.

AWS is a clear example of transformation B in action. It solves a fundamentally different problem from the one addressed by Amazon's core business. It features a fundamentally different business model. It clearly sprang from, and therefore is related to, that core, but moving in a different direction has allowed Amazon to create an impressive growth engine that has the potential to be as big as its current core business.

More generally, an appropriately expansive view of its core business has been a key to Amazon's success over the past two decades. If Amazon had defined itself by the products it sold, it never would have expanded to cloud services, digital publishing, and streaming content. Similarly, if it had confined itself to its current competencies, it would not have pushed into new markets. Bezos has said that the key is to have a relentless focus on the customer and to balance innovation efforts between improving today and creating tomorrow.

"If you want to really continually revitalize the service you provide the customer, you can't stop at 'What are we good at?'" he told us. "You have to ask, 'What do our customers need and want?' And no matter how hard it is, you better get good at those things."

Higher Education: From Integrated Campus Educators to Online Skill Builders

Along many dimensions, higher education seems to be on an unstoppable growth tear over the past few decades. Demand seems impossible to satiate. There seems to be no ceiling to what people will pay to get a coveted degree. Yet many pundits view the higher education system in the United States as being on the brink of crisis. Many of the world's top-ranked universities call the United States home, but spiraling costs place these schools out of the reach of many students or require them to take on crushing debt.

Some of the cost increases relate to research or overall physical plant upgrades, and others involve an escalating competition in campus amenities. Just as one school touts "workout facilities with climbing walls and 'lazy rivers,'" another highlights a residence hall with a "2,100-gallon aquarium, a relaxation room with futuristic 'spherical nap pods,' big-screen televisions, and more." It's little wonder that by 2015, aggregate student loan debt in the United States exceeded $1 trillion. Student outcomes have not matched cost increases, and this means that the return on investment in education is decreasing. In 2013, disruption guru Clayton Christensen predicted that 50 percent of universities could fail over the next fifteen years.

In parallel, the rise of high-speed networks, the improvement of video compression technologies, and the emergence of new delivery mechanisms raise the possibility of systemwide disruptions to the way education is delivered. There will always be people who go to two- or four-year universities to have an impossible-to-replicate life experience where they meet new people and discover their passions. And the clustering of high-quality educators on a physical campus will make campuses ideal locations for students to coalesce to receive guidance for some period of time. But new online models are emerging at a breakneck pace.

Transformation at Arizona State University

In the face of these challenges, a small number of schools are pioneering powerful new growth strategies that allow them to effectively and affordably educate broader populations of students. One example is Arizona State University. Upon becoming ASU president in 2002, Michael Crow launched a comprehensive transformation program. Historically a school more known for its laid-back atmosphere than its academics, ASU quadrupled its research investment (while holding constant the size of the faculty), with a specific focus on areas where ASU had location-based advantages, such as water and resource management and solar technologies.

By 2016 the National Science Foundation reported that ASU had soared from eighty-fourth in 2005 to forty-ninth in the ranking of research expenditures in more than six hundred US universities between 2005 and 2014. In parallel, ASU used technology to fundamentally transform its traditional campus-based education program. For example, in 2007 it launched eAdvsior, a sophisticated data-driven advising platform and has created assorted partnerships with innovative companies like Knewton, a leading education data analytics company, and Pearson, the top provider of education technology platforms.

While ASU was working on these efforts, a number of leading universities began edging online, largely by providing access to lectures from famous professors online in so-called massive online open courses. Then ASU did something very different. In 2009 it launched ASU EdPlus, a separate operating unit focused on providing custom-created degree programs online. Using a platform originally created to allow campus-based students to augment courses with online modules, EdPlus began offering fully accredited degrees online. From 2009 to 2016, EdPlus grew from four hundred students to more than twenty-six thousand.

In describing the different ways that ASU has grown, Crow does not distinguish between online and offline education. Rather, he describes how technology plays a different role in four "realms" of education. The first is on-campus learning, enhanced by more than a hundred digital partners. The second is what Crow calls "digital immersion, enhanced by online technology" where ASU takes the "same faculty, their research material, their labs, our library, every mission we have taken, every event that we have, and we have found a way to technologically link it to into 140 degree programs." The third realm is "full digital immersion," using "open-scale technology to remove structures around the size of the class." The first project in this realm is a global freshman academy with about two hundred thousand students. Finally, the fourth realm is "education through exploration" that blurs the line between game playing and education. "You've played games like SimCity, SimAnt, and Spore, right?" Crow says. "Imagine playing a game that by the end of it you have mastered college chemistry, college biology, and college physics."

ASU has also used technology to target nontraditional students that would never consider touching foot on its traditional campus. For example, in 2014 it announced a deal with Starbucks that allowed Starbucks baristas to receive degrees through the program for free. By 2025 Starbucks expects to provide tuition support for twenty-five thousand employees to use the program to receive degrees.

"There is a whole movement among some major American corporations into conscious capitalism, where capitalists that are creating wealth also advance human capital and advance and maintain natural capital," Crow says. "Starbucks is one of the companies that wants to advance human capital for their corporation and their communities. We said we would produce twenty-five thousand college graduates from their American employees that started but didn't finish university. Six thousand of those will graduate from our online programs with no costs. This is growing as we speak. In fact, half the people who went to college who are alive have no degrees because they didn't finish their program."

Innovation at BYU-Idaho

Similarly, in 2006 then BYU-Idaho president Kim Clark invited coauthor Clark Gilbert to launch an online learning arm. Between 2006 and 2009 Gilbert's team built an online learning organization that allowed students to learn targeted skills and earn certificates and associate degrees, while on-campus education continued to focus on providing bachelor's degrees.

In 2009 BYU-Idaho launched Pathway, a one-year program to prepare students for college. It taught students how to study, write cogent resumes, and manage family finances. It augmented interactive, cohort-based online courses with face-to-face small group gatherings all around the world. The program started with fifty students in three pilot locations. By 2016, it reached tens of thousands of students in four hundred locations around the world. In total, BYU-Idaho's online degree programs reached thirty-five thousand students by 2016, exceeding the thirty thousand students who attend its traditional residential campus.

Disruptive Education at Southern New Hampshire

Southern New Hampshire University serves as the East Coast representative in the small cadre of schools pushing education in new, disruptive directions. Under the guidance of President Paul LeBlanc, SNHU has aggressively expanded the school's online offerings to the point that what once was a fringe offering now constitutes the school's true core.

SNHU founded its online program in 1995, and it slowly grew over the next decade. Over the ensuing decade, it exploded. By 2014, some 80 percent of SNHU's students are fully online, with fewer than 5 percent on campus full-time. In 2014 SNHU launched College for America, a complementary online institution that focuses on skill building, with students advancing by demonstrating capabilities and competencies on specific projects.

The three schools profiled here constitute a small fraction of the expansive US higher education apparatus, but they demonstrate the power of creating new growth by finding new ways to serve customers who are not adequately served by the core offering.

Keys to Transformation B Success

The examples in this chapter, and indeed in this book, all involve large companies. You might think that weird. After all, disruption is a startup game. Right?

Well, not entirely. A few years ago, we built a database highlighting all the major disruptive developments. From 1950 to 1980, disruption was indeed dominated by startups. In fact, startups launched about 85 percent of disruptions during that period. In the past few years, however, momentum has shifted, with roughly 40 percent of disruptions launched since 2000 driven by large companies.

What explains the change? One plausible explanation is that the more the idea of disruption is documented and the more we understand the markers of disruptive change and how to manage it internally, the more that big companies have at least a fighting chance.

Transformation B is about finding a new way to solve a different problem. Success therefore comes from identifying problems that the target customer historically has wanted to solve but can't, iteratively fine-tuning the business model to best the competition, and using partnerships, acquisitions, and external hires to accelerate the development of capabilities required to win against a new competitive set.

Identify Constrained Markets

The reason disruption always grows markets is that making the complicated simple or the expensive affordable breaks constraints that historically bottled up markets. Spotting a transformation B opportunity requires finding a problem that a significant group of customers *wants* to solve but can't because it lacks specialized skills, sufficient wealth, or the time to go to inconvenient, inaccessible locations.

Higher education is a clear example of a constrained market. ASU, BYU-Idaho, and SNHU historically educated only those people who could afford to pay tuition and who had the time to come to a centralized location. Online learning allows these providers to make education much more accessible and affordable.

Another clear example of a constrained market is health care. There are some health conditions that individuals can self-diagnose and manage, but in many cases we must seek help from someone with specialized skills. Training alone is insufficient, because health care professionals rely on sophisticated tests to determine how best to intervene. Family physicians (formerly called general practitioners) are reasonably widely dispersed in most mature markets, but seeing a generalist can involve frustrating waits followed by lightning-fast encounters. Specialists are even harder to access, because they are time pressed and tend to cluster in a handful of centralized facilities.

Of course, technology is changing much of this. Many patients now come to a consultation armed with advice from what physicians derisively call "Dr. Google." Websites such as patientslikeme.com allow individuals to share unorthodox ways to address difficult-to-treat conditions. As wireless solutions become truly ubiquitous and processing power increases, embedded and wearable technologies will increasingly allow self-diagnosis and management.

In short, health care is on the brink of systemwide disruption as technological developments obliterate barriers that historically constrained the market. The opportunity for this kind of disruptive growth is immense, as is the need. People in the United States spend far more on health care than those in any other country, but the system doesn't produce great outcomes; nor is patient satisfaction high. Pulling health care into lower-cost locations lowers system costs while potentially increasing patient satisfaction by increasing convenience.

Walgreens is one company seeking to realize the opportunity this disruption creates. Charles R. Walgreen Sr. opened his first store in 1901. It measured a mere fifty feet by twenty feet. Between 1901 and 1984, Walgreens grew to one thousand stores. It accelerated its expansion, opening its six-thousandth store in 1996.

Walgreens's aggressive expansion strategy helped the company, which mixes sales of prescription and over-the-counter medications with snacks and household care items, grow from a midsized company to one of the fifty biggest companies in the United States over four decades. As a result, more than 75 percent of Americans live within a five-mile radius of a Walgreens, so future growth required a different approach. Further, the rise of online shopping opened the door to an entirely new class of competitors. Certainly Walgreens could grow by finding ways to expand beyond its historical home market. In 2012 Walgreens purchased 45 percent of Switzerland-based Alliance Boots, which operates in more than two dozen countries, fully merging with the company in 2014. But what other paths to growth could it chart?

Beginning in 2009 under the leadership of CEO Gregory Wasson, the company formed a strategy encapsulated by its tag line "At the corner of happy and healthy." The company's transformation A strategy involved, among other things, reimagining the role of its twenty-seven thousand pharmacists. Typically, pharmacists focused on behind-the-scenes tasks of processing paperwork, dealing with insurance, and dispensing drugs. With the help of Innosight and IDEO, a leading design company, Walgreens removed barriers between pharmacists and patients by creating semiprivate spaces to facilitate direct discussion. Patients received better treatment, leading to a higher number of repeat visits, and the pharmacists' job satisfaction went up.

Transformation B involved transforming Walgreens stores into the front line of defense for the beleaguered US health care industry. What does Walgreens have that few other companies have? More than eight thousand stores, where people come to fill prescriptions and buy other sundry items. That physical infrastructure could also be used to address simple, everyday conditions that clog up primary care offices, such as strep throat, flu shots, and ear infections. Also in scope were patients suffering from chronic conditions, such as high blood pressure or diabetes, that needed routine monitoring and face-to-face consultations. Now Walgreens has four hundred clinics staffed by trained professionals that serve as an affordable, effective way to provide basic health care.

Not every move made by Walgreens has worked. Notably, a partnership with Theranos—a hotly hyped startup that purported to do single-blood-drop diagnostics radically faster and cheaper than historical market leaders—fizzled. But Walgreens will no doubt continue to explore multiple paths to pull health care from hospitals and the home to its retail locations.

Identify Consumption Barriers

The media examples in the beginning of this chapter also demonstrate the power of overcoming consumption barriers. Although most people think of Google as a search engine, its core business is advertising. As mentioned earlier, its AdWords program allows companies to bid on keywords and tie advertisements to users' searches using those keywords. Google's do-it-yourself auction model opened advertising to small businesses that historically found newspaper or television advertising to be too complicated or expensive. eBay looked at the time-consuming task of finding rare collectibles and made it as easy as clicking a button. How did we share news about ourselves before Facebook? We made a succession of telephone calls, took pictures, developed them, and shared them, or, in more recent years, sent out email blasts. In each case, making the complicated simple and the expensive affordable dramatically increased consumption.

Our book *The Innovator's Guide to Growth* suggests a range of analysis you can use to identify barriers to consumption. Consider, for example, creating the following.

- A *consumption pyramid*, which looks at consumption by wealth or size of business to highlight disproportionate spending by large businesses or wealthy households. When spending is concentrated among a small number of purchasers, it suggests opportunities to grow markets through simplification.

- A *consumption chain* of a good or service, which shows the steps the end customer takes to obtain a product or service, revealing where expertise is required to solve a problem. Any opportunity to take a link out of a chain has the potential to drive new growth.

- A *consumption map*, which shows where and when consumption happens. When consumption is confined to narrow parts of the day or can take place only in specific locations, disruptors can drive growth by expanding accessibility.

Beware Illusionary Nonconsumption

One word of advice when you're looking for nonconsumption. Sometimes, the real reason people don't consume is that they don't care very much about the problem, or they have figured out a perfectly adequate solution. In other words, not all "white spaces" want to be filled, and some "blue oceans" are crystal clear for a reason.

We learned this lesson the hard way when we tried to build a business called ChoiceMed. If you walk into a Singaporean hospital—as coauthor Scott Anthony did in August 2011 to welcome his third child to the world—you are immediately struck by its high quality. The doctors have been to some of the best schools in the world. The hospitals are clean and have modern medical equipment. Yet, somehow, Singapore is able to do something miraculous. Whereas the United States spends almost 20 percent of its gross domestic product on health care, Singapore spends about 5 percent, and the average Singaporean lives eight years longer than the average American.

The idea of ChoiceMed was to find people in the United States who were undergoing an elective procedure, such as a knee or hip replacement, fly them to Singapore, have the procedure done, put them up in a six-star hotel to recuperate, and fly them back to the United States—all the while saving thousands of dollars. A great idea, right? Prospective customers told us they thought so, promising to sign up in droves. Buoyed by positive feedback, we raised a few hundred thousand dollars and began to work in earnest to get our first paying customers. We went to "prospect rich" environments—retirement communities in Florida—to run seminars.

The result? Nobody showed up. It turned out that when they were faced with the very real prospect of getting on a thin metal tube and flying almost ten thousand miles to a place that, honestly, most of them had never heard of, the stated interest dissipated.

The best predictor of future behavior is past behavior. If people are spending significant time and money trying to solve a problem, that's a good signal they will welcome cheaper or more accessible solutions. If they *say* the problem matters to them but their behavior shows otherwise, you can expect to struggle.

Iteratively Develop the Business Model

Chapter 2 recommends executing transformation A aggressively. Transformation B, on the other hand, is best done through more of an iterative, test-and-learn approach. What's the difference? Remember, in transformation A the *what* doesn't change materially. You know there is a market; you are changing only the way you approach it. For transformation B, both the *what* and the *how* are changing. With two variables in play, it makes sense to follow a more prudent path to commercialization.

Consider the approach Xerox took to develop its services arm. It started in 2001 when Xerox agreed to invest $100 million to set up

Xerox Global Services (XGS). Naturally, XGS started by focusing on document management. Xerox's far-flung salesforce and powerful brand allowed it to immediately access senior leaders at significant corporations, and it won meaningful deals with organizations such as health care company Baxter International. Under the leadership of Jim Joyce, who came to Xerox when the company acquired his small IT services company, XGS began acquiring small companies to drive further process automation.

Early, small-scale successes emboldened Xerox to make a big bet, acquiring Affiliated Computer Services (ACS) for more than $6 billion in 2009. Overnight, XGS went from a relatively minor piece of Xerox's total business to a $3 billion business with more than eighty thousand employees. Xerox's R&D prowess, along with its powerful brand, convinced companies like P&G and Dow Chemical to sign long-term deals that allowed them access to XGS's leading-edge solutions.

Note that Xerox didn't start by splashing out billions on ACS. Rather, it ran a series of small experiments in the market to validate that there was an opportunity in the services space. Many of these experiments didn't work, but enough of them did to give Xerox confidence that it was moving in the right direction. It had validated the *what* and narrowed in on a sustainable *how*. The ACS acquisition, then, dramatically accelerated its growth.

It is critical to discover this path by action and not by analysis. Every idea to create new growth is partially right and partially wrong. The problem is that you don't know which part is which. The default way that most large companies confront this problem is to seek truth through analysis. They interview potential customers, create detailed forecasts, interview experts, and hold internal discussions to build alignment. Finally, they launch what they think is a perfect plan. But there's no such thing. Inevitably, they learn a life lesson taught by the great American philosopher, actor, and occasional boxer Mike Tyson, who once said, "Everybody has a plan, until they get punched in the face." The innovator receives the punch when the plan that looked so good on paper ends up resting on shaky assumptions. Indeed, no business plan survives first contact with the marketplace.

Successful innovators smartly manage risk through disciplined experimentation. Before the Wright brothers built a plane, they flew a kite. The great thing about kites is that, when they crash, no one gets hurt. To optimize the kite, the Wrights built a simple wind tunnel, which made it much easier to run experiments. Fortunately, the past decade has concurrently seen an explosion of tools to help design and execute experiments and a rapid decline in the cost of these experiments. Books like Steve Blank's *Four Steps to the Epiphany*, Eric Ries's *The Lean Startup*, and coauthor Scott Anthony's *The First Mile* provide practical toolkits to systematically de-risk an idea. The basic idea behind all these books is to apply the scientific method to strategic uncertainty.

The First Mile uses two acronyms to explain the process. The first is DEFT, which stands for document, evaluate, focus, and test. First, document your idea thoroughly to make sure you have thought through all of its components. Evaluate it via multiple lenses to identify uncertainties and weak points. Focus on the most critical areas. Then test rigorously and adapt quickly.

The second acronym relates to the testing process. Whenever you innovate, you never can be sure about the assumptions on which your business rests. So, like a good scientist, you start with a hypothesis. Then design an experiment. Make sure the experiment has clear objectives (why you are running it and what you hope to learn). Even if you have no idea what the right answer is, make a prediction. Finally, execute in such a way that you can measure the prediction, such as running a so-called A/B test in which you vary a single factor. Again, you can never know for sure, but you can have HOPE: hypothesis, objective, prediction, and execution plan.

Part of the magic of doing this well is to reverse engineer a business. Instead of trying to assemble historical data and extrapolate into the future, you start by asserting what a good idea must look like. What must revenues be to be material? What level of net income moves the needle? What costs are therefore allowable to let the model hang together? Then you determine the assumptions that would need to be true for those answers to be feasible. Columbia professor Rita McGrath calls this *discovery-driven planning*, and, in our experience, it is one of the most powerful tools for successfully managing transformation B opportunities.

The approach feels familiar to any venture capitalist who knows that financial forecasts are only a bunch of guesses. As Gilbert and our former colleague Matt Eyring described in a 2010 *Harvard Business Review* article, innovators should address risks that have the highest impact on their business as soon as possible. The first focus should be on *deal killers,* which are binary make-or-break issues. Then there are *pivot points,* when answers have a big impact on multiple pieces of a business. For example, a business that sells to consumers is vastly different from one that sells to a national government; figuring out the commercialization path for an idea early is critical. Third on the list is what you might call *confidence boosters,* which don't have an outsized impact but build team members' confidence in the belief that they're moving in the right direction.

The notion of iterative development also fits with our general guidance to move *toward* white space but don't try to jump to it too fast. There are a number of cautionary case studies of companies struggling as they've tried to venture into markets that have a tenuous connection to their core business. Seek a stepping-stone or lily pad strategy: look for a starting point where you can keep a foot in today's world as you venture into a new space. The destination is a very different place, but the path to get there has a degree of coherence that minimizes its risk.

Accelerate Capability Development via Acquisitions and External Hires

Generally, a company pursuing transformation B needs to assess the new competitors it will encounter. If your competitive set isn't changing, after all, it suggests you aren't stretching far enough. For example, in its core retailing business, Amazon competes against other retailers, such as Walmart and Barnes & Noble. Its Amazon Web Services business has a completely different set of competitors, such as Infosys, Accenture, Microsoft, and IBM. It's easy to discount the challenges of moving into new markets with a different set of competitors, particularly in a disruptive circumstance, when many of the competitors will be fast-moving entrants. Triumphing over these new competitors requires humbly recognizing the limits of your current capabilities and aggressively closing critical capability gaps.

Of course, given an infinite amount of time you can develop new capabilities, but the accelerating innovator's clock simply suggests that acquisitions are likely to be a key success factor. Indeed, many examples of transformation B involve significant acquisitions or strategic partnerships. SingPost made several acquisitions and created a strategic relationship with Alibaba. Arizona State University partnered with Knewton, Pearson, and Starbucks. Xerox made a big bet on ACS.

Another example is Adobe. Recall that its transformation A involved shifting from packaged software to software subscriptions. Its transformation B was moving from software to marketing services. Its insight was that many core buyers of its software were in creative industries such as advertising. Adobe's role, however, was limited to the creation of an advertisement. The advertising industry involves so much more. In particular, technology has created the ability to fight against the old problem highlighted by retailer John Wanamaker's famous quip: "Half the money I spend on advertising is wasted; the trouble is I don't know which half." In 2009, Adobe purchased Omniture, a leading online marketing and web analytics business, and used it as the anchor of a suite of digital marketing solutions. Then it added other acquisitions, such as Day Software (in 2010) and Efficient Frontier (2011).

Depending on the size of your company or your transformation B ambitions, you might need to develop a capability to ingest a stream of new companies. Consider Apple. The company is famous for its insular approach to innovation, wherein it seeks to assert end-to-end control as much as it can. Between 2001 and 2010—as it introduced the iPod, iPhone, iPad, Apple TV, and its retail stores—the company made at least twenty-six acquisitions, including Quattro Wireless to rev up its advertising business; Siri to develop its voice recognition capabilities; and a variety of software companies to add to its product suite.

Outside hiring is another way to rapidly inject fresh capabilities. That's how Gilbert accelerated the growth of Deseret Digital's transformation B. Historically, the digital side of the newspaper simply replicated online the print version of the newspaper. Gilbert, along with Chris Lee, president of Deseret Digital, mixed a small number of staff-reported pieces with crowdsourced and curated pieces to develop a wide portfolio of digital sites. Some looked like traditional content websites. Others were much more community oriented, such as multilingual Facebook pages that housed FamilyShare, one of the largest global communities of mothers. To target these online audiences, the

Deseret team built demographic and behaviorally targeted advertising platforms that had no analogue in print.

Even more important, Deseret Digital diversified its revenue streams into digital marketplaces that were less ad dependent. These digital marketplaces, under their KSL.com brand, were ideally suited to capture the new revenue streams that were emerging online, such as daily deals (a la Groupon), job postings, and home and automobile listings. By the time Gilbert left in 2015, these digital transformations meant that Deseret Digital contributed more than half of Deseret Media's in-market combined net income, up from less than 20 percent in 2010.

When Gilbert was forming his digital team, he largely avoided people who grew up in the core business. Rather, he looked for people who "didn't come to work for a newspaper." For example, he hired people who had worked at companies like Yahoo, Omniture, AOL, and Overstock.com. These people weren't smarter or intrinsically more talented than Gilbert's core staff. They simply had developed grounded intuition in the new market. And while there remained continued pressure from dominant players such as Google and Facebook, who would you rather have competing: People who grew up selling print and TV ads or digital natives? One of Gilbert's mantras was, "A digital buyer needs a digital seller."

More generally, our advice is that transformation B should involve a careful blend of people we dub "aliens" (who will push you in a new direction) and "diplomats" (who will help negotiate bilateral relationships). First, the aliens. In 1962, Thomas Kuhn's classic *The Structure of Scientific Revolutions* highlighted what Kuhn dubbed *paradigm shifts*, which always came from outside the established orthodoxy. If you don't bring in aliens, it is unlikely that you'll be able to push the innovation frontier.

However, the diplomats—who can speak core and alien and can arbitrate differences between the two—also play a critical role. The magic of transformation B is that you borrow just enough from the core to create competitive advantage without crossing a line that opens the door to the innovator's dilemma (this is the focus of chapter 4). The savvy veteran—a person who knows the people to call to get things done, recognizes the unstated assumptions that lead to what looks like odd behavior to aliens, and knows how to influence critical executives—can help make this combination happen.

Team dynamics are important, and it goes without saying that you need to balance aliens and diplomats carefully. If you have too many aliens, you're likely to struggle to successfully interface with the core. If too many diplomats, you're unlikely to develop anything compelling, and you run the risk of playing politics rather than moving ideas forward.

What Could Netflix Do Next?

One hesitates to give unprompted advice to a company that has had as much success over the past two decades as Netflix. Yet looking at it through the lenses of this book, and as good a job as Netflix has done in transforming its current business, it seems to us that it has opportunities to layer on top a transformation B strategy to create growth in new markets.

What might that look like? In chapter 2 we say that the core job Netflix does for its customers relates to entertainment. As it has evolved its core business from DVDs to streaming media, it has developed the ability to seamlessly deliver online content and capture and analyze the revealed preferences of its customers. What new markets could Netflix pry open if it fused those capabilities with emerging disruptive technologies?

One possibility would be primary education (K–12 in the United States), an area of personal passion for founder, CEO, and chairman Reed Hastings. A decade ago we tried to build a business called Guaranteach. The theory was to address a fundamental gap in the education market: everyone learns differently, but it is very difficult to materially customize K–12 education. We created a platform where teachers could submit short videos teaching various subjects. We then had students go through a simple diagnostic test to identify their preferred learning style. Did they prefer pictures or words? Analogies or step-by-step instruction? We could then serve up a custom video to meet their needs. Although the theory was solid and we were able to get teachers to submit more than twenty thousand videos, we never cracked the code of a high-engagement platform. We sold the business to another provider in 2011.

What if Netflix rose to the challenge of delivering compelling educational experiences at scale, customized to the preferences of individuals? The efforts detailed by ASU, BYU-Idaho, and SNHU are having a significant impact, but compelling, customized education at scale still presents substantial opportunities. Why not Netflix? Remember the scene in *The Matrix* when Keanu Reeves's character, Neo, "plugs in" and learns how to fly a helicopter? In our view that capability is very likely to remain science fiction, but there will be ways to teach people what they need, when they need it, in a way that maximizes their ability to learn it. Education will increasingly move from something that is done at a specific point in people's lives to something that is truly perpetual.

Let's dream a little bigger. What if Netflix and IBM were to pair up to fundamentally disrupt health care? IBM's Watson platform is best known to many people for its appearance on (and domination of) the popular quiz show *Jeopardy*. But IBM is working hard to apply Watson's supercomputing brainpower to complex problems such as addressing difficult-to-diagnose health conditions. Imagine Netflix tuning its discovery and recommendation power to help individuals make all the day-to-day behavior modifications required to live healthier, happier lives?

Education and health care are massive, complex industries, and Netflix would need a serious dose of outside capabilities to succeed in either one. But the rewards could be massive.

CHAPTER SUMMARY

SingPost went from basic mail delivery to logistics and e-commerce solutions. Deseret Digital went from an online replica of the print newspaper to a collection of communities and marketplaces. Amazon.com went from a retailer to an IT services company. Arizona State University went from a campus educator to an online juggernaut. Adobe went from software to marketing solutions. Each company created a dynamic new growth business by taking advantage of underlying disruptive trends to solve a distinct but related problem in a distinct but related way. To successfully drive transformation B, remember to do three things:

1. Identify constrained markets.

2. Iteratively develop the business model to serve those markets.

3. Use partnerships, acquisitions, and new hires to succeed against a new competitive set.

4. The Capabilities Link between A and B

What career should you choose if you want to change the world? Over the past few years, we've presented five options to almost five thousand people around the world. The majority, about 35 percent, choose starting a company. The next most popular answer is becoming a teacher, drawing 30 percent of the vote. About 20 percent think that the best path is to join a not-for-profit. Another 10 percent believe that working for the public sector is the route to impact (interestingly, this holds relatively constant across cultures). There's only 5 percent left. What haven't we said?

Joining an established company.

Indeed, the prevailing view is that big companies are where innovation goes to die. In the 1980s, Richard N. Foster (a long-time McKinsey & Company director who served on Innosight's board for seven years and helped to develop some of the ideas described in this book) released *Innovation: The Attacker's Advantage*. A cover note promises that the book will describe "why leading companies abruptly lose their markets to new competitors." In the 1990s, Innosight cofounder Clayton Christensen published *The Innovator's Dilemma*, whose cover proclaims that the book will show readers how "new technologies cause great companies to fail." The titles grow more ominous over time. In 2013, Dave Ulmer drew on his experience at several large companies to detail *The Innovator's Extinction*. His cover blurb? "How natural selection and best intentions will drive your company into the grave."

Another voice is that of Paul Graham, the founder of Y Combinator, a leading incubator that helped spur Dropbox, Airbnb, and hundreds of other companies. Graham perhaps summed up the zeitgeist best when he said, "Running a startup is like being punched in the face repeatedly, but working for a large company is like being waterboarded."

Coauthor Scott Anthony believed all this when he packed up his family and moved them to Singapore in 2010. He didn't come to Singapore to expand Innosight's consulting operations to Southeast Asia (although that's what he ended up doing). Rather, he "retired" from consulting and shifted his eyes to Innosight Ventures, a separate company that incubated and invested in startup companies. That's what you do if you want to change the world, right? You search for what the world has termed *unicorns:* privately held companies worth more than $1 billion.

A Tale of Two "Startups"

In October 2010, Anthony had a pair of contrasting experiences that showed him he had framed the issue incorrectly and that impact came from seeking a different beast: a big company that combined assets of scale and entrepreneurial behavior to drive massive impact.

The first experience was hearing a pitch by a couple of young kids for a business called Plunify. The basic idea was to democratize the tools used by programmers of field-programmable gate arrays. Sold yet? It turns out it is a big market, with a couple of billion-dollar-plus companies that looked ripe for disruption. The finer details of Plunify aren't important. What matters is that it was the first time Anthony recalls entrepreneurs pitching for funding not with a business *plan*, but with a *business*. What's the difference? A business plan is words, pictures, and spreadsheets. A business has a functioning website, customers, and revenues. The Plunify team had gotten its business off the ground essentially using nothing more than their parents' credit cards.

Then a few weeks later, Anthony found himself in Durgapur, a small city nestled in the eastern part of India. He was visiting the pilot project of an idea that an Innosight consulting team had cocreated with Medtronic, the world's largest independent medical device manufacturer. Medtronic had asked Innosight for help with its pacemaker business in India. Now by all accounts, India should have been a leading market for Medtronic. After all, its people have more heart disease than those of any other country. A pacemaker—a small, implantable device that regulates the flow of electricity to the heart—would benefit millions of Indians. Yet Medtronic struggled in the market. It doesn't take a health care expert to understand why. The majority of Indians pay for pacemakers out of their own pockets, and the device's $1,000 price point rendered it unaffordable for most potential customers. But constraints to growth went beyond the product itself. The primary care market in India is stretched to capacity, meaning many patients who might have benefited from a pacemaker didn't even know they needed it.

Over time, Medtronic could address the affordability problem with a radically cheaper pacemaker, but that would take years, if not decades. So the team designed a novel business model to increase the pacemaker's accessibility and affordability. The business model, called Healthy Heart for All, included direct-to-consumer marketing through billboards and a website; diagnostic camps, in which a small team would go to a village and diagnose hundreds of people in an afternoon; consultative work with hospitals to streamline the implantation process and make it more affordable; and, most critically, the world's first loan program for an implantable medical device. Think about that for a second. If you take out a loan for a car and you don't pay it, the lender takes back the car. If you take out a loan for a device that gets implanted in your chest and you don't pay it, well, repossession presents obvious challenges. But by applying principles that had enabled microlenders like Grameen Bank to serve previously unserved low-income consumers, Medtronic was able to address this challenge. As of this writing, the program has touched tens of thousands of patients, with hundreds of loans provided to lower-income patients and almost no defaults.

The Benefit of Incumbency

At first glance, the Plunify story seems to confirm the hopelessness of big company innovation. After all, how can big companies compete if kids can use cloud solutions, do-it-yourself tools, and online marketplaces to launch businesses for almost nothing? But wait. If you had a glance at the Plunify website in its early days, what would stop you from copying it? You, too, could access the cloud solutions, do-it-yourself tools, and online marketplaces. And in its embryonic stage Plunify would struggle to differentiate itself against competitors.

It's never been easier to *start* a business, but that means it also has never been easier to *replicate* one, and arguably that makes it harder than ever to effectively *scale* one. Despite falling costs, startups are spending more than they ever have before, because the second a startup gets a whiff of success, the race is on. Sure, enduring companies can emerge from this fierce competition, but it is brutally hard. And, ironically enough, it means startup companies increasingly face the exact kinds of short-term pressures that make innovation so hard for big companies.

Contrast Plunify with Healthy Heart for All. Even if we shared every single detail of what Medtronic did, you couldn't hope to copy it, because Medtronic has things you don't have. These include relationships with doctors and hospitals in India, regulatory clearance, existing technology, a robust balance sheet to back the loan program, an understanding of local markets, and more.

This is the incumbent's opportunity: drive growth by combining unique, difficult-to-replicate assets with just enough entrepreneurism. It's the corporate equivalent of Muhammad Ali's "Float like a butterfly, sting like a bee": the might of the megacompany and the energy of the entrepreneur.

Christensen has famously noted that the only way for incumbents to succeed with disruption is by creating a separate organization having substantial freedom. We agree. But it's not easy. You could of course create a spin-off company with completely separate staff, systems, and structures. But if you are going that far, why not simply give the capital to a venture capital firm to invest? In reality almost any new growth businesses launched by an established company feature some point of interface between today and tomorrow or, in the language of this book, transformation A and transformation B.

There is widespread agreement about the need to separate and carefully manage overlap between these areas, but anyone who has been through the process knows that the devil is truly in the details. We've done our share of exorcisms as advisers to companies and actively participating CEOs and board members. We share that experience in this chapter by detailing the "C" of the transformation equation: the capabilities link that connects transformation A and transformation B and flips the innovator's dilemma into the innovator's opportunity.

Whenever we describe the idea of dual transformation to companies, we observe that the idea of transformation A and B sticks and is adopted as a language system quickly. The "C" in the transformation equation, which is admittedly subtler and harder to explain, doesn't stick as well. That's unfortunate, because that link is actually the most important part of successfully driving dual transformation. Dual transformation is not about unrelated diversification. Rather, it is about thoughtful, logical expansion into markets that historically were difficult to serve, if not nonexistent.

The challenge of the capabilities link is that it requires striking a careful balance. If you link A and B too tightly, the gravitational pull of today's business means you end up replicating today versus creating tomorrow. If you keep A and B too separate, you create an undernourished orphan that lacks the ability to survive in a tough world. If you strike the balance correctly, you create an unfair advantage—one that you need to win in a fiercely competitive world.

There are three keys to seeing what would otherwise be invisible and doing what would otherwise feel impossible. First, stock the link selectively with capabilities that will truly give you an unfair advantage over current and potential competitors (versus capabilities that either aren't unique or aren't meaningful). Second, manage interfaces strategically by using structured mechanisms such as clear decision rules or a formal "exchange team" (discussed a bit later). Finally, actively arbitrate between A and B, standing ready as a leader to demonstrate a strong bias toward transformation B.

Stocking the Link Selectively

One metaphor that helps explain the capabilities link is to see it as an *air lock* in a spacecraft or a submarine: a passageway between the exterior doors. When you exit the craft, you first enter the air lock and close the door behind you. You select any equipment you need and then exit the ship. When you come back you replace the equipment, close the door to the outside, disinfect, and only then carefully reenter the ship. The air lock creates a safe space to trap contagions, water, or the suction power of a space vacuum from damaging the ship.

The constrained space on a ship places a premium on carefully choosing the equipment that stocks the air lock. Similarly, you should carefully choose the organizational capabilities that you will stock in your capabilities link. One simple question guides this selection: what truly gives you a competitive advantage in driving transformation B?

For example, as coauthor Clark Gilbert started to pursue the creation of digital platforms for Deseret Media, there were three capabilities that mattered to him. First, a subset of the content produced by traditional journalists could be repurposed for his digital audiences. Second, Deseret's corporate brand and its connection to the organization's mission helped reach consumers and advertisers. Third, data about customers, and their reading and purchasing behavior, could help arm the special-purpose digital salesforce Deseret created.

The fundamental mistake organizations make is to borrow capabilities because they are there and appear to be free. If a capability is not going to create real competitive advantage, be careful. It's entirely possible that the capability in the core will not help you win in transformation B. It is also possible that the capability from A may actually *hurt* your efforts in B. For example, why didn't Deseret simply use the existing salesforce to sell digital advertising? One challenge was the different economic model. The best sales rep for traditional media would flog full-page, color advertisements that might sell for tens of thousands of dollars to a handful of traditional advertisers. In contrast, hitting an online target might mean finding hundreds if not thousands of advertisers willing to pay hundreds of dollars for an ad.

That's a no-win situation. If you shift incentives away from your current business, you hasten its decline and threaten investment-supporting profits. If you don't shift attention away from your current business, you miss meaningfully participating in tomorrow's profit streams. Also, recall Gilbert's mantra from chapter 3: "A digital buyer needs a digital seller." Digital advertising increasingly involves mastering complex algorithms and engaging with an emerging ecosystem of players, such as real-time bidding platforms that continuously update prices. A traditional sales rep might at best lack relationships with more analytically sophisticated buyers and, even worse, might lack the skills and training to connect with and serve these buyers.

Consider, for example, what the team at Deseret Media ended up dubbing "the parable of the eleventh floor." A leading automotive dealer had paused advertising with Deseret Media. When the dealer's CEO gave the green light to restart spending, the sales manager from Deseret's traditional sales team suggested connecting with the dealer's advertising agency to map out an advertising campaign. The dealer's CEO said that would be fine for TV and newspaper campaigns, but anything digital would require working with the dealer's digital team, located on the eleventh floor. "My sales manager had never even heard of, and certainly had never visited, the eleventh floor," Gilbert recalls. "You can bet our digital competitors like Autotrader.com and Cars.com knew exactly where the eleventh floor was located. This represented a turning point in our transition to establishing a separate digital sales team for transformation B."

Finally, the entire paradigm of a "salesforce" runs counter to the way online leaders win. As Google's popular search-based advertising began to take off about a decade ago, many newspaper executives said they weren't worried because they had something Google didn't: feet on the street in local markets. However, one of Google's big advantages was a self-service platform that allowed small business owners to easily customize campaigns. Innosight has been a customer of Google's for more than a decade, and no one from Innosight has ever spoken to a human being from Google.

Gilbert tried at one point to integrate the Deseret salesforce. However, he found that even when the A salesforce hit its targets for traditional products to traditional customers, it would always be 15 percent to 20 percent under plan for new products to new customers. He recalls telling one of his traditional sales leaders, "Look, if you are an entrepreneur and your sales organization is constantly coming under plan, what would you do?" The response was that you'd fire them and hire someone else. And that's what Gilbert eventually did when he and his team peeled off responsibility for B and parked it in a separate salesforce. The new organization doubled growth from the start. "When we pulled B away from the A sales leader, he was mad, and he thought we were making a big mistake," Gilbert reflects. "Not only did we threaten his leadership, he thought we were doing something bad for the company. Even today as digital sales now exceed sales in the traditional business, he still believes we were wrong. It's almost impossible to overestimate the persistence of this world view."

Also, seemingly free capabilities might come with hidden costs or limitations. Even things as innocuous as forecasting spreadsheets and presentation templates carry core DNA. For example, in the book *Good Strategy/Bad Strategy*, UCLA professor Richard P. Rumelt describes how, shortly after the United States deregulated the airline market in the late 1970s, his analysis suggested that fares for long routes would drop and those for short routes would increase. The planning models used by Continental Airlines, however, predicted the opposite, so it planned to invest heavily in large, long-haul planes.

As Rumelt dug in to the details, he found planners were using a tool provided by Boeing (called the Boeing Planner) that played a part in negotiating fares with the board that regulated the industry. "This projection had nothing to do with competition, supply, demand, capacity, or market forces," Rumelt writes. "It took costs and added a markup. *It 'predicted' what the [regulator] would do in setting fares*. The Boeing Planner was a fine tool, but it wasn't a fare predictor unless you had a regulator."

When you consider key capabilities, recall that they can be things, such as a technology, internal experts, brand names, or stores, or they can be know-how, such as product development, manufacturing, or the ability to work with regulators. Detailing capabilities is easy enough, but understanding truly unique ones is harder than it looks. After all, we also suffer from a range of biases that inhibit our ability to accurately assess strengths and weaknesses (which explains why 90 percent of drivers self-report being above average). When we ask most companies what allows them to win in business, the most common response, after a spell of awkward silence, is, "Our brands." Then we innocently follow up by asking the last time an industry upstart called, looking to license a corporate brand (typical answer: "Never"), or we ask them their estimated net promoter score (typical answer: either "What's that?" or a negative number). The next contender typically is scale. But even though scale can create significant advantage, it also can carry downsides, such as molasses-like decision-making processes or inflexibility.

For example, during the height of the internet boom, Intel and SAP formed a joint venture called Pandesic. The goal was to fuse Intel's processing power and SAP's enterprise resource planning (ERP) software to create a new e-commerce venture. One of the venture's executives said, "We are a blue chip startup: all of the upside, and none of the risk." After losing several hundred million dollars in invested capital, the venture shut down. Pandesic had selected capabilities from its parents that caused the startup to invest heavily in what proved to be the wrong assets. The assets worked for the parent sponsor, of course, but were either unneeded or in some cases unhelpful for the new market opportunity. By imposing assets and capabilities on the new venture, the "blue chip" advantage became a liability.

We saw this when we discussed the concept of dual transformation with a book publisher considering whether to create a new division for digital publishing. When she heard us describe a carefully managed capabilities link, she said, "Oh, so the new venture is really just a hybrid organization." No. Transformation B is a separate entity, with a separate target market and a separate business model. Only after that is clearly established can the B leadership clearly determine which capabilities from A will end up being a comparative advantage to B.

One way to identify the unique capabilities you should stock in the link is to conduct a simple role-playing exercise. First, imagine working at the largest natural competitor for transformation B. Which core capability do you have that the competitor will look at with envy? If you happen to have hired someone from that organization, sit her down and get her honest perspective. Then imagine you leave your company to start a company targeting the transformation B opportunity. What core capability would you as an entrepreneur knock on the door of your former company and ask about? The kind of external orientation generated by this role play helps combat the biases that blind even the savviest strategist.

After identifying which capabilities you should stock in the link, next assess *when* they should be made available. Borrowing from the core almost always slows you down. A decade ago we were working with a team at Procter & Gamble to explore a highly disruptive idea in the diaper category. P&G's largest brand globally is—you guessed it—Pampers, which now represents more than $10 billion in annual sales. The team working on the idea had lots of questions, such as whether the problem they hoped to solve for the customer truly mattered, whether success would cannibalize current diaper sales or would grow the category, and how competitors would respond.

To test its key assumptions, the team planned to run a quick-and-dirty market test. But because team members planned to use the Pampers brand on the trial version of their product, they were stuck. Several committees needed to review the look and feel of promotional copy and to ensure Pantone colors conformed to global brand standards. Then, of course, there was concern about the impact on the brand if P&G ultimately killed the product. But there was absolutely no doubt that the Pampers brand, if ultimately stamped on the product, would boost sales. If the product succeeded in test markets, sure, then borrowing the brand made sense, but at this stage of development all it did was slow down the team. The team launched the product in nondescript packaging without the Pampers seal and learned that the problem it addressed simply wasn't deep enough for customers to change their behavior and buying habits. The team quietly shut down the project and moved on to its next idea.

Innovating faster than the market is next to impossible. Innovating *better* than the market is not. A grounded, externally oriented perspective on your unique capabilities is a critical starting point to fighting an unfair fight.

Managing Interfaces Strategically

"We're a very collaborative company," one of our clients told us. "When we start to pursue new things, we're sure we can just talk it out." People may be collaborative. But systems are not.

Systems—such as how you budget, how you allocate people between project teams, how you gather customer feedback, how you create products, and how you measure and reward people—are optimized to achieve specific outcomes. By definition, that means they're not optimized to achieve *different* outcomes. Thus, a key to successfully managing the capabilities link is to develop distinct systems, create formal exchange teams, and institute transfer pricing to handle the challenge of the interface between A and B.

Develop A and B Systems with Different Rules

A portfolio management system is a popular way to manage an interface. A robust portfolio management system clearly outlines that projects that look like *this* get evaluated using one set of criteria and funded from one bucket, and ones that look like *that* get evaluated using a different set of criteria and are funded from a different bucket. Robust portfolio management systems are key enablers of dual transformation for three reasons. First, they help ensure congruence between the stated strategy and the actual work being done in an organization. Second, they serve as an early warning signal that a key project is falling behind schedule. Finally, they help ensure that the right resources make it into the right projects.

Our 2012 ebook, *Building a Growth Factory*, details the characteristics of effective portfolio systems. Effective systems should do the following:

- Separate a portfolio into meaningfully different buckets (such as core improvement, adjacency, transformation A, and transformation B)

- Be comprehensive, covering all of a company's or business unit's growth ideas

- Provide nearly real-time data so that executives have timely information to make decisions

- Feature multimodal data, with both quantitative and qualitative metrics

- Be at least somewhat automated, allowing information to be gathered without extensive intervention

Another example of a distinct system for transformation B comes from a chemical company that hoped to create a strategy to mix and match inputs from small suppliers to quickly create custom products. Its scale and sophisticated supply chain relationship skills, the company believed, allowed it to break historical trade-offs between speed, customization, and price. Hence, successful execution of the strategy required it to tap in to the department that qualified and managed relationships with suppliers. However, that group had developed a set of procedures and decision-making criteria based on safety and compliance, and qualifying a new supplier took months. That would kill the speed benefit.

The head of the group worked with the project leader to come up with a program they called "fast pass," in homage to the program that allows visitors to Disney parks to, in certain circumstances at predetermined times, jump to the front of the line. The chemical company's program was essentially based on a simple checklist. For example, had the supplier worked with another large company? Had its processes been audited by a third party? Had it existed for a certain number of years or sold a certain amount of cumulative volume? When the conditions were met, the potential supplier could go through a lighter, faster version of the qualification process.

Create a Formal Exchange Team

At Deseret, Gilbert kept his digital businesses largely separate from his traditional publishing business. But he knew that the selective insertion of core capabilities would give him an advantage over fierce competition from digital entrants, and there were some tasks that would benefit both A and B. So he created what he dubbed *exchange teams* tasked with things such as these:

- Developing a shared editorial voice to help ensure brand consistency across the print and digital businesses

- Creating editorial constructs for user-generated content, lists, and content curated from third parties to further reinforce that consistency

- Sharing content between the print newspaper and the digital businesses

- Collating customer research to gain underlying facts and figures that informed new product development and sales efforts

- Establishing frequency ratios and change rules for categories of home page stories to inform the pace at which online content would rotate on the website

- Creating core navigation tags that would create brand equity between the print and online products

These exchange teams were not ad hoc, nor were they formed in response to random requests from employees in either the A or the B organization. Rather, leadership established specific teams and determined clear mandates and governance. Each team had a specific target benefit, with measurable results. Those results ran no risk of pitting transformation A against transformation B; success would help both sides.

These small teams had a hand-picked mix of people from A and B. For example, the shared content team had the print features editor, the director of Deseret Connect (described in chapter 2), and the web traffic manager from Deseret Digital. The team pulled resources in either direction, such as managing the process by which the print operation used stories from the network of digital contributors. Leadership designed the teams to be temporary; team members would solve the problem, develop repeatable rules of engagement, and then return to their traditional organizations.

The development of *listicles* (articles that basically are detailed numerical lists, such as "17 Slightly Odd Things Every College Student Has Done") shows an exchange team in action. The web team from transformation B loves listicles, because they drive engagement and provide advertising inventory. The traditional publishing team from transformation A hates listicles, because they look like low-quality journalism. The brand exchange team doesn't arbitrate on whether listicles are good. But it does develop guidelines to make sure listicles don't violate the overall brand positioning around thoughtful faith and family media. For example, a listicle detailing the most attractive cheerleading schools in America wouldn't pass the exchange team's guidelines, while a list of the most family-friendly movies would.

A few words about leading exchange teams. It presents significant challenges, because it requires a unique blend of capabilities. Notably, exchange team leaders need to balance the *initiative* to get people moving and find solutions against the *deference* to let other people work through challenges and feel their effort is valuable (both their effort on the exchange team and the broader efforts within their home organization). The typical forceful leader who spikes an initiative backfires by isolating either the A or B side of the organization, reducing information flow and cooperation. An exchange team leader needs to artfully compromise, validate the personal and organizational sense of identity in some team members, and defuse heated moments. But too much deference mires the team in gridlock. Striking this balance without losing patience and getting pulled into emotional, self-preserving arguments is extremely difficult.

For example, at Deseret Media, Jake Hancock and Matt Sanders managed the exchange team handling the interface between Deseret Connect—the low-cost platform Deseret Media built to reduce the cost of producing stories—and the core newspaper. Having nonjournalists contribute to the news product was threatening to many of the traditional journalist staff. The feeling of vulnerability was particularly acute not only because these outside individuals did not have the same training, but also because many journalists were seeing staff positions reduced in the core newspaper business. The exchange team leader helped ensure that Deseret Connect complemented, but didn't replace, the traditional newsroom by focusing on features, sports reports, and columns versus the hard news reporting that was core to the newsroom. By repeatedly recognizing and validating the unique work of the newsroom while remaining firmly committed to the growth of Deseret Connect, Hancock and Sanders ensured the initiative's success.

Similarly, after Gilbert became president of BYU-Idaho, he had another dual transformation challenge on his hands. Transformation A involved strengthening the in-class experiences, while transformation B involved dramatically expanding online learning. Gilbert formed an exchange team focused on curriculum development. Exchange team leader Jon Linford spent considerable time validating the traditional faculty-centered classroom model, reaffirming that the campus faculty would remain in charge of course learning outcomes, course content, and assessment. But he diligently emphasized the value of the new online organization in the design and execution of online experiences. It turns out that a professor at the head of a classroom with a blackboard behind him is a bad metaphor for online courses. In fact, when campus faculty got too involved in online course design and online pedagogy without proper training, the student experience frequently suffered.

In summary, the deferential but firm exchange team leader validates what is uniquely strong in A, while not compromising the principles that led to a separate organization for B in the first place.

Institute Transfer Pricing

Basic economics holds that dropping prices raises demand, and raising prices lowers it. One reason companies, in our view, overborrow capabilities is that it appears to be costless. A simple answer to this challenge, then, is to institute what's known as *transfer pricing*, which involves essentially making a market in capabilities. The transformation B team wants to tap in to the HR team to create employee agreements? Then the borrower team pays for a fraction of the lender team's time. The new growth group wants IT to modify a core system? That comes with a charge. Most companies don't have the information at their fingertips to determine those kinds of charges precisely, but even the notion that capabilities carry charges can be sufficient to get people to think closely about whether it truly makes sense to tap in to it.

For example, Deseret Digital paid a licensing fee for content it borrowed from the print publication (the digital side could keep advertising revenue tied to the content). Similarly, BYU-Idaho transferred tuition revenue to the campus budgets to pay for faculty expertise and time on course development exchange teams.

That said, Gilbert is not a fan of proportional allocation of fixed costs, such as office rents and salaried functions that the new organization doesn't tap in to directly. He describes it this way.

Early on, A wants the B organization to share all of the fixed, corporate costs. But if B was a true startup it wouldn't have carried those costs. If you give the CFO the right to allocate costs from A to B, he will always overallocate, even if it is "fair" allocation. This is really, really critical. The finance people will say, "That's unfair. They are benefiting from free rent." I tell them that if B went away we would still have those costs, so without B their fixed costs would be even higher. Once B is mature, sharing some of that fixed burden makes sense, but not until B progresses past its startup phase and A has undergone its own transformation. Otherwise A will use the newfound revenue stream to avoid the hard decisions around transformation. We saw this at Deseret Media when our legacy team wanted to divert digital profits so they could put off the hard choices required in the face of declining traditional advertising. Let B grow independently and then have the corporate leadership—not A—decide how to allocate—or not allocate—surplus profits.

Arbitrate Actively

Inevitably, when you concurrently drive transformation A and B, it leads to conflicts. Turf wars and related intercompany squabbling certainly happens, but many of the conflicts are natural results of people trying to optimize different outcomes. In the early days of dual transformation, transformation A will naturally trump transformation B. After all, A is where most of the people sit and where most of the profit is derived.

Leaders can't ignore these conflicts. Rather, they must identify them early and then actively intervene to ensure they don't slow down progress or result in suboptimal outcomes. Chapters 8 and 9 talk more about the specific crises the dual transformation leader needs to be prepared for, but our general counsel is that leaders should show strong bias in favor of transformation B to counter the bias against the new and different that implicitly exists in most systems.

For example, Xerox invested to create its services arm while it was executing significant cuts within the core. Salespeople who were asked to open doors for XGS did so hesitantly. The first victory, a $67 million contract with Baxter International, was considered a fluke even though it was huge compared with a typical copier sale. Anne Mulcahy (CEO from 2001 to 2009) and her successor, Ursula Burns, had to intervene to favor the services salesforce whenever there was a squabble over who controlled an account. "I had to make calls on who covered what account," Burns said. "For *Fortune* 500 clients, most of the engagement is a services discussion, not, 'Will you buy a color printer from me?'"

Notice Burns's use of the first person in that statement. Managing the capabilities link should not be done by a group or in a distributed manner. At Deseret Media it was done by Gilbert, who controlled both organizations, and Christopher M. Lee, the head of digital. "The CEO has to dive down and be involved, even if he might normally not go three levels deep in the operating organization," Gilbert says. "There are times when the CEO has to come down and be the tie breaker, and generally bias in favor of B."

Also, Gilbert's experiences have taught him the importance of actively supporting exchange team leaders, who are put in unenviable positions. Some of that support is simply showing active empathy for the challenging nature of the role played by the exchange team leader. "A little bit of understanding from the senior executive can go a long way in helping the exchange team leader manage this difficult, but critical, organizational role," Gilbert notes.

The need for personal involvement of senior leaders also holds true for organizations much bigger than Gilbert's. For example, health care and related benefits giant Aetna has more than $60 billion in revenue and fifty thousand employees. CEO Mark Bertolini has driven an aggressive dual transformation program that we discuss in more detail in chapter 5. He told us, "The more significant the new project and the shift is, the more the CEO should be driving it."

CHAPTER SUMMARY

You flip the innovator's dilemma into the innovator's opportunity by smartly blending together the power of established assets and the energy of entrepreneurism. The final component of the core dual transformation framework is the capabilities link, which thoughtfully manages the tricky challenge of combining pieces of A and B. Remember three guiding principles.

1. *Stock selectively.* Most of your core capabilities won't help, and could hurt, your transformation B efforts. Remember Gilbert's mantra: A digital buyer needs a digital seller.

2. *Manage strategically.* Develop systems, create formal exchange teams, and institute transfer pricing to ward off the innovator's dilemma.

3. *Arbitrate actively.* Top leadership needs to actively arbitrate the interface between A and B, with a bias to protecting transformation B.

Part Two. Leading Dual Transformation

Part I describes the dual transformation equation: $A + B + C = \Delta$. The next five chapters describe the leadership behaviors that maximize the chances that your dual transformation will succeed. Chapter 5 describes how spotting early signs of disruptive change can give you the courage to choose to start the dual transformation journey before your platform is on fire. Chapter 6 details how a "future-back mindset" provides the clarity to focus on a select few corporate moonshots that combine an unsolved problem, a conceivable solution, and a compelling business model. Chapter 7 explains how to relax implicit blinders that constrain your thinking and embrace the curiosity to explore new frontiers. Chapter 8 explores how to gain the conviction to persevere, even in the face of crises of commitment, conflict, and identity. Finally, chapter 9 shares firsthand reflections from a handful of leaders about their own experience with dual transformation.

5. The Courage to Choose

In 2010, Nokia's board appointed Stephen Elop to the role of CEO. Elop, a well-known executive at Microsoft, was a bold choice. After all, Nokia, the famously Finnish company, had never had an outsider, let alone an American, as CEO. But the board members knew that the changes shaking up Nokia's core cell phone business required doing something dramatic. At the time, interestingly, Nokia's cell phone business still showed significant signs of strength. Apple's iPhone had the hype, and Google's Android operating system was experiencing explosive growth, but Nokia still dominated the market. In fact, 2010 set a high-water mark for the unit, with sales volume of more than 100 million handsets (by 2012 that number would be almost 25 million).

After six months on the job, Elop gave an internal speech describing his view of the situation. He drew on the well-traveled metaphor of the burning platform to urge the company to change radically.

A man working on an oil platform in the North Sea woke up one night from a loud explosion, which suddenly set his entire oil platform on fire. In mere moments, he was surrounded by flames. Through the smoke and heat, he barely made his way out of the chaos to the platform's edge. When he looked down over the edge, all he could see were the dark, cold, foreboding Atlantic waters. The man had mere seconds to react [and] he decided to jump.

In ordinary circumstances, the man would never consider plunging into icy waters. But these were not ordinary times—his platform was on fire. The man survived the fall and the waters. After he was rescued, he noted that a "burning platform" caused a radical change in his behaviour. We, too, are standing on a "burning platform," and we must decide how we are going to change our behaviour.

There's little doubt that Nokia needed to change radically in 2011. But consider the options you have when the platform is truly on fire: get burnt to a crisp, or jump and pray. Those are not good strategic alternatives. Leaders need to have the courage to choose when the spark is lit or, even better, at the moment when it's clear that the conditions mean that a future spark could have a meaningful impact.

When was that moment for Nokia? In hindsight, the entrance of Apple and the Android platform in 2007 was an industry watershed. But let's go back to the end of 2005. Motorola and Apple partnered to introduce the Motorola Rokr handset. (In 2011 Motorola sold its mobility business and a treasure trove of patents to Google, which subsequently sold the unit to Lenovo in 2014.) At the time, the partnership seemed like a winning combination. Although Motorola wasn't the leader in the handset market, its iconic Razr brand of thin devices was on its way to true blockbuster success. Apple had the shine from its booming iPod business and increasing momentum in its still core computer business. But the result of the collaboration was a compromised product that flopped in the market. Commercials, hilarious in retrospect, touted the fact that Rokr was the first handset that integrated Apple's iTunes music software. Popular artists like Madonna and the Red Hot Chili Peppers poured into a phone booth and the voice-over intoned, "One hundred tunes in your pocket, baby." One hundred tunes. Wow.

It was clear from the beginning that then-Apple CEO Steve Jobs was ambivalent about the partnership. Just two weeks after the commercial launch, Jobs noted publicly, "We see it as something we can learn from. It was a way to put our toe in the water." Apple had also filed a number of patents that would enable it to create a simple, elegant phone, such as its 2004 filing (granted in 2010) for a "capacitive touchscreen." It also was rumored to be releasing a version of its iPod music player with a screen that allowed it to play videos. The signs of what would come next were in plain sight.

Of course, companies explore new market opportunities all the time, and many hotly hyped technologies end up fizzling. The fundamental challenge for leaders is that the data showing disruption under way is always opaque. By the time it is crystal clear, it is too late to do anything about the disruption. This means that decisions can't be guided purely by historical data, because if data drives you, you can only go backward. The following three case studies show organizations that demonstrated the courage to choose before convincing data had arrived. Then we describe the seven specific early warning signs of disruptive change.

Netflix

Legend has it that Netflix's founding traces to Reed Hastings's frustration borne of incurring ridiculous late fees for forgetting to return his *Apollo 13* DVD. Recall that the original idea was to allow people to rent and return videos through the mail. The rise of the DVD format, which could be easily mailed in slim envelopes and delivered by the US Postal Service, along with the adoption of monthly subscription fees (described in more detail in chapter 2), gave the idea additional juice. The DVD itself was clearly a cornerstone of Netflix's initial strategy. It partnered with DVD player manufacturers (such as Toshiba and Sony) as well as movie studios to drive adoption of DVDs, and adoption rose quickly, helping push Netflix into the mainstream.

However, Hastings began quickly to plan for a world without DVDs. "From the beginning, DVD by mail was seen as a temporary play to stimulate a digital network, to build up all the other Web infrastructure, and build the brand," he said. This isn't ex post facto rationalization after a successful transition. Hastings said this in 2008 at a private CEO forum organized by Innosight. "It has lasted longer than we ever thought," he added. "If you'd asked me when we started in 1997, 'In ten years, what percent will be downloading and streaming?' I would have said, 'Oh, a majority.' And, in fact, it's microscopic compared to DVD.

And DVD continues to have lots of life. So even I overestimated the pace of change."

The challenge in Netflix's early days was that the commercial internet didn't offer speeds that would provide a good user experience. But as the years passed and new technologies such as fiber, fourth-generation mobile networks, and higher-speed Wi-Fi became more ubiquitous, and as video compression techniques improved, it was time to begin the shift. In 2007, Netflix began offering free streaming to mail subscribers and then introduced a streaming-only plan in 2009.

At the time, Netflix's core business was healthy and growing. In hindsight, moving to streaming video allowed Netflix to accelerate growth, get ahead of its competition, and expand its business outside the United States. The last point is critical. The cost of replicating Netflix's DVD infrastructure globally would surely be substantial. The ability to essentially flip a switch and be present in a new country accelerated Netflix's growth dramatically. It began its international expansion in 2010 and, by 2016, had expanded to almost two hundred countries, with almost half of its subscribers outside the United States.

At the time, however, none of these benefits was obvious. In fact, if anything, Hastings and team had too much courage. In 2011, Netflix announced plans to split the company into two parts. One company, which would carry the Netflix name, would focus purely on the web streaming business. The other company, to be named Qwikster, would focus only on the mail-based DVD business. But customers weren't ready for that radical a shift, and they rebelled. The company also tried to raise prices by 60 percent. The move enraged subscribers. Netflix lost 800,000 subscribers, and its stock price dropped 77 percent in four months.

Chastened by the rare management misstep, Netflix scrapped the plan and decided to keep offering different options under one corporate roof. Hastings later admitted, "My greatest fear at Netflix has been that we wouldn't make the leap from success in DVDs to success in streaming. In hindsight, I slid into arrogance based upon past success."

Nonetheless, Hastings remained firm in his conviction that the future for Netflix would be streaming. "Eventually in the very long term, it's unlikely that we'll be on plastic media," he said in 2011. "So, we've always known that, [and] that's why we named the company Netflix and not DVDs by Mail."

Turner Broadcasting System

Not surprisingly, you meet a cast of characters when you work with a company founded by legendary iconoclast Ted Turner, even a decade after he sold his namesake Turner Broadcasting System to Time Warner for more than $7 billion.

Return with us to 2006. Stepping into a meeting of the leadership team of Turner Entertainment Networks (TEN) in Atlanta, the first person you meet is most likely Laz. More formally known as Mark Lazarus, the charismatic leader has responsibility for TEN's stable of channels such as TNT, TBS, and Cartoon Network. Laz (who left Turner in 2011 to become head of NBC Sports) is quick with a quip and able to incisively cut through to the heart of issues. When a consulting team member, for example, talks about not being thrilled to be in a Friday meeting with a young child at home, Laz's eyes narrow and he says, "You do know what business you chose to get in, right?"

Next you meet the King of May, or Steve Koonin. The King bears some physical resemblance to Wayne Knight, who famously played the character Newman in *Seinfeld*, but one shouldn't underestimate Koonin, who has an industry reputation for unveiling winning programs, such as the Kyra Sedgwick drama *The Closer*, during the vital period in May called *upfronts*, where networks promote shows and try to woo advertisers. To Koonin's right you see his trusted adviser the Drama Mamma, a nickname Jennifer Dorian earned when leading a highly successful effort to come up with a motivating theme and tag line for TNT: "We Know Drama." And let's not forget the New York contingent: the advertising sales team led by Barry Fischer, dressed in black and waiting eagerly to get back to the center of the universe, otherwise known as Manhattan.

We swallow hard and prepare to tell this group that it needs to accelerate the pace of transforming a model that is, by all accounts, wildly successful.

A Simple, but Powerful, Business Model

First, a bit of context. Ted Turner's insight when he founded his company in the late 1970s was that the proliferation of cable networks created the possibility to bring many more channels into individuals' homes beyond a handful of big networks. If you flipped on one of Turner's channels in about 2000, you were likely to encounter reruns of the police procedural powerhouse *Law & Order*, the bubbly comedy *Friends*, or an Atlanta Braves baseball game. TEN's basic business model was to be a financial intermediary between, on the one hand, studios that had content sitting on the shelf and, on the other hand, companies that needed programming to beam from satellites or run over coaxial cables. These companies, known in industry parlance as *affiliates* or *multisystem operators* (MSOs), would pay TEN for prepackaged channels.

Anyone who watches television knows the other key component of revenue: advertising. The more interesting the content, the more viewers TEN generated, and the more advertisers would pay to reach those coveted eyeballs. In 2005, TEN's revenue was split roughly evenly between those two categories.

TEN crunched the numbers and found opportunities to arbitrate the difference between what content owners wanted and what TEN could make selling the content to cable and satellite companies and advertisers. The simple beauty of the business model was at least one reason Time Warner happily paid billions for the company in 1996, and largely left it alone to generate substantial profits that helped offset the bleeding in its ailing magazine arm (which was spun off in 2013).

In this environment, it's no surprise that TEN followed a linear strategy planning process: start with today's business. Detail modest year-by-year changes in revenues and costs. Compare results to the overall target. Make modest adjustments. Repeat.

Disruptive Challenges

But nonlinear shifts emerging in the market led the team to consider a different approach. In 2005, Chad Hurley, Steve Chen, and Jawed Karim founded a company that allowed users to upload video clips. Playing on the slang word for a television set—the boob tube—they called their business YouTube. As a bizarre mix of endless cat videos and pirated professional content began to populate the site, search titan Google took notice. In May 2006—less than twelve months after the company was founded—Google snatched it up for almost $2 billion. The industry wondered whether so-called user-generated content on topics aimed at the "long tail" of users interested in arcane topics could undermine a decades-long focus on blockbuster hits.

In the third quarter of 2006, another important milestone occurred. Netflix, less than ten years old, announced that its quarterly revenues had crossed $300 million, meaning it was well on pace to become a billion-dollar business. In 2006 the popular press got wind of a rapidly growing trend among high school and college students: the use of what we now know as social networks. News Corp septuagenarian Rupert Murdoch shocked the industry by paying $580 million for social media pioneer Myspace. That move ended up being a boon to then twenty-four-year-old Mark Zuckerberg by giving him space to continue the relentless growth of Facebook.

Turner could look to its cousins in the newspaper business to get a glimpse of the future. Although newspapers still appeared to be on stable financial ground, industry analysts increasingly—and correctly—worried that the industry was about to fall off a cliff. When Knight Ridder, America's second-largest newspaper company and the publisher of the *Miami Herald* and the San Jose *Mercury News*, put itself up for sale, few buyers stepped forward. McClatchy purchased the company in 2006 for "just" $6.5 billion (a price that in hindsight was probably ten times too high).

These trends weren't having a meaningful impact on Turner's business in 2006, but Laz and team worried about the degree to which the long-range planning exercise they were working on, which looked at the business stretching out to the year 2011, was built on a solid foundation.

A Perfect Storm on the Horizon

During our meeting with the Turner executives, we shared the results of our analysis. We had built a simple model that used so-called Monte Carlo techniques to look at thousands of scenarios. Given the underlying trends in the industry, the analysis showed significant risk that TEN would encounter what we called a perfect storm: cable and satellite broadcasters would consolidate and increase their power as disruptive content offerings proliferated, decreasing the relevance of TEN's business model. We didn't expect that the business would disappear, but we did project a more than 20 percent chance of a wide enough miss on the long-range planning target that it could lead TEN's corporate parent to consider drastic options, such as a reorganization or a divestiture.

TEN's leadership agreed that these early warning signs warranted an aggressive response. Specifically, the TEN team developed five key strategic thrusts to help respond to the trends in the industry, each of which TEN would execute against in the years to come.

1. *Invest in original content.* The King of May—a prescient industry observer if ever there was one—got ahead of key industry trends. TEN struck innovative deals with personalities like Tyler Perry and Conan O'Brien. For example, after a successful ten-episode pilot on independent TV stations, TEN ordered one hundred episodes of Perry's *House of Payne*, a sharp break from typical practice of ordering shows in batches of twelve to twenty-four per year. TEN earned the reputation as a place where stars had the freedom to explore creative paths and potentially keep a piece of the upside they created.

2. *Strengthen the ability to negotiate with affiliates.* As cable operators and satellite broadcasters continued to consolidate, TEN knew it had to find ways to ensure it maintained bargaining power. So it invested in a unique collection of rights to broadcast major sporting events, augmenting its relationship with the National Basketball Association, Major League Baseball

playoff games, and pieces of the NCAA men's college basketball tournament.

3. *Do digital differently.* TEN knew it needed to work hard to further its digital presence. As it built up its sports library, it also obtained rights to run the digital properties for the NBA and the Professional Golfers' Association (PGA).

4. *Innovate the advertising model.* Traditional thirty-second spots increasingly felt like an anachronism in an age of time shifting and binge watching. In 2007, TEN began to experiment with something called TVinContext. The service offered companies the ability to match their advertisement with a particular moment in a show or movie. Imagine, for example, an exciting car chase followed by an advertisement for BMW's latest offering. Academic research showed that such pairings had substantial impact on customer recall. Turner also began experimenting with sponsored content and in-show product placement.

5. *Innovate the business model.* TEN wanted to find ways to augment its revenue streams beyond selling commercial airtime and receiving fees from network operators. It began to explore options such as using its Turner Classic Movie brand and content library to run offline events such as film festivals or even branch into physical retail stores.

Not everything TEN did was successful, but if you flipped on one of its channels in 2011 you saw a station transformed. Instead of rerun after rerun with the occasional Braves game, you would see fresh, original programming and major sporting events. Its online presence grew substantially, and TVinContext received significant industry acclaim as TEN rolled it out.

Aetna

Harvard economist Michael Porter has made a number of contributions to the field of corporate strategy. One of the most seminal was his theory that outperformance comes from picking industry circumstances in which five forces (barriers to entry, supplier power, buyer power, competitive rivalry, and threat of substitution) support success. In 2011, health insurance companies certainly appeared to have the Porterian wind at their backs. Spending on health care had grown from roughly 6 percent of gross domestic product in the 1960s to almost 20 percent, a number that dwarfs the spending of any other country in both absolute and relative terms.

Although the 2010 Affordable Care Act, colloquially known as Obamacare, had the potential to put pricing pressures on pharmaceutical and medical device companies, it looked like a panacea to insurance companies. After all, a key provision of the act was that every American needed to have health insurance, which meant that roughly fifty million uninsured people became target customers.

In the face of all of this, Aetna CEO Mark Bertolini decided to blow the company up.

The need to do so, from the outside at least, wasn't obvious. Before Bertolini had become CEO in November 2010, Aetna had grown through the 2007–2009 economic downturn; and with the economy picking up, in 2011, Bertolini's first year as CEO, net income was almost 40 percent higher than it was in 2009. But Bertolini and his leadership team believed that inexorable forces would lead to long-term industry transformation. Consumers were increasingly arming themselves with information from WebMD and related websites. Wearable technology created the possibility for more-advanced diagnostics and remote monitoring. Big data analytics and behavioral economics could change the face of prevention.

As Bertolini and his leadership team sifted through these trends, three opportunities emerged. First, the company could shift from selling insurance policies and administrative services to large companies, which then provided them to their employees, to directly targeting consumers. (In a quirk of history, in 1946 the United States made employee health insurance a tax-deductible expense for companies, so many individuals get benefits from their employers.) Specifically, Aetna started creating a consumer-facing marketplace that would make shopping for health insurance as simple as buying a book at Amazon.com. Second, it could help health care providers change their fundamental pricing approach from fee-for-service to fee-for-value.

Then, for its transformation B, Aetna committed to providing new services to doctors and hospitals. Historically Aetna's only relationship with the providers themselves was reimbursing them for service. But as technology advanced and competition increased, Aetna knew these providers needed to improve their ability to manage their costs and risks and improve health outcomes. Bertolini's vision was to become the "Intel inside" of new provider networks via a new business it pieced together through acquisitions and investments called Healthagen. Bertolini publicly proclaimed that success would "destroy the insurance industry as we know it."

As of the writing of this book, Aetna is well along the path of fundamentally transforming itself in five ways.

- Move from the business of pricing risk to the helping members manage their health.

- Drive the "retailization" of health care by empowering consumers to make informed decisions and support them in their ongoing health care journey.

- Make health care more affordable while improving quality by enabling providers to take on risk and practice population health management.

- Help governments and employers take better care of their beneficiaries and members by offering cost-effective access to high-quality care.

- Helping providers move their core business model toward fee-for-value; by 2020 Aetna expects that 75 percent of its members will be under value-based contracts.

The disruptive forces that are driving change in the health care industry promise long-term pain for insurers and other participants that try desperately to cling to yesterday's model. As Bertolini put it, "You can be like the steel industry and go into fetal position, and hope to be the last one standing. Or you can systematically look at your whole value chain." The courage to choose gave Aetna the time and space to experiment with different approaches, line up the right resources, get organizational alignment, and get ahead of fundamental industry change.

Bertolini says that the CEO plays a critical role in making these kinds of choices: "The CEO's responsibility is to create a stark reality of what the future holds, and then to begin to build the plans for the organization to meet those realities."

Early Warning Signs

Dual transformation is the corporate equivalent of highly invasive surgery. It carries substantial risk. Not only can efforts fail, but also the organization can become distracted, creating opportunities for eagle-eyed attackers. A company should always be exploring new and different paths to growth, but those with substantial room to expand their core business without facing the existential threat posed by disruptive change should put the lion's share of their efforts in the basics.

On the other hand, the Nokia case highlights the importance of not waiting too long. When it is obvious that you need to transform, the degree of freedom you have to successfully execute goes way down. As your core business begins to decline, you naturally have to turn an overwhelming amount of attention to mitigating the impact of that decline. The sense of urgency, sometimes bleeding into a sense of crisis, leads to significant rigidity.

Netflix, TEN, and Aetna all managed this balance well, investing early enough that they had space to explore but not so early that they got too far ahead of the industry. Each case featured a courageous leadership team, because making the case for change isn't always obvious. In the face of all the disruptive change TEN's leadership team was reading about, the core business was blistering hot. This is common. The seeds of transformation typically take root well outside a company's mainstream. Early developments tend to have little or no impact on a company's financial statements. After all, by 2005, online marketplaces (such as eBay and craigslist) and employment sites (such as Monster.com) had eviscerated the *need* to buy a classified ad, which, industry insiders knew, was the real profit generator for most newspapers; but many buyers did so out of habit, so newspaper companies still had healthy profit margins.

Although grounded intuition has a role to play in making decisions in the absence of convincing data, our study of historical patterns of industry disruption highlights telltale signs of impending change. Specifically, we watch for seven warning signs, which can be grouped into three stages. Next, we describe these warning signs in depth, explain how to identify them, and explore why they suggest Clayton Christensen's fears about the future of Harvard Business School's flagship two-year MBA program have merit.

Stage 1: Circumstances

Forest fires are more likely, and have a more devastating impact, when dry weather has created large amounts of natural kindling. The closer together trees are, the more likely it is that a fire can spread. Similarly, certain initial conditions increase the possibility of disruptive change.

Decreases in Customer Loyalty, Driven by Overshooting

The story of every successful company is basically the same. Try a bunch of things. Find something that works. Execute and expand.

The trick, and the essence of the innovator's dilemma, is that doing everything you are supposed to do—listen to your best customers, produce the best products and services you can, push prices up, earn high margins, and have your stock price surge—sows the seeds of disruptive change. At some point customers say, "The last thing you gave me was more than good enough. I'll take this new version, but the extra features don't matter to me, so I don't want to pay any more for it." This is called *overshooting*: providing a given market tier performance it can't use. Your television remote control probably serves as a daily reminder of overshooting. Each of those buttons can do wonderful things, but would you pay extra fees for yet another button? Probably not. When overshooting begins to set in, customer loyalty decreases, creating conditions in which an entrant can gain traction with a simpler, cheaper solution.

Significant and Lasting Investments by Venture Capitalists

What venture capitalists are funding today can be tomorrow's disruptive change. For example, during much of the 1980s and 1990s, many parts of the startup ecosystem focused on communications, technology, and health care. Those industries then became hotbeds of disruption in the past two decades. Similarly, in the past few years there have been significant investments in markets like data analytics, 3-D printing, renewable energy, and financial services.

Most of the individual startups will fail, of course, and the winning technologies will unfold in surprising ways. As futurist Roy Amara once noted, "We tend to overestimate the effect of a technology in the short run and underestimate the effect in the long run." In the afterword, we talk more about specific industries we are watching.

Stage 2: Catalysts

The next set of early warning signs relates to triggering events that drive the transition from circumstances conducive to disruption to the beginning of disruptive impact.

Policy Changes Open the Door to New Entrants

Governments are often portrayed as inhibitors of innovation, but that's not fair. Many commercial innovations, including the internet, mobile technologies, and countless lifesaving drugs, have their roots in government research. That said, there is little doubt that governments can curtail both the motivation and the ability of innovators to drive disruption. When governments change the rules or focus their ample buying power in new directions, it can also accelerate, or at least influence, the pace of industry change.

Entrants Emerge at the Low End or Market Fringes
with Inferior-Seeming Solutions

Remember when the iPhone first came out? It was a fantastic handheld computer. It was not a fantastic phone. Its battery life and call quality were pitiful compared with the performance of Nokia's phones. Similarly, the first wave of digital disruptors in media had serious limitations. You had to wait to get your movie from Netflix. The quality of content on new media providers was laughable compared with what you would get in a well-run newspaper or magazine. YouTube primarily showed videos of cats, for goodness' sake.

But it's wrong to say that a disruptor is inferior. Disruptors do it differently. They trade off raw performance in the name of simplicity, convenience, affordability, or accessibility. By necessity, first customers tend not to be mainstream. Perhaps it is an undemanding customer who is happy to trade performance for price. Perhaps it is a customer who historically lacked the skills or wealth to use existing solutions, or a so-called early adopter who cares more about novelty than perfection.

The innovator uses this foothold to improve the product and service so that it meets the needs of broader customer groups, until an innovation that was once dismissed as inferior becomes perfectly adequate for wider use. When upstarts following this game-changing strategy begin to emerge, it's time to stand up and take notice.

Customer Habits and Preferences Show Signs of Shifting

When customers begin to display lasting shifts in behavior, it opens the door for changes in the basis of competition. For example, one trend that has changed the market for business technology is the so-called consumerization of the enterprise. Employees used to have little choice except to use computers and cell phones mandated by corporate IT departments. After all, these technologies were relatively expensive and hard to integrate into corporate systems. But as companies like Apple and Dell increased usability and decreased cost, consumers increasingly showed up to work toting their favorite devices. Companies whose success was predicated on strong relationships with corporate buyers faced an onslaught of competitors that played the game in a very different way.

Companies often miss behavioral shifts because they start, not among mainstream customers, but with people at the fringes of the market. But remember, the quirky behavior that teenagers follow now (a hundred text messages a minute!) becomes mainstream only a few short years later.

Stage 3: Impact

Until this point, it is easy for incumbents to still feel safe. Venture capital investment? Maybe that will impact us in a decade, but we have time. Wacky behavior at the fringes? Interesting, but immaterial. A ground swell of changes in customer habits? OK, that's pretty serious, but we have the resources, we have the brand, and we have the capabilities to fight back. If you respond in a serious way before you get to stage 3, you often indeed have sufficient time. But if you don't have the courage to choose, you can expect to see the final two warning signs of change.

A Viable Competitor Fine-Tunes a Disruptive Business Model

Google. Amazon.com. Netflix. Tencent. All these are giants of the internet era (in case you aren't familiar with it, Tencent is a massive digital company in China). Each is portrayed as a high-tech company. And indeed, technology is at the core of the way each creates value for customers. But what has made each of them a powerful global force is the business model it followed, which made incumbent response difficult.

We've described how feet on the street are no match for Google's ad-auction model and how Netflix decimated Blockbuster's key profit driver: late fees. Amazon.com flipped the traditional retail model on its head by optimizing its supply chain to the point that it receives money from customers before it places an order with a supplier, giving it negative days working capital in its core retailing business.

For its part, Tencent zigged where most similar companies zagged. The dominant business model for online providers is to build audiences and then sell advertisements. Tencent built a huge audience via its free QQ messenger service, but it built its business on microtransactions, in which customers buy credits to advance in a simple game or add a scarf or hairstyle to their messenger's avatar. By 2015 the company had annual revenues of more than $10 billion, more than 75 percent of it from these kinds of small purchases. Tencent further diversified its business model by integrating payments into its WeChat messaging platform. By the end of 2016 Tencent had emerged as Asia's most valuable publicly traded company.

Technologies can be copied, but business models persist. When a competitor develops a model that decimates a heretofore dominant profit stream, allows it to prosper at price points the market leader can't match, or involves an integrated network of unique suppliers and partners, disruption is nigh.

Slowing Revenue Growth Is Coupled with Increased Profit Margins as Leaders Exit Volume Tiers and Cut Costs

Perhaps most paradoxically, when incumbents begin to feel the pain from disruption, it doesn't always feel very painful. The slowing growth that comes with overshooting feels like the natural result of an industry maturing. Emerging disruptors grow in a seemingly disconnected market, and, if they pick off customers, often they are ones the incumbent doesn't care much about anyway. Of course, slowing growth at the high end, coupled with customer flight in volume tiers, sets off financial alarm bells that draw out the cost cutters. Analysts applaud the focus on efficiency, setting off improvements in the stock price that convince leaders that more systematic action is unnecessary. But when the company runs out of costs to cut, and can't figure out how to grow the top line, the applause turns to dismay as the full force of disruption becomes increasingly obvious.

Table 5-1 shows the three examples in this chapter along with some of the early signals that helped leaders at Aetna, Netflix, and Turner demonstrate the courage to change. Note that in each case the respective company responded before a truly disruptive business model emerged with corresponding negative financial impact.

How to Spot Early Warning Signs

The seven signals of disruptive change are straightforward, but they aren't always easy to see. We have five tips to help you spot early warning signs.

Go to the Periphery

The periphery is the edges or fringes of your industry. It might include extreme customer groups, such as those in particularly demanding circumstances or those that have demonstrated they can be satisfied with very little. It might include people historically locked out of the market

TABLE 5-1

Early signals of disruption at three companies

Early warning sign	Aetna (2010)	Netflix (2008)	Turner (2007)
Change in customer loyalty	Not material, but insurance providers generally are not "loved" brands	Not material	Channel proliferation driving decrease in ratings
Venture funding	Health care IT had been funded aggressively for 10+ years	New content models had been funded aggressively	New content models had been funded aggressively
Policy change	Affordable Care Act	Nothing material	Nothing material
Emergence of disruptors at the fringes	Google and Microsoft attempting to create electronic medical records, new online-only insurance models	YouTube, Hulu, and other online streaming services emerging	Netflix, YouTube, and Facebook present but nascent
Customer habit change	Customers using web to diagnose; postrecession cost consciousness	Fringe customers with high bandwidth watching on laptops and phones vs. TVs	Fringe customers with high bandwidth watching on laptops and phones vs. TVs
Competitor business model	Not yet viable	Not yet viable	Not yet viable
Financial impact	Not material	Not material	Not material

because they lack skills, wealth, or sophistication. It might include the teenagers and hackers who love to play. In a business-to-business context, it might include smaller businesses, or businesses in poorer markets. It certainly operates in global innovation hot spots where new businesses incubate and early adopters proliferate, such as Silicon Valley, Shanghai, Berlin, and London. As legendary science fiction writer William Gibson famously noted, "The future has already arrived. It is just not very evenly distributed."

Pay Attention to Small Things

During a 2005 presentation at Turner, coauthor Scott Anthony highlighted the disruptive potential of YouTube. One audience member commented, "YouTube is great, but if you add up every video that anyone has ever watched on it, it is less than the lowest-ranked prime-time show on a Tuesday night." True—in 2005. Less true in 2010. And certainly not true in 2016.

Anything that is growing rapidly bears attention. Karl Ronn, a Procter & Gamble executive who helped that company launch three billion-dollar disruptions before leaving to create his own disruptive ventures, told us his rule of thumb: "Anything that has doubled its size is a potential disruptor, regardless of size." Those fast-growing companies, he noted, "are running the test market we should have run. This is a simple way to not ignore small stuff."

Not every early-stage development pans out, of course; Murdoch's bet on Myspace serves as only one example. But identifying peripheral developments early through the disruptive lens maximizes your chances of identifying a serious disruptive change with enough time to respond appropriately.

Think about What Could Happen in the Future, Not What Is Happening Now

For a range of psychological reasons, it is hard for even the most sensible executive to point out the fatal flaws in what a company is doing today. But if you step out into the future, executives can take a more clinical perspective. For example, TEN put itself far enough into the future that no one felt a personal risk in pointing out that there might be cracks in the business model.

The right range depends on your industry. Consider a multibillion-dollar defense company we advised. The company had just lost a critical contract to a rival, but its five-year growth plan still looked solid, because development and procurement cycles in the defense industry stretch over decades. When the company expanded the range of its growth projections from five to fifteen years, a mission-critical problem came into view. Changing customer needs due to geopolitical forces, defense budget crunches, and technological disruptions meant that the defense company faced a massive revenue shortfall that would challenge the organization to transform itself and create new growth.

Involve Outsiders

A telling example of how hard it can be to identify problems in your current business comes from an experience coauthors Clark Gilbert and Mark Johnson had at Harvard Business School in the early 2000s. The two were participating in a colloquium about responding to disruptive change. Leadership teams from a half-dozen organizations, such as Intel, Kodak, and the US Defense Department, attended the event. Fitting the HBS theme, researchers wrote twenty-page case studies describing a disruptive development in the respective industries. Companies had to listen quietly while their case study was discussed. Here's how Gilbert describes it.

> I thought this was going to be the most boring event ever. We basically had written five versions of the same case. But it was remarkable. Every time when the discussion ended and the company could comment, they would patiently explain how they were different. Kodak could instantly see Intel's problem with low-end microprocessors. The defense guys could see Kodak's challenge with digital imaging. But none of the companies could see their own problem. It really showed me how hard it can be to identify your own problems.

Assess the Cost of Inaction

TEN's analysis focused on how its business could erode if it didn't change and if disruptive developments continued. Most companies take the opposite approach. They consider various response strategies, often building detailed spreadsheets to project the required investment and impact of each strategy. A popular approach involves calculating the net present value (NPV) of an investment proposal by discounting future cash flows using an agreed-upon rate. A basic rule of finance is that positive NPV projects should be approved, and negative ones should be rejected. However, most people who follow this technique make an implicit assumption that the base case is zero, an assumption that biases them against doing projects that require up-front investments and might not generate returns until a few years into the future. When you recognize the cost of inaction, it raises the imperative of response.

Is Christensen's Fear Justified?

In 2014, Clayton Christensen gave the annual management lecture for the Singapore Institute of Management to a thousand-person audience. He described the disruptions taking place in education, saying he was worried about the future of his employer, the Harvard Business School.

In particular, he questioned the long-term viability of the school's core two-year MBA offering. He ended his speech by saying, "I will pray for Singapore's future if you will pray for the Harvard Business School's."

Are there early warning signs of impending disruptive change that could affect an institution like HBS? The short answer is yes. Table 5-2 is a simple tool we use to assess the presence of the warning signs described in this chapter (this tool and other key tools appear in the appendix and at dualtransformation.com). It provides qualitative choices for each of the seven warning signs to help identify how pressing the threat is.

Let's look at each row.

- *Changes in customer loyalty (moderate risk).* The number of people signing up to take the Graduate Management Admission Test (GMAT), a prerequisite for admission to a two-year MBA program, declined by 33 percent between 2009 and 2015. That's at least one sign that customer loyalty is decreasing.

TABLE 5-2

Tool to assess the warning signs of disruption

	Sign	Low risk	Moderate risk	High risk
Stage 1: Circumstances	*Customer loyalty*	Stable or increasing	**Slow decline**	Rapid decline
	Venture investment	Little or none	Substantial seed and early-stage activity	**Substantial growth-stage activity**
Stage 2: Catalysts	*Policy changes*	Little or none	**Under consideration or discussion**	In the process of being implemented
	Industry entrant activity	Little or none	**Growth at the low end or fringe of the market**	Entering or present in the mainstream
	Customer habit shifts	Habits are stable	**Change at the fringes**	Change in the mainstream
Stage 3: Impact	*Business model innovation*	Entrants optimizing existing models	**Entrants experimenting with different models**	Entrants successfully executing different models
	Profit margins	**Stable or increasing**	Slow decline or increasing due to cost management	Rapid decline

- *Venture investment (high risk).* It's hard to get precise figures on venture investment, but at least two sources suggest that US venture capitalists invested about $2 billion in education-related startups in 2014, up from less than $500 million in 2009.

- *Policy changes (moderate risk).* As the cost of higher education has risen substantially over the past few decades, a growing number of students are graduating with crushing debt burdens. Politicians have taken notice, and although major reform hasn't happened, there are signs it could be coming.

- *Industry entrant activity (moderate risk).* Over the past few years a number of new models have emerged as viable ways to provide business education. This includes platforms that offer access to massive open online courses (MOOCs) and improvements in employer-driven education programs.

- *Habit change (moderate risk).* Online education clearly involves a set of habits distinct from traditional classroom-based education. These habits haven't crossed over to mainstream behavior, but as more children grow up digital, the teaching paradigm could transform.

- *Disruptive business model (moderate risk).* Emerging players in the market are clearly experimenting with radically different business models, an action that could present significant challenges to HBS and other mainstream schools. These business models haven't yet shown commercial viability, but they could do so in surprisingly short order.

- *Financial results (low risk).* The last time we checked, Harvard's endowment still looked pretty solid. In 2014 HBS launched a $1 billion, five-year fund-raising campaign. The campaign quietly started in 2012 and had already raised $600 million when the official announcement came. By mid-2016, HBS announced that it had raised $925 million.

Overall, there is reason to worry. And there are reasons to be encouraged that the school that houses the father of disruption is indeed responding. Harvard's publishing arm has a corporate learning arm that provides customized education programs to mid-level managers at corporations, using a blend of case studies, online modules, and web-based lectures. In 2013 it created a separate group called HBX to develop online courses. In 2014 it rolled out a three-week program that teaches basic business skills, such as financial analysis. In 2015 HBX launched an immersive version of Christensen's class that can be taken by individuals or teams at companies for less than $2,000 per person.

Time will tell, of course, whether Christensen's prayers are answered.

CHAPTER SUMMARY

By the time the platform is on fire, dual transformation is next to impossible. Leaders need to follow the lead of Reed Hastings at Netflix, Mark Lazarus at Turner Entertainment Network, and Mark Bertolini at Aetna and summon the courage to choose to transform before the need is obvious. Keep your eyes open for the seven early warning signs of disruptive change: decreases in customer loyalty, spikes in venture capital investment, policy changes, fringe entrants, changes in customer habits, formation of new business models, and a shift of financial focus from revenue growth to margin protection. To spot these signals, live in the periphery, pay attention to anything growing rapidly, plant yourself in the future, involve outsiders, and estimate the cost of inaction.

6. The Clarity to Focus

In 1961, US president John F. Kennedy stood before a joint meeting of Congress. The young president had a job to do. Sixteen years after the end of World War II and eight years after the cessation of hostilities in the Korean War, the country was teetering between optimism (from dominating the global economy) and despair (from falling behind in the critical space race with the Russians). Few people doubted the country's technological prowess. After all, the Manhattan project had famously developed a nuclear weapon in a shockingly short period of time. The world was beginning to see the changes that stemmed from Bell Labs' invention of the transistor in 1947. But it was the *Russians* who had sent the first satellite into orbit. The *Russians* who had sent an animal into orbit. And the *Russians* who seemed positioned to win the next great world race.

After a short preamble, President Kennedy made this famous declaration.

> I believe that this nation should commit itself to achieving the goal, before this decade is out, of landing a man on the moon and returning him safely to the Earth. No single space project in this period will be more impressive to mankind, or more important for the long-range exploration of space; and none will be so difficult or expensive to accomplish. We propose to accelerate the development of the appropriate lunar space craft. We propose to develop alternate liquid and solid fuel boosters, much

larger than any now being developed, until certain which is superior. We propose additional funds for other engine development and for unmanned explorations—explorations which are particularly important for one purpose which this nation will never overlook: the survival of the man who first makes this daring flight. But in a very real sense, it will not be one man going to the moon—if we make this judgment affirmatively, it will be an entire nation. For all of us must work to put him there.

After this, the term *moonshot* entered the lexicon as shorthand for a difficult or expensive task expected to have great significance.

Kennedy's speech was no idle, pie-in-the-sky promise. Before making it, Kennedy had Vice President Lyndon Johnson carefully study the feasibility of the proclamation. And it was smart strategy as well. As Johnson explored how the United States could beat the Russians into space, rocket scientist Wernher von Braun wrote a memo describing how the Russians' current lead in heavy rockets made it hard to beat them in launching satellites or exploring the edges of the Earth's atmosphere. However, getting to the moon required a tenfold performance improvement over current technology. Here, the Americans had an advantage, with a broader and deeper technological set of resources. As Richard Rumelt writes in *Good Strategy/Bad Strategy*, "von Braun recommended a preemptive announcement of the more ambitious objective because the United States had a good chance of beating the Russians to its accomplishments. Kennedy's speech was delivered one month after von Braun's memorandum arrived."

Kennedy's clear focus drove resource allocation and ultimately accelerated one of the twentieth century's signature achievements.

This kind of strategic clarity is an absolute imperative for dual transformation, given its complexity. And that is the clarity to choose what to do as well as what not to do. After all, the essence of strategy always has been, and always will be, choice. One of the great Steve Jobs's most-cited quotations is, "I'm actually as proud of the things we haven't done as the things I have done. Innovation is saying 'no' to 1,000 things."

Yet most companies don't turn to Kennedy for inspiration for innovation. Rather, they turn to China's longtime leader Mao Zedong. Mao is not a natural go-to source for innovation. Yet if you've ever heard or uttered the phrase "Let a hundred [or a thousand] flowers bloom," you are (probably unwittingly) channeling the chairman. The phrase traces to a 1956 speech by Mao. He used the phrase during a brief spell of openness, when the regime encouraged dissident opinions. It was known as the Hundred Flowers Campaign. However, as criticism of his regime mounted, Mao changed course in less than a year, with critics publicly castigated and sent to prison labor camps. He later boasted that his campaign "enticed the snakes out of their lairs."

That is not good inspiration for innovation.

Many of the case studies we feature in this book involve a laser focus on a handful of strategic moves. Xerox streamlined its core business and created a business-process outsourcing business. SingPost made its core postal delivery offerings more convenient and created outsourced logistics and fulfillment capabilities. Adobe shifted from selling packaged software to offering subscriptions and built a suite of offerings around marketing services. Turner Entertainment Networks had five strategic thrusts, such as increasingly producing original content and playing digital differently. No doubt, there were significant numbers of experiments within those broad choices, just as Kennedy described alternating between two fuel boosters until scientists were certain which was better, but each example is significantly closer to a moonshot than to planting a hundred seedlings.

This chapter provides a front-row seat as Manila Water, the water utility provider for the six million people who live in the eastern part of metro Manila in the Philippines, demonstrates the clarity to focus. We then describe three keys to success: using what we call a *future-back* approach, managing across three different time frames simultaneously, and being willing to walk away from pieces—if not all—of the historical core.

Strategic Choices at Manila Water

Manila Water is a public-private partnership formed in 1997 to improve the quality and reliability of the water infrastructure in the eastern portion of metro Manila. When the company—which is more than 50 percent owned by the Ayala Corporation, one of the Philippines' largest conglomerates—received the license, only about one in four households in east Manila had reliable access to drinkable water. By 2013, an injection of fresh talent and modern management techniques into a decrepit government bureaucracy had increased that proportion to almost 100 percent.

CEO Gerry Ablaza and his management team now faced the paradox of success: investors expected the company to continue to grow given its successful history, but its success meant it had to look in different places to find that growth. The company started its search for new growth from a position of strength, with 2013 producing record revenues of about $400 million and a net income of about $125 million.

The team followed a three-step process to make clear strategic choices. First, it determined its growth gap (explained next), which clarified the problem it had to solve. It then determined the goals and boundaries of its new growth efforts. Finally, it short-listed two strategic opportunity areas that it believed had the most potential for new growth.

Step 1: Determining Your Growth Gap

Our experience is that almost every organization has a gap between its future desires and its present reality. The bigger the so-called growth gap, the more you have to step up investment in growth and the further you have to push the boundaries of your current business to find growth. Manila Water followed four steps to determine its growth gap.

1. *Set a target.* Manila Water set a goal of doubling net income in five years. It was a specific goal that lay far enough in the future that people felt safe discussing what would need to have happened by then, but not so far that uncertainty about technological or market developments rendered a discussion meaningless. We've seen companies consider slightly shorter horizons, but never shorter than three years, and as much as thirty years in slower-changing markets like defense. Manila Water chose to ground its target in net income, a tactic that has an advantage over the default choice of absolute revenue size, because it frees you up to look at different business models.

2. *Estimate the potential of current operations.* Manila Water projected that its base business would remain relatively stable, which was no surprise because it was ubiquitous in the geographies in which it operated. Thus, typical techniques to grow top-line

revenues—by reaching new customers in current markets or stealing share from existing competitors—weren't relevant. It did see room for net income growth by operating its core business more effectively. Specifically, it estimated that it could close about 20 percent of its net income gap through operational improvements.

3. *Estimate the potential of existing investments in new growth.* In 2013, Manila Water launched an ambitious plan to create a "water utility as a service" business for municipalities in other parts of the Philippines and in reasonably proximate neighbors Indonesia and Vietnam. The theory was that, having solved the challenge of world-class operations in an emerging market context, Manila Water could grow in these adjacent regional markets. It had scored some early wins and projected that this strategy had the potential to close about 60 percent of its target net income gap. Although Manila Water was focused on a single investment, some companies have many new growth efforts under way. If you are in that circumstance, in this step you should develop a complete list that details each idea, its financial potential, and the required investment to realize that potential. Then estimate the risk-adjusted value of your list by multiplying the financial potential of each investment with its probability of success.

4. *Calculate your growth gap.* The final step is simple enough. Manila Water added the results from steps 2 and 3, compared them to its target in step 1, and identified that it had a growth gap of about 20 percent of its net income target.

The process Manila Water followed sounds simple enough, but our experience points to four pitfalls. First, leaders tend to overestimate the degree of people's alignment with the future target. Getting a group with diverse perspectives to form a consensus view is harder than it looks. Consider starting by asking key members of the leadership team to write down their own view of the future target. Most teams find that estimates vary, often by large amounts. You don't have to have perfect alignment, because subsequent work often makes clear what really could be feasible, but directional alignment obviously helps.

Second, companies tend to underestimate the presence of disruptive warning signs (discussed in chapter 5). These signs, at the very least, herald tougher times ahead. Most companies do a fairly good job of monitoring their direct competitors, but they underinvest in monitoring and interpreting telltale signs of future threats from substitutes and existing or yet-to-be-born disruptors.

Third, when companies make a list of new growth projects, they often create "Potemkin portfolios." The name refers to the Russian prince who was fond of building villages that were nothing more than facades to fool visiting officials about his region's prosperity. In plain terms, no one is actually working on projects that leaders diligently describe during annual planning meetings. Portfolios that look robust on paper are often worthless.

Finally, people tend to be wildly optimistic about the returns promised by their current investments in growth. People generally underestimate the time and cost involved in efforts, even if they are experts in their field. Psychologists call this the *planning fallacy*. The problem is even worse for new growth efforts, which involve many new variables. A new growth effort might involve, for instance, targeting a new customer set, working on an unproven technology, interacting with new partners, and trying out a new revenue model. If the probability that each of those four areas will work out as planned is, individually, 80 percent, the overall chances of success are only 40 percent.

Bring rigor to the analysis. For example, look at past growth initiatives. How many of them delivered as much as predicted? You can also use publicly available industry benchmarks or draw on data from the venture capital industry. For example, research by one academic found that roughly 75 percent of ideas fail to return capital to investors.

Generally, rigorous analysis leads an organization to surface previously hidden risks to current operations and to lower expected returns from planned investments. This need not be a cause for alarm. If calculating a growth gap is approached honestly and openly, it can galvanize the need for change and ensure ongoing attention to the long term. An accurately calculated growth gap will not only enable you to make more-accurate investments in future growth but also may highlight the need to make strategic acquisitions to buy further time or perhaps (softly) communicate different growth targets to external analysts and stakeholders.

The overall goal here is to gain insight not precision, so our final piece of advice is not to spend much time on this effort. Manila Water, for example, developed the first estimate of its gap in about two weeks. Sometimes an afternoon at the white board can give you at least a directional estimate. If you spend more than a month in all but the most complex circumstances, you are likely overthinking the problem.

Step 2: Determining Goals and Boundaries

The world is a big place, and the hunt for ideas to transform your business could take you seemingly anywhere. One of the first things we advise senior leaders is to set clear and strict rules for the hunt. Think about the broad choices facing Manila Water.

- *What type of service should it consider?* Clearly the company would consider anything related to water or related utility services. Leadership determined that other infrastructure-related services could be considered. It decided to take energy generation off the table, under the theory it was simply too different for the company, and its parent Ayala had a separate business focused on energy.

- *How much was it willing to spend pursuing new opportunities?* Manila Water believed it had developed skills related to working in high-fixed-cost environments and wasn't afraid of making further investments. But it set an upper bound to the amount it was willing to invest.

- *How long was Manila Water willing to wait before a given idea had an impact?* Ideally, an idea would begin to have an impact within twenty-four months of commercialization. But Manila Water would be willing to wait up to five years in the right circumstances.

- *What geographies should it target?* Historically, Manila Water's operations were focused on the eastern portion of metro Manila. The leaders decided that any idea had to have some relevance for customers within the current geographic scope, but they were interested in exploring opportunities that also had the potential for national, or even international, expansion.

- *Was it willing to pursue other regulated areas?* Because it was historically a heavily regulated company, the leaders believed one key competency was managing the regulator, so they were happy to pursue new areas that would require significant lobbying in addition to unregulated areas.

- *Were areas replete with bribery and corruption worth considering?* A reality of operating in the Philippines is that bribery is simply the cost of doing business in particular markets. Manila Water took off the table any market where corruption was core to the business.

We call this exercise creating your goals and boundaries for growth. Beyond what Manila Water considered, you also could think about things such as the following.

- *Which customer group can you target?* If you are a consumer-focused company, can you consider business customers? If you are a business-focused company, could you consider targeting consumers? If you target large companies, could you target small ones? If you typically serve service providers, can you go directly to end users?

- *Which distribution channel can you use?* If you typically use a retail channel, can you consider direct sales? If you typically use mass channels, can you consider using niche ones?

- *What revenues must you reach at steady state?* Is it $100 million? $50 million? $5 billion? What constitutes steady state?

- *What kind of margins do you need to obtain at steady state?* Above your current margins? On par with your current margins? Below your current margins?

- *What is the offering you will provide?* If you typically sell products, can you sell services? If you typically sell services, can you sell products?

- *How will you generate revenues?* If you sell products, can you consider leasing or a subscription model? Could you consider a platform in which you make money in transaction fees? Or other models?

- *Which suppliers and partners will you use?* Can you consider using new suppliers? Can you consider outsourcing tasks you normally do yourself? Can you consider owning tasks that you would normally outsource?

- *What tactics will you use?* Can you consider acquisitions and partnerships?

- *What go-to-market approach will you use?* Can you consider test markets with preliminary prototypes that aren't perfect?

The output of the process should clearly summarize what you desire for each area, what is off the table, and what you would consider in the right circumstances.

The appendix and dualtransformation.com have a simple template to capture the output from this exercise. One way to translate the template into a high-impact visual is to create a bullseye diagram with green in the center, yellow in the middle, and red at the outer fringes.

Completing the template need not be an arduous or overly scientific activity. Have your top leadership team complete a short survey, and then hold a two-hour meeting to discuss areas with the strongest disagreement. Remember, you are under no legal requirement to hold to your initial goals and boundaries. As the world changes and you see what works and what doesn't work, you can and should go back and revise the rules of the game.

It typically isn't hard to define what is clearly in bounds. And what you would consider usually comes pretty easily. Codifying and communicating these "consider if" areas can be liberating for an organization, because often the rank and file apply stricter filters than top leaders intend. The biggest challenge is taking things off the table. It feels as if it runs counter to what innovation is all about, but without constraints you are likely to end up with too many subscale experiments.

Step 3: Determining Your Strategic Opportunity Areas

With the rules of the game determined, the final step for Manila Water was to identify the areas that had the greatest potential for growth, the corporate equivalent of moonshots. We call these *strategic opportunity areas.* They are strategic because they fit within the strategic goals and boundaries of your organization. They are opportunities because they present possibilities to create new growth. And they are areas because they are broad enough to explore in multiple ways.

That last part merits extra emphasis. The clarity of focus is not about aligning immediately on hyperspecific tactics (that comes later). Rather, in the parlance of *Playing to Win* by Roger Martin and A.G. Lafley, you are making "where to play" choices.

To assess a potential opportunity area, you need to ask four questions.

1. Is the *what* compelling? How important and unsolved is the problem you are targeting?

2. Is the *who* sufficient? How many people face the problem?

3. Is the *how* believable? To what degree is a solution imaginable without any miracles?

4. Is the *why* convincing? To what degree does it fit your capability set and market trends?

Companies can spend years trying to define future opportunities (the phrase "Boil the ocean" comes to mind), but our experience is that a focused sixty- to ninety-day effort in most cases can develop a short list of high-potential opportunity areas. In Manila Water's case, it took a small, dedicated team working with Innosight consultants about two months.

It started with the team blitzing the market, conducting about fifty visits with consumers and business owners. The exercise's stated goal was simply to talk to individuals about the problems they faced that might suggest a solution fitting within Manila Water's goals and bounds. The market blitz was intentionally diverse; visits ranged from business leaders in palatial residences with teams of servants to some of the poorest consumers in the world.

In parallel, the team conducted secondary research to identify the areas other global utilities had recently considered and to identify interesting startups in or around broad themes that began to emerge from the discussion. Then, through facilitated brainstorming activities, the team summarized its work in the form of about fifty potential opportunity areas. As team members worked to detail those areas, they thought a half-dozen had the highest potential. Through a series of open-ended discussions with top leadership, spearheaded by project sponsor Ferdz dela Cruz (Manila Water's head of operations and CEO Ablaza's right-hand man), the team ultimately put those ideas into three buckets.

Move Forward

The first bucket contained two areas that looked to be a good fit against all the criteria, with no obvious deal-killing risks. Manila Water decided to form teams to explore and ultimately develop a commercial business in each space.

The first area targeted commercial wastewater. Businesses such as restaurants create significant dirty water through daily operations. This water ideally should be treated to remove waste elements. However, in 2013 estimates suggested that more than half of the commercial and industrial companies in Manila defaulted on environmental regulations. To mitigate this situation, government agencies had begun to step up the enforcement of wastewater regulations, with companies increasingly faced with surprise site inspections, fines, stop-operations orders, and media exposure of default. Companies were increasingly looking for experts who could help them mitigate the operational, financial, and reputational risk associated with noncompliance and help them set up long-term compliance solutions for treating industrial and commercial wastewater. Quick-service restaurants and industrial food-processing companies were the most noncompliant and faced serious operational and reputational risks. This area looked attractive to Manila Water, because it could leverage largely off-the-shelf solutions the company already used in residential areas to provide commercial and industrial establishments with affordable solutions that ensured government compliance.

The second opportunity area was packaged water. Although Manila Water provides high-quality water through its infrastructure, poor plumbing inside apartment and office buildings meant that there was a vibrant group of private water-refilling stations that generated about $30 million in annual revenues in the eastern portion of metro Manila alone. Estimates suggested that six out of ten households visited a refilling station at least once a year. These refilling stations largely took tap water from Manila Water, ran it through an "ionizer" (which has questionable benefits in water quality), put it in a large plastic bottle, and sold it at a 500 percent to 1,000 percent markup.

Many consumers reported frustration with the hassle of getting bottles, and offices and high-end residential customers expressed frustration with the challenges of storing bottles. Manila Water imagined offering a low-cost, high-quality model by centralizing manufacturing and building a robust distribution system across Manila, work that would set the stage for it to expand across the Philippines.

Keep in Inventory

A few of the areas had potential to be sizable, but presented a critical risk that gave Manila Water pause. The company decided to keep these in the equivalent of work-in-process inventory. If it turned out that circumstances changed in ways that made these areas more feasible, or if the other areas stalled, the company would accelerate exploration. Otherwise, it would focus on other areas.

An example idea in this category was flood control. Climate change and massive urbanization have worsened Manila's perpetual flood problem. Reports suggest that Manila has lost almost half of its metropolitan canals and waterways, with those that remain chock-full of informal settlers. During rainy periods, major roads are regularly blocked, and 300,000 people living in low-lying areas are impacted annually. This causes significant social and economic problems.

Government agencies have indicated a willingness to invest as much as $10 billion to improve flood infrastructure but as of 2013 had not formulated a specific program. Manila Water has long discussed pursuing a public-private partnership with government agencies to improve the infrastructure development, operations, and maintenance of Manila's flood management system. Although a solution would be technologically challenging, Manila Water's existing infrastructure would be a critical component of a solution. Manila Water decided to hold off on this area until a more specific initiative emerged from the government.

Stop Exploration

There were dozens of ideas that Manila Water investigated but ultimately decided fell short in too many ways to burn more time and money investigating. The decision to stop exploring areas—some of which Manila Water had been talking about for years—was clarifying for the organization.

For example, an idea that Manila Water had often considered was advertising. Manila Water prints and circulates close to three million invoices every month to a captive audience across all social-economic, commercial, and residential sectors. At the time, the advertising market in the Philippines was relatively small and primarily focused on affluent customers, which constituted a subset of Manila Water's customers. Manila Water could either sell empty spaces in the invoices to advertisers or stuff marketing leaflets in with its paper bills. It would need to invest significantly in systems to better understand its customers because advertisers would want to be able to target messages. The small market size, coupled with the complexity of delivering a compelling solution, led Manila Water to decide to stop exploring this idea.

Outcomes for Manila Water

Project ET (east zone transformation) started in August 2013. By December, the team had clarified the goals and boundaries for growth, identified two high-potential opportunity areas, and formed small, dedicated teams to begin pursuing those areas under the overall guidance of Robert "Boogz" Baffrey, an up-and-coming leader who was pulled from his previous role leading wastewater operations to spearhead Manila Water's new growth efforts.

Sharon Marcial led the first pilot of the packaged water business in December of that year under the name Healthy Family. The pilot continued throughout the first half of 2014, before the project was formally launched in August 2014. By early 2016 it had built five plants and sold more than one million bottles, with Marcial serving as a full-time general manager. Then it began to expand beyond Manila Water's home base in eastern Manila, creating new challenges and opportunities. Robbie Vasquez led the development of the commercial wastewater solution, experimenting with three commercial models in 2014 before launching the business formally in January 2015.

In an interview in August 2016, Ablaza and dela Cruz reported being pleased with the progress to date, while noting that they considered the company still no more than halfway along its transformation journey. The new businesses in which it had invested had made good progress, and new innovation and growth mindsets had spread throughout the organization.

"When I first joined Manila Water in 2010, we were for all intents and purposes a single-trick pony," Ablaza noted. "Today, we have a portfolio of businesses. This year we expect non-east zone businesses to contribute something on the order of 15 percent of total enterprise profitability. That is no small achievement. The east zone is such a large business that any new effort looks so puny by comparison."

Ablaza also commented on the cultural change that has come along with Manila Water's efforts to transform itself.

> The organizational culture coming from the privatization days was basically a mindset of let's go for excellent operating efficiency, top-of-the-line customer service, responsiveness, but, most of all, compliance to regulation. It is a mindset where we would say, "Let's manage or minimize our risk and make sure our oversight authorities don't call us out on any major issue." It is almost everything that an innovative culture is the opposite of. I think we have, or at least have started, to develop a mindset that we need to embrace change if we are to grow. We need to be a different business if we are to create shareholder value.

For his part, dela Cruz highlighted the new disciplines the journey has built. "I believe we have a more systematic, programmatic way of transforming the operating model and have really institutionalized an innovation discipline," he said. "One thing you can say about Manila Water is when we do this type of project, we really internalize it."

Chapter 9 has further reflections from Ablaza, dela Cruz, and other leaders who have gone on the journey of dual transformation.

Keys to Success

The clarity to focus is a critical enabler of dual transformation. The best way to develop such clarity is to use a future-back approach, think concurrently across three time frames, and be willing to walk away from substantial pieces of the historical core.

Adopt a Future-Back Mindset

Companies, particularly large, established ones, tend to follow "present-forward" approaches to strategy. That is, they start by detailing today's business, then project what next year will look like, then look at the year after that, and so on. This data-driven approach results in a business that looks very much like today's business, with a couple of minor tweaks. The unstated assumption that governs this process is that the future will resemble the past. When you're planning in times of disruption, however, this approach not only fails but also underplays the biggest threats and obscures the biggest opportunities.

Instead, you should take a future-back approach. Imagine that you and your leadership team board a time machine. You get out at some future date; as before, that might be three to five years in the future in fast-moving industries, and twenty to thirty years in slower-moving ones. Inexorable trends will have affected everyone in and around your industry. Many of these trends aren't hidden. And how they'll affect the industry isn't a mystery. The question is, When you open the door and walk the halls of tomorrow's business, what do you and your team want to see? Data should inform the effort but not drive it.

This future-back approach has both a quantitative and a qualitative component. Quantitatively, you should have at least a rough view of how much of tomorrow's organization is A versus B, and a rough sense of the quantum of investment required to execute a dual transformation.

We believe, however, that the qualitative view is much more important. What will tomorrow's organization feel like? At a cocktail party, how would you tell a story about what you're doing? Many of the examples in Part I of this book had from/to statements describing the core of the transformation. What will be your *transformation blurb* (a short description of what your company will look like after the transformation)? Having alignment on a simple but meaningfully different direction for the company is critical.

Rather than develop blurbs and stories, many organizations ground efforts purely in financial terms. Perhaps they aspire to boost total shareholder returns into the top quartile of an industry (no one ever aims for the second quartile, do they?). Or a goal might be to increase return on invested capital by a couple of percentage points. It is no surprise that the corporate machinery stutters in the face of an ill-defined transformation, particularly one that has almost no motivational hook. Make no mistake—transforming an organization is hard work, and if there isn't a more convincing reason than to spur greater financial returns, it can be hard to redirect corporate machinery.

We don't recommend setting up a special committee to develop the essence of your future story. Rather, have your key executives craft it via a set of ongoing dialogues about the future. And when we say dialogues, we mean it. In his 1996 classic *On Dialogue*, physicist David Bohm detailed the value of dialogues as a way to drive a collective group in a new direction. Rather than a "Ping Pong game, where people are batting the ideas back and forth and the object of the game is to win or to take points for yourself," a good dialogue needs "a common participation, in which we are not playing a game against each other, but with each other. In a dialogue, everybody wins."

The value of this approach is that it builds a shared view of five key topics:

- The most likely future environment

- The desired state of the future company

- The most critical strategic initiatives

- The most critical assumptions

- Critical near-term action items to start the journey

And somewhere along the way—you never know exactly when it will happen—the pieces of the puzzle click together and you and your team will land on a fewer-than-ten-word description of the future company.

Consider Jarden Consumer Solutions (JCS), a multibillion-dollar consumer products company. Historically, the company viewed itself primarily as a business-to-business appliance manufacturer. That is, it saw retailers as its main customer. As a result, Jarden's relationships with individual consumers tended to be highly transactional. A consumer who buys a Mr. Coffee machine or Crock-Pot slow cooker will typically own it for five or more years and will yield no added revenue for Jarden over that time.

By spending more time talking to consumers and observing how they use appliances on a day-to-day basis, the Jarden team began collecting new insights on the underlying jobs that people wanted to get done in the face of trends such as the rise of health consciousness. This knowledge opened new avenues for the company beyond satisfying retailers by improving existing appliances. How could it satisfy a person's desire to save time, lose weight, cut down on cholesterol, or entertain friends? What can be done about a mom's or dad's desire to be a good parent? A series of discussions helped crystallize the company's transformation blurb: "We were a business-to-business appliance manufacturer, we must become a business-to-consumer health and wellness solutions company." As CEO Andy Hill noted, "Being consumer centric is a big transformational concept, and it represents a major cultural change for us."

A future-back orientation helps with the next key to success: thinking concurrently across three time frames.

Think across Three Frames

Clarity of focus is meaningless without a robust plan to achieve it. As the saying goes, "Strategy without execution is hallucination." And driving a company in a fundamentally new direction presents complicated challenges. You probably have heard F. Scott Fitzgerald's famous line, "The test of a first rate intelligence is the ability to hold two opposed ideas in the mind at the same time and still retain the ability to function." In our experience, moonshot-oriented leaders need to hold not two but *three* frames in their mind simultaneously:

- The *moonshot* frame, where they conceive of and describe an inspirational future state that captures the organization's attention

- The *lunar module* (or launch pad) frame, where they think about the components and building blocks that will move the moonshot from dream to reality

- The *Tuesday lunch* frame, where they think about the specific thing they will do tomorrow to make sure they're making progress. The name refers to the fact that engineers can't design modules that enable moonshots if they haven't eaten, or if they don't have the right equipment or training.

Look back at the excerpt from Kennedy's speech. Although the most cited line is about sending a man to the moon (and, importantly of course, bringing him back), the president also described critical steps along the way and mentioned specific enabling technologies.

As you think across these three frames, you naturally begin to think about what you need to do and when you need to do it, so that you can make the desired future state happen. How much do you need to be investing in B? How can you tell whether it is going too slowly and requires intervention? Flipping back and forth and managing activities appropriately help turn inspiring visions into tangible progress.

Be Willing to Wave Good-Bye to the Past

We haven't spent much time in this book detailing perhaps the most iconic transformations of the 1990s (IBM) and early 2000s (Apple). Both examples are well documented and indeed are powerful examples of dual transformation. And in both cases transformation A involved jettisoning key parts of the historic core business.

In IBM's case, over the past two decades, beyond substantial investments to create a services arm, the company exited the hard disk drive, printer, and personal computer markets. Apple cofounder Steve Jobs was known as a creation maestro, but his first set of actions when he returned to Apple in the late 1990s wasn't to create; it was to destroy. He consolidated Apple's complicated product portfolio to four products. The resulting simplicity created organizational capacity to invest in the resulting wave of transformation Bs (iPod, iPhone, etc.).

A more recent example of a company willing to walk away from its heritage is Intuit. The company, founded by Scott Cook in the early 1980s, helps individuals and companies bring discipline to their finances. The product that made the multibillion-dollar company was Quicken, a software package targeted at individuals. But over the years Quicken's role in the company atrophied, surpassed by QuickBooks (for small businesses), TurboTax (to help individuals manage the complexities of the US tax code), and emerging offerings such as Mint, a company Intuit acquired that makes it easy for web-savvy customers to identify savings opportunities.

By 2015, the historic core of the business was down to $50 million in annual revenues. In August 2015, Intuit spun off Quicken to a private investor. These kinds of decisions can be heartbreaking but are a natural component of corporate transformation, because they can free up talented employees and create more mental space for the pursuit of the new and different.

CHAPTER SUMMARY

In 1961, John F. Kennedy demonstrated the clarity to focus by asking Congress to support a mission to send a man to the moon by the end of the decade. Leaders driving dual transformation need to bring similar clarity to critical strategic choices. To identify your moonshots, follow a three-step process.

1. Identify your growth gap.

2. Determine your growth goals and boundaries.

3. Align on a handful of strategic opportunity areas.

To enhance your clarity and to ensure it translates into impact, remember to adopt a future-back mindset. Think simultaneously across the moonshot, lunar module, and Tuesday lunch time frames, and be willing to say good-bye to legacy businesses.

7. The Curiosity to Explore

No one knows exactly how the fire started. The regulator concluded that its source was the use of an unauthorized blowtorch to seal a duct. Regardless of the cause, at 2:02 p.m. on October 9, 2013, fire broke out at a cable chamber of the Bukit Panjang exchange. Extensive damage impacted internet access for more than a quarter-million subscribers across all service providers, including government agencies.

As soon as the fire department declared the area safe, Singtel quickly sprang into action. A key part of the response strategy was figuring out how to divert traffic around the affected cables. The company's intricate knowledge of how the network operated allowed it to solve that problem quickly. Then it had to fix the cables themselves. Experts estimated it could take months.

But this was Singapore, and this was Singtel, one of its crown jewels. Singtel restored more than 40 percent of the fiber connections within twenty-four hours, and repaired the damaged cables within two days. It declared full service restoration on October 14, only 120 hours and 58 minutes after the incident. Tay Soo Meng—a long-time Singtel veteran who at the time headed the network group—and his team did more than diligently attack the problem; they went days with virtually no sleep until they fixed the problem.

The local regulator fined Singtel about $4.5 million because it lacked a specific contingency plan for an outage of this scale. But the regulator acknowledged the company's efforts to provide compensation to users and proactive and transparent response. Over the next eighteen months, Singtel implemented a comprehensive fire prevention and suppression system.

Singtel is an operating machine like few others in the world. It was spun out from government ownership in 1992 but stayed a regulated monopoly until the local industry was deregulated in 2000. Although Singtel is publicly traded, its majority owner is Temasek, an investment company owned by the Singapore government. Singtel's Group CEO at the time of deregulation was Lee Hsien Yang, the second son of Lee Kuan Yew, the founder of modern Singapore. Chua Sock Koong, who previously was deputy Group CEO and chief financial officer, became overall Singtel Group CEO in early 2007.

By 2010 Singtel had become Southeast Asia's largest mobile provider. At the time Singtel reached more than 400 million subscribers through wholly owned operations in Singapore and Australia as well as its significant ownership stakes in providers in Southeast Asia and Africa. Like all mobile providers, Singtel built and operated communications networks that historically were used by consumers to make voice calls. At first, the shift from voice calls to messages and other data services was a boon for the industry. However, it created opportunities for new competitors like Skype, WhatsApp, Facebook, and others to ride over the top of the communications networks and provide competing services. The industry had nightmares of becoming a so-called dumb pipe, bearing all the costs of building expansive, expensive networks but seeing the returns go to these upstarts.

Singtel has a deep finance function, plans rigorously and thoroughly, and regularly wins awards for having the best corporate governance in Asia. Since 2010, in parallel with efforts to streamline and shift its core business from voice to data, something interesting has happened. The company has invested in dozens of startups and built several substantial new growth businesses. Senior leaders have all but given up wearing ties. Leaders have traveled to far-flung places such as Tel Aviv and

Silicon Valley—not to visit Singtel operations in those geographies, but to get firsthand exposure to startups.

In short, Singtel has demonstrated the curiosity to explore.

Problems of Predictability

One of our favorite party tricks is to come into a company we've never met before and proclaim omniscience. We announce that, without having prepared for the meeting at all (which of course we have) or reading anything about the company, we can predict its strategy. The proclamation typically leads to puzzled glances. Then we say, "Your strategy is to continue to do precisely what you are currently doing."

Protests ensue, as audience members describe how they're boldly moving into this market and investing in that technology and partnering with this well-known startup company and have brought in this hot talent. All true—but generally meaningless unless the company is matching bold proclamations and piecemeal moves with the hard work of rewiring the underlying systems that determine how the company allocates resources on a day-to-day basis. After all, your strategy isn't what you *say* you do; it is what you *actually* do, which is driven by how you spend your time and money. And over time, the day-to-day engines that drive resource allocation become optimized to do what has allowed you to succeed, only better.

But even though finely tuned operating engines bring significant benefits, they also present serious challenges in the face of disruptive change. Consider a conversation we had with a top executive at Procter & Gamble more than a decade ago. The company called us in early 2004 saying it needed help with innovation. That wasn't at all obvious from the outside. After all, the company had just launched category-creating products like Febreze (removes malodor from room air and fabric), Swiffer (enables quick cleaning), and Crest White-strips (allows individuals to whiten their teeth themselves). P&G was expanding rapidly in emerging markets, and global revenues were surging. A.G. Lafley was earning acclaim for bringing the spring back in P&G's step after the previous CEO surprisingly resigned in 1999. The company's stock price was surging.

Yet.

P&G's leaders were worried. They peered into their development pipeline and saw a problem. Line extensions and other incremental ideas crowded the pipeline. That meant the company faced the prospect of declining growth. Not in the next year, and maybe not even in the next decade—but leaders decided P&G had to improve its ability to more systematically and reliably create ideas that had the potential to create new brands and indeed new categories.

We were talking to a top executive about what was holding the company back. "We are organized to deliver consistent, reliable results," he told us. "And that's exactly the problem."

P&G's systems prioritized predictability and reliability. In 2016, P&G increased its dividend for the sixtieth straight *year.* Why is pursuing predictability a problem when it comes to driving new growth? As much as we understand innovation better than ever before, success stories almost always have twists, turns, false starts, and false steps.

How Predictability Interferes with Innovation

Let's turn from the P&G story to consider Odeo, a company founded to help consumers organize podcasts on their Apple iPods. A good idea, perhaps, until Apple built into its software the functionality Odeo was seeking to create. In desperation, company founder Ev Williams broke the company into teams of two. He asked each team to spend two weeks developing something—anything—that might allow the company to succeed.

Jack Dorsey and Biz Stone had an idea. What if, they wondered, we created a way for people to update their status? And we intentionally constrained their postings to no more than 140 characters? Yes, Twitter emerged as a side project from a company going down the drain.

Odeo's original investors, including Charles River Ventures, had the opportunity to invest in this new idea but passed, because its commercial potential was unclear. As of the writing of this book, Twitter has 300 million active users and is worth more than $10 billion. A perfectly predictable company shuts down side projects.

Or consider the story of UK-92480. Pfizer was exploring the sexily named drug about twenty years ago. Pfizer hoped it would lower blood pressure in patients. It didn't work. End of story, right? It turned out, however, that the drug had a side effect, one that led male patients in particular to come back and ask for more. Pfizer studied the side effect and optimized it, and the erectile dysfunction category and multibillion-dollar blockbuster Viagra were born. A perfectly predictable company shuts down failures and doesn't study side effects.

Finally, step back to the 1920s. The mind of British scientist Alexander Fleming is brimming with ideas about ways to kill bacteria. Perhaps because his mind was so crowded, he left his lab in shambles when taking a vacation in August 1928. When he returned he found something he didn't expect: a petri dish festering with bacteria—except for one particular part of the dish. Yes, at least one reason Fleming discovered penicillin was that he was a bit of a slob. A perfectly predictable company certainly cleans its laboratories.

The Challenge of Balance

Business leaders have two fundamental challenges. They must exploit what they currently have, and they must explore to develop what they don't have. Predictability helps with exploitation, but it can choke off exploration. And both transformation A and transformation B require a heavy dose of exploration, because, by definition, the precise way to win along either vector can't be completely certain. Leaders must therefore balance two things: the reliability and predictability that is core to playing today's game with greater degrees of precision, and the curiosity that helps organizations explore and find new paths to success.

Curiosity and Decision Making

As the collective parents of seventeen children (Gilbert with eight, Johnson with five, and Anthony bringing up the rear with four), the three of us can attest that human beings are born curious. As most of us go through the educational system and workforce, however, reliability is drilled into us to the point that curiosity is buried, if not destroyed.

Standard operating procedures exist for a reason. There's a right answer. A right way to do things. We're taught that the best way to answer a problem is to gather data, analyze the data, and make a decision based on the results of the analysis. Roger Martin, former dean of the Rotman School of Management at the University of Toronto, has spent much of the past two decades exploring problem solving approaches. He argues that this rational, data-based approach traces back to Aristotle's early writing more than two millennia ago. The basic idea is that there is a universal truth, and the right analytical approach can bring out that truth.

In many contexts, this kind of rational approach makes perfect sense. Consider the story that started this chapter. A rational approach to problem solving helped Singtel determine how to repair a potentially catastrophic problem. Extreme discipline allowed Singtel to surface and rapidly apply optimal solutions. Many of the problems a telecommunications operator faces, such as optimizing network design, running billing systems, and installing new technologies, are perfectly suited to rational, data-driven problem solving approaches.

Curiosity is critical, Martin argues, when the imperative question isn't, "What is true?" but rather, "What is possible?" The latter question can't be answered purely by gathering data and building intricate spreadsheets. Instead, it requires intuition and judgment.

"Think of a sommelier," Martin says. "What is their skill set? Is it anything about the manipulation of quantities? How many people get to be a sommelier by measuring the alcohol content of wine? No, you get it by being able to make fine distinctions between wines in a blind test. It's art, based on experience."

There's a fundamental difference in mindset between a corporate planner optimizing resources within an existing business, on the one hand, and a venture capitalist hoping to discover the next big thing, on the other hand. The corporate planner expects every investment to work out. He places a premium on making detailed analyses and delivering against milestones. Exceptions are highlighted and punished.

The venture capitalist, however, knows that statistically, any time she makes an investment it is unlikely to work out. Because 75 percent of venture capital investments fail to create any kind of commercial return, the mode and median return of most investment portfolios is a big fat zero. The only way to generate returns is to learn whether a particular company could be a positive outlier in as resource-efficient a way as possible. Those that look promising get further investment.

Those that don't, don't. There's a brutality to the process, because, after all, the venture capitalist has a portfolio of investments but the startup entrepreneur can realistically pursue only one significant idea at a time.

If you demand that every idea succeed, you will be consigned to work on incremental improvements within the confines of your current business. After all, that's the only place where you can approach absolute certainty that customers will do what you expect, that you can deliver what you hope to, and that the components of the business model will come together in the right way.

More specifically, having the curiosity to explore impacts three key components of developing new ideas.

The Funding Component

How does a well-run business make decisions about investments related to its core? It carefully gathers data, analyzes the data, considers strategic alternatives, develops a recommendation, and builds consensus around that recommendation before finally presenting it to top brass. Decision meetings rarely decide things, because, when the process is run well, the decision has been made through a carefully orchestrated set of pre-meetings. Debates are settled by data; if leaders aren't satisfied by what they see, they instruct their team members to go back and conduct more research, sharpen their analysis, or talk to industry experts. The decision is made, and that's usually the end of it. Discussions then turn to execution, measuring progress against predetermined milestones, spending against budget, and so on.

Explorers recognize they can't know the right answer, so they want to invest as little as possible in learning which of their hypotheses are right and which ones are wrong. Discussion is much more focused on critical uncertainties, optimal testing mechanisms, and emergent learning versus the sanctity of data.

The Focus Component

Chapter 6 describes how leaders need the clarity to focus on the highest-potential opportunity areas. One of the paradoxes of dual transformation is that leaders need to become less focused as they go about developing winning strategies in those areas. After all, history shows us that sustainable strategies for disruptive innovations emerge from a process of trial-and-error experimentation.

The Failure Component

A strange idea that has blossomed over the past few years is that failure is generally good. Not so—failure is bad. Who wants to have something not work out? Many types of failure are bad and should be avoided. Imagine a heart surgeon talking proudly about a patient he killed because he made a mistake during an operation. That's not good. When something doesn't work because you were stupid, sloppy, or hadn't invested enough time to develop a learnable skill, that's bad.

When people say that failure breeds innovation, they are talking about a very specific thing in a very specific circumstance. When you are in exploration mode, by definition you don't know what the answer is ahead of time. So you figure out the best hypothesis you can and then find a way to test it. When it doesn't work, you figure out why it didn't work and go back to the drawing board. When this process is executed in the right way, it is indeed not a failure; it is a step on the way to success.

Chapter 6 describes how Manila Water clarified its new growth strategy by focusing on a handful of growth opportunities. Its senior leaders argued that treating new and core ideas differently helped it advance those opportunities without distracting efforts to reposition its core business. As CEO Gerry Ablaza describes it, "We set up a separate governance structure so that the programs, the capital investment, and the people decisions can be made separately from the main business or the core business. So it sets it free in a manner of speaking from the usual institutional processes that we have in place."

Infusing Curiosity at Singtel

The trends affecting the telecommunications industry are inescapable, so Singtel, with the urging of its board chair, Simon Israel, knew it had to improve its ability to respond to change. As Group CEO Chua said in the company's 2012 annual report, "Embracing a culture that allows innovation to flourish is important. This will require a shift in our collective mindset—away from failure aversion to one of constant experimentation."

An uncertain future world meant that its historical disciplines had to be augmented with an injection of curiosity. Chua, Israel, and the Singtel leadership team did three things that helped bolster the organization's ability to discover disruptive paths to success.

Create Safe Spaces for Innovation

In 2010, Singtel announced plans to invest S$200 million (about US$150 million at 2015 exchange rates) in startup companies through an investment vehicle called Singtel Innov8. Of course, part of the rationale was to generate financial returns, but an even more important purpose was to provide a vehicle to brush up against the world's innovation energy.

In 2012, Edgar Hardless took over as the new leader of the fund. Over the next few years Innov8 expanded to become a global team that included representatives in Tel Aviv and Silicon Valley. Innov8 scoured the globe to find interesting investment opportunities that fit emerging themes around mobile advertising, big data analytics, cyber security, the internet of things, and more. By 2015, Innov8 had invested in more than fifty companies and was well established as a go-to investor in both the region and the industry.

One of Innov8's early investments was in Viki, a video-streaming website based in Singapore that offers on-demand video of TV shows, movies, and music videos from around the world. Rakuten Group of Japan acquired that business for $200 million. In 2014, Innov8 backed Jasper, a hyped company that created a platform to help companies manage services related to the internet of things. In 2016 Cisco Systems acquired Jasper (the name refers to the operating system created by Tony Stark, otherwise known as Iron Man) for $1.4 billion.

Among Singtel's regional associates (companies in Southeast Asia in which Singtel holds a significant, but noncontrolling, stake), Globe Telecom in the Philippines has been the most aggressive in developing a similar structure. In 2012, Globe CEO Ernest Cu backed a proposal from Minette Navarrete to create a separate investment vehicle called Kickstart Ventures, jointly owned by Singtel and the Ayala Corporation, the family-controlled conglomerate that constituted the other significant investor in Globe. One of Kickstart's missions is to develop the entrepreneurial ecosystem in the Philippines, a country with a young, technologically savvy population. Between 2012 and 2015 Kickstart made twenty investments in early-stage companies in the Philippines. Impressed by the progress, in early 2015 Cu convinced his board to set aside $50 million to expand Kickstart's investment activities.

Increasingly, companies have decided that this kind of corporate venture capital is critical given the pace and scale of change in the global market. This is arguably the third wave of the formation of these kinds of funds. The first came in the 1980s, as venture capital began to enter the mainstream. The second was in the late 1990s in the midst of the dot-com bubble. Interestingly, the first two waves were early signs of the market turning: companies jumped into venture capital after booms had created big returns for venture capitalists and then were left gasping for air as bubbles burst and returns stagnated.

The third wave started about a decade ago and survived the global financial crisis in 2007–2008 and the worldwide turbulence that has continued since, something that suggests this time corporate venture capital might be here to stay. If you decide to follow in Singtel's path, you should heed the guidance of academic experts to first clarify your strategic intent. Do you want to maximize financial returns? Have a listening function that gets an early look at interesting startups? Have a more direct window into emerging technologies? Identify acquisition targets early? Then make sure you match your structure to your strategic intent. If you truly want to maximize returns, for example, hire talent comparable to what you would find in leading venture capital funds, and ensure they have the chance to earn competitive financial returns. If you want to identify acquisition targets early, ensure that you structure investments in a way that simplifies the consummation of a deal.

In 2012, two years after starting Innov8, Singtel reorganized to reflect its dual transformation agenda. It set up a special-purpose organization called Group Digital L!fe (yes, that's an exclamation point—another countercultural element) to incubate new businesses that went beyond Singtel's historic core. To demonstrate the importance of these efforts, it asked veteran Allen Lew to lead "GDL." Prior to the reassignment, Lew ran the Singapore business for Singtel. He went overnight from commanding a staff of thousands delivering billions in revenues to a staff of hundreds delivering tens of millions in revenues. And most people on that staff weren't homegrown Singtel talent. Rather, in conjunction with the new organization, Singtel announced its first big acquisition in mobile advertising: a $321 million deal to acquire Amobee, a leading digital marketing business.

In 2013 Singtel publicly committed to spend $1.6 billion over the next few years to pursue strategic acquisitions in the digital space. Reflecting on that commitment in 2015, Israel noted that the plan was big enough to demonstrate a commitment to do something significant, but not so big that it posed a fundamental risk to the company. (Indeed, in 2016 Singtel announced its intent to spend close to $2 billion, an amount that exceeded its aggregate investment in new growth from 2010 to 2015, to acquire a stake in companies that would nudge its stake in mobile operators in Thailand and India by several percentage points.)

From 2012 to 2014 Lew and his team were clearly in exploration mode, dabbling with ideas such as mobile payments, local information guides, and even a smart phone app custom-designed for the unique patois in Singapore known by locals as Singlish. Lew built a team that blended longtime Singtel staff having a passion and proclivity for innovation, young energetic hires, and experienced innovators from unrelated industries.

In late 2014, Singtel consolidated GDL's efforts into a handful of main strategic areas, such as digital marketing (with further acquisitions added to Amobee), big data analytics, and cyber security (with an $800 million acquisition of US-based Trustwave in early 2015). With substantial investment capital still to follow, those areas were set up to be significant growth drivers for Singtel.

Furthermore, the capability to explore emerging areas such as smart, connected devices will pay dividends in the years to come. In late 2014 Lew moved on to his next assignment: taking over Optus (Singtel's wholly owned subsidiary in Australia). In 2014 Optus had revenues of about $8 billion and almost nine thousand employees.

Expose Leaders to New Thinking

Every year, the top one hundred leaders from Singtel in Singapore and Australia gather for what is called the top management workshop

(TMW). In 2011, Singtel held the three-day TMW in Beijing. On the first full day, the group broke into small teams and visited local startup companies. One of us (coauthor Scott Anthony) provided outside stimuli, leading the group through case study discussions about Procter & Gamble's systematic approach to innovation and Netflix's disruptive business model.

All this was in a place where Singtel had no consumer presence at all (its enterprise business, which provides connectivity and related services to businesses, had some business in China, with clear aspirations to do more). Why Beijing, then, if it was commercially irrelevant to most of the audience? It was an intentional effort to expose Singtel's top leaders to new ways of thinking, where they could brush up against new cultures and see the surprising startup energy in what was perceived at the time by many outsiders as a staid Communist country.

Then in 2012, Singtel held TMW in Manila, with teams conducting field visits with consumers across all social strata in and around the city. In 2013, the location was New Delhi. Singtel's board of directors joined the act as well, holding meetings in Silicon Valley, Israel, and Boston.

Group CEO Chua describes these visits as important components of strengthening her team's understanding of local markets. "We can always get any number of speakers to come out here to speak, and give the board any amount of literature. But nothing beats going to the markets in which we operate, visiting the shops and talking to customers, or traveling to tech innovation hubs like Israel, Silicon Valley, or Boston to see what big tech companies and small startups are doing."

In parallel, Singtel's human resources team regularly brings in fresh thinking. Rita McGrath of Columbia University, Vijay Govindarajan of the Amos Tuck School of Business, and Linda Hill of Harvard Business School ran interactive sessions attended by hundreds of Singtel employees. In 2008, Singtel's HR team began organizing a multiday event called the Singtel Learning Fiesta, which exposes thousands of Singtel employees to new ideas, as well as vendors that can help with everything from organizing hackathons to managing social networks. By 2015, the event had grown to more than twenty thousand "learning spaces" for 170 courses (both live and virtual) in Singapore, Australia, Malaysia, Hong Kong, the Philippines, and the United States.

These are concerted efforts to expose leaders, and the broader organization, to fresh ideas and new ways of thinking. This tactic fits one of the most persistent findings in the innovation literature: magic happens at intersections where different mindsets and skills collide. The curious organization plants itself at the intersections by taking road trips, bringing in outside speakers, and regularly rotating people between functions and roles.

Reinforce Curiosity in Routines and Rituals

Most organizations, particularly large ones that have existed for decades, often admit that curiosity isn't in their culture. What is a culture? Borrowing from MIT's Edgar Schein, we define a culture as a set of assumptions, often unstated, that govern the way people think and act. Those assumptions typically are about causality: we do *this* because we know it leads to *that*. Assumptions form because a group tries various ways to solve a problem that occurs frequently, and it replicates the things that work and stops the things that don't. Over time, it becomes "the way things are done around here."

Developing a culture that is more conducive to curiosity, therefore, requires finding ways to reinforce it in day-to-day routines and rituals so that it ultimately disappears into unstated assumptions. Members of the Singtel family, and other companies discussed in *Dual Transformation*, have found various ways to do that.

Understand Your Customers

Optus has had thousands of its workers participate in what it calls "customer close ups." Workers spend a day in a store and a day with the customer relations team. The in-store day starts by workers spending an hour as a shopper, making a purchase, and reporting what is "good, curious, and interesting." In the next two hours, participants introduce themselves as Optus employees and shadow a sales rep. After a lunch break they put on a trainee badge and spend two hours as a store representative (with a regular employee helping out, of course). Finally, they end the day by having direct interactions with customers.

These kinds of immersive programs are great ways to develop deep empathy with customers and lead participants to question underlying assumptions they have about the business. The larger a company is, the wider the gap typically is between its leaders and its customers. Leaders spend an increasing amount of time looking inward, attending approval meetings, reviewing employee performance, and so on. Walking a mile in the customer's shoes helps bridge that gap by giving people, especially leaders, firsthand exposure to what life looks like for normal customers. In particular, this kind of firsthand experience often gives leaders a deeper appreciation for key points of customer frustration.

Shape the Physical Environment

Anyone who has worked in a range of offices knows that the physical environment matters. You can feel it when you walk into a company. Innovative environments have colors and pictures and sights and sounds and, yes, foosball tables and other forms of play. Environments that aren't innovative have thick carpets and closed doors and dark lighting and a serious but stultifying air. The former environments help encourage innovation by pulling diverse groups of people together and reinforcing experimentation and play.

Singtel's GDL had a special-purpose space designed on the principles of transparency and collaboration. Globe took advantage of the need to move into a new office building in 2013 to reinforce its own cultural shift by creating a bustling cafeteria, plentiful meeting rooms, and open offices that favor chance encounters.

Simplify Experiments

A few years ago, Adobe started a program called Kickbox. Participants receive a red box that's about the size of an encyclopedia (if you're younger than thirty, ask your parents). When employees crack open the box, they find a range of tools designed to facilitate developing prototypes for ideas. Most critically, the box contains a prepaid $1,000 debit card that workers can spend without asking for anyone's approval.

As of 2015 some one thousand people had received a kickbox. That's a $1 million investment, but it is also a thousand experiments that otherwise would not have been run. Many of those experiments have gone nowhere, but some have informed new product development efforts or highlighted acquisition opportunities.

Share Rough Ideas

Exposing half-baked ideas early, rather than waiting for an idea to be "perfect," generates useful, usable feedback. It also has positive spillover effects as people in other corners of the organization can take fragments of an idea in new directions or can avoid wasting time on things that are similar but not as good. Singtel uses its top management meetings to share ideas with wide groups of people. Optus went even further in mid-2015, running a full-day session on innovation with its top four hundred people. One key component was a walk-through that allowed people to see innovation in action at the company.

Celebrate Desired Behaviors

Our final example comes from a company not otherwise mentioned in this book, but it fits too perfectly not to share it. Tata Sons is India's largest conglomerate, with business units ranging from tea to IT consulting to automobiles. Collective revenues across its sprawling collection of businesses exceed $100 billion. Every two years, it holds an awards ceremony to fete its innovation accomplishments. One of the most coveted awards is called Dare To Try. As the name connotes, the award goes to a team that tried something that did not work. As the summary of the 2013 ceremony notes, "Showcasing a growing culture of risk-taking and perseverance across Tata companies, the Dare To Try category at Tata Innovista saw over 240 entries. The Dare To Try category recognises and rewards most novel, daring and seriously attempted ideas that did not achieve the desired results. The award went to Tata Consultancy Services." The number of submissions crossed three hundred in 2015.

Whenever you innovate, two good things can happen. Of course, you can create value. But you also can learn something that opens future avenues to create value. As serial innovator Thomas Alva Edison noted, "If I find 10,000 ways something won't work, I haven't failed. I am not discouraged, because every wrong attempt discarded is often a step forward."

Operational machines don't become tap dancers overnight, but from 2010 to 2016 Singtel clearly strengthened its curiosity quotient. In

August 2016, CEO Group Chua reported being pleased with Singtel's progress.

> Change is not new to us. Over the last three decades, we have re-invented ourselves many times over: from a statutory board, we were corporatized, then publicly listed. Today, we have moved well beyond simply being a telco offering connectivity. We have become a regional communications and ICT [infocomm technology] solutions company with a presence in some 23 countries globally. How did we get here? Each and every transformation we went through required a corporate tenacity that wasn't afraid of change nor what the future would bring. As technologies changed, as the industry changed, as what customers wanted were changing, we responded each time with forward-looking actions. I believe this mindset of change and adaptability is what has taken us from leadership position in Singapore to the forefront in the region.

Becoming a Curious Leader

Problems of predictability don't rest only within a company's systems. We suspect that at this stage you are feeling vaguely uncomfortable. Making the kind of courageous decisions described in chapter 5? Well, that's the essence of leadership. Bringing the kind of clarity to complex problems described in chapter 6? Surely you got to where you are by making tough calls and giving clear direction. Sure, what we have described before this chapter might involve a bit more art than usual, but it's nothing you can't handle with sufficient focus and attention.

But being curious. Fumbling. Flailing. Playing. That's behavior you might have followed when you were younger. But that's not what got you to the position you're in now. And the mentors who helped you along the way are likely little help. So how can you become a more curious leader? That's a book-worthy topic in itself, but we end this chapter by providing four specific tips.

Find an "Inverse" Mentor

When you think of a mentor, you naturally think of someone with gray hair who has seen it and done it. You turn to these mentors because they've stared down the problem you're facing, and they bear the scars from their struggles and the trappings of their successes. But when you're confronting disruptive change, you need a very different sort of mentor. You need someone who is plugged in to the disruption. Odds are high that person has *less* experience, at least in terms of years on the earth.

Marc Benioff, the founder and CEO of Salesforce, makes a point of developing an eclectic network. He has *reverse* mentors, who have grown up living with new technologies, such as Dropbox cofounder Drew Houston. "He grew up in the internet. I didn't," Benioff said. "So he can see things in ways that I don't. That perspective is really important. I can't sit in my headquarters and pretend I'm in touch." Benioff also has *inverse* mentors, with completely different experience sets, such as Black Eyed Peas superstar and music entrepreneur will.i.am. In times of disruption, reverse and inverse mentors will help you see things you couldn't otherwise see.

And yes, parents, this is your excuse to play Minecraft with your kids.

Learn to Code

In 2008, Dave Gledhill became the group executive and head of group technology and operations at DBS Bank, a leading Singapore-based bank that, as of the writing of this book, had more than S$400 billion in assets and a market capitalization of about S$50 billion (roughly US$300 billion and US$35 billion). One year later, Piyush Gupta took over as CEO and began pushing an aggressive transformation agenda, with a specific focus on embracing digital technologies.

An obviously important emerging area for any bank going digital is the smart phone, and DBS has aggressively explored mobile-only banking offerings in markets like India. Although Gledhill is a fourth-generation engineer with a degree in computing and electronics, his formal education was decades ago, well before the rise of smart phones and related apps.

"My coding days were twenty years ago, and none of this stuff existed then," Gledhill said. "I was struggling to understand at a deep level what was happening inside the phone, which made it hard to function as a leader of technology."

So Gledhill committed himself to develop an app. An evening event provided the inspiration. In Singapore, every car is required to have a reader with a smart card that interacts with the city-state's smart toll system and almost every parking garage. One time Gledhill found himself at an event where the host provided complimentary parking. Unfortunately, Gledhill forgot to remove his smart card from his car, so classic Singaporean efficiency rendered the complimentary parking moot.

Gledhill wondered, what if he could create an app that provided location-based reminders, which reminded you to do a certain thing only when you were in a certain location? "How often do you find yourself saying, 'When I get here I must remember to . . .'?" Gledhill asked himself.

He downloaded Apple's developer kit and started watching videos from Apple University while exercising. After "teaching myself C++ all over again," Gledhill developed a functioning version of the app, which he called, simply, Reminder. The app proudly sits on his phone's home screen, with Gledhill noting how the icon (which resembles a shoelace knot) actually was a strand of pasta.

Gledhill didn't pursue formally publishing the app on Apple's store, but he considered the experience invaluable. "It has given me such a depth of awareness about how devices operate and what they are capable of," he said. "It has made me better able to provide guidance for the digital bank at a very technical level because I really understand what is going on."

For example, making a location-based app work requires understanding precisely where a user is located. The most reliable way to do so is via a GPS signal. However, a GPS doesn't work indoors, so it would require a creative workaround if you were to deliver against Gledhill's original use case. That firsthand knowledge aids Gledhill in decision making, problem solving, and discussions with vendors.

Several of Gledhill's direct reports followed his lead and started developing their own apps. "When a leader does this," he said, "it sets the attitude that everyone in the organization better be learning about how to be a leader in the digital space."

Leaders seeking to bolster their capacity to lead a culture of innovation should follow Gledhill's lead. After all, it is hard to make decisions about technologies or business models with which you have no firsthand experience.

Get Out of the Building

Steve Blank teaches at Stanford University and the University of California at Berkeley, but he is hardly a traditional academic. Rather, in his career Blank has actively participated in more than a dozen startups and by now has mentored hundreds more. Over the past decade he has emerged as a prominent thought leader, describing how to take a more scientific approach to the creation of new businesses. One of his mentees, Eric Ries, wrote the 2011 book *The Lean Startup*, which has become a must-read for almost any entrepreneur.

The epigraph in Blank's 2013 book with Bob Dorf (*The Startup Owner's Manual*) says it all: "Get out of the building!" It is hard to become more curious when the stimuli you receive is limited to the thick carpets of the executive floor or the five-star hotel you stay at on road trips. Take any excuse you can to get out of the building to do the following:

- Visit a customer in her natural habitat.

- Spend time with a team working on a new growth venture, not in an orchestrated review but in the field.

- Call on an interesting startup in your area, not to sell, but only to learn.

- Just *go out* and explore when you are on the road.

These activities bring to mind the famous line from spy novelist John le Carré: "A desk is a dangerous place from which to view the world."

Embrace Transparency

When Alan Mulally took over as CEO of Ford in 2006, the American icon was on shaky ground. The company had a culture filled with politics and positioning. It would go on to declare a $20 billion loss in the first quarter of Mulally's watch.

Determined to turn the company around, Mulally, an engineer by trade who had spent thirty years at Boeing, instituted weekly meetings where his team had to present reams of performance data. Charts were color coded, with the usual green (good), red (bad), and yellow (bears watching). During one of the first review meetings, Mulally found himself in a sea of green.

He stopped the meeting. Either we are *trying* to lose billions of dollars, or someone is not telling the whole truth, he said. One of his mantras is, "You can't manage a secret." Transparency is a critical component of curiosity. Look, not everything you do will work out. When you as a leader show that you are fallible, and when it becomes clear that the organization is more interested in getting to truth than in saving face or managing internal positioning, it helps release often latent organizational curiosity.

CHAPTER SUMMARY

Futurist Alan Kay once said, "The best way to predict the future is to invent it." No matter how clear your focus, dual transformation will require that you have the curiosity to explore multiple paths, even when the outcome of any given one is likely failure. That runs counter to the machinery that powers most organizations, which is designed to remove variation and deliver predictable results. Singtel's journey shows how to boost your curiosity quotient by:

- Creating safe spaces for exploration
- Exposing leadership to new stimuli
- Incorporating curiosity in day-to-day routines

Individual leaders seeking to reignite latent curiosity should find inverse mentors, learn new skills, deliberately get out of the building, and embrace transparency.

8. The Conviction to Persevere

Transformation is the toughest job a leader will ever face. Picture the choice facing J. Stewart Bryan III. It was early 2012, and in his hand the ever-polite septuagenarian held something that seemed to represent hope for Media General, the organization that had been in his family for almost 150 years. The letter was an offer from an organization owned by no less than the Oracle of Omaha himself, Warren Buffett, to purchase the vast majority of Media General's thirty newspapers.

The Bryan family's connection to the company traced to the 1870s, when a friend of Stewart Bryan's great-grandfather gifted him the *Daily Times* in Richmond, Virginia. The company expanded its newspaper operations when it purchased the *Tampa Bay* [Florida] *Tribune* in 1927 and spread to other parts of the southeast United States over the subsequent decades. The company—as it turned out, very wisely—diversified into television broadcasting when it launched its first local station, WFLA, in Tampa Bay in 1955. Between 1999 and 2006, Media General took advantage of its ample cash flows and strong balance sheet to further diversify, spending more than $1 billion purchasing a string of additional stations across the Southeast, bringing its total to eighteen.

In 2003 Bryan stepped down as CEO, appointing Marshall Morton as his successor. Bryan continued to come into the office frequently and served as an active chair of the board of directors. By 2006, despite the technological changes ripping through the industry, Media General seemed to be on solid ground. The company had about $800 million in annual revenue and a market value of more than $1 billion, and it employed seven thousand people. Bryan was worth tens of millions of dollars, on paper at least.

It was clear to Bryan, Morton, and the rest of the leadership team that the pace of industry change required aggressive investments in transformation, but industry change kept outpacing the team's well-intentioned efforts. A deep recession in 2007–2008 brought the entire media industry to its knees. A hedge fund took over three board seats in 2007 and tried to force aggressive cost cuts. With control of voting stock, Bryan was able to rebuff them (coauthor Scott Anthony replaced one of those directors in 2009 and served on the board until 2013), but the intervention began what would become a series of layoffs as Media General cut its costs to match the decreases in its revenues.

By 2012, Media General was staggering. Successive rounds of layoffs had reduced the workforce to about four thousand. Bryan, known for his kindness, quick wit, pitch-perfect Southern accent, and ever-present bow tie, had to let go friends with whom he had worked for decades. The company's market capitalization sank to less than $100 million. With substantial debt needing to be refinanced in 2013, whispers began suggesting the company might need to file for bankruptcy protection.

In the rational part of his brain, Bryan knew that there was only one answer to the offer from World Media Enterprises, a wholly owned subsidiary of Buffett's Berkshire Hathaway. In essence, Buffett wasn't paying anything for the newspapers; he was simply removing the millstone that was dragging down Media General. After the transaction Media General would have a stable, cash-producing broadcast business, with the financial freedom to find a path for future growth.

But leaving behind a family legacy that stretched back decades! No matter how clear the analysis, that kind of move is emotionally draining.

With a heavy heart, Bryan and the board approved the deal.

The story turned out reasonably well for Media General. Later in 2012 the company sold its last newspaper, the *Tampa Bay Tribune* (which Buffett had avoided because he wanted to focus on newspapers in smaller geographic areas). Media General merged with Young Broadcasting in 2013, acquired Lin Media in 2014, and was acquired by Nexstar Broadcasting Group in 2016 (after a fierce fight with Meredith Corp.)

for almost $5 billion. After the transaction, Nexstar became the third-largest broadcast company in the United States, with about 175 television stations across the country and more than $2 billion in revenue.

But the process to get to that end point was brutal on the organization, its leaders, and the thousands who lost jobs. In early 2014, in response to an email from coauthor Anthony congratulating Media General on the Lin merger, Bryan noted the following.

> Our structure is now 180 degrees removed from where it was, in both operations and governance; and, while it appears to be the best solution for shareholders, it has, also, some sad and poignant side effects for me and some other long-term employees and colleagues. As you know so well, however, the world has changed—some say for the better, others don't—but many of the old ways of dealing with others, in business and society in general, leave me wistful for the old ways.
>
> But then, I'll be 76 in a month, and I've had much fun while being involved in a business I've always thought was good for the country and the world.

Sadly, Bryan died in early 2016 before the completion of the Nexstar transaction due to complications from injuries he suffered from a fall in his home.

As we've said, executing a dual transformation is the hardest challenge leaders and their teams will ever encounter. But, increasingly, there is no alternative. In this chapter we describe the final piece of the puzzle: the conviction to persevere in the face of predictable crises. Although every transformation journey we've studied is unique, our frontline experience teaches us there are always, somewhere during the journey, three categories of crises: crises of commitment, crises of conflict, and crises of identity. After describing these three crises, we explain how the disciplined separation of transformation A from transformation B, and a grounding in a motivating purpose, provides the best inoculation against these crises.

The Three Crises of Dual Transformation

There isn't a strict recipe for how to fundamentally change a company, and every dual transformation story has its twists and turns and unusual characters. Yet in the same way that many great movies follow basic templates (such as the hero's journey), the dual transformation journey has predictable moments when leaders face a crisis that will challenge their convictions. To bring these moments to life (without betraying individual confidences), we illustrate these crises here through a composite case study.

"George" is the leader of Partzelg, a $2 billion company based in the US Midwest that makes components used in a wide range of motorized vehicles, such as automobiles and airplanes. The business has performed well over the past two decades, but growth has slowed, and projections show that the core business will begin to decline in twelve to eighteen months.

Sensing the early warning signs of disruptive change, George and his team decided to launch a dual transformation effort. He asked Andy, a twenty-six-year veteran, to lead transformation A, in which Partzelg's core business would shift from a traditional sales model to a leasing model. Andy's plan promises to minimize sales declines and dramatically boost profit margins and cash flow. It requires radically reconfiguring the organization, however, and laying off about 30 percent of staff.

Bernadette is driving transformation B. After considering several options, she and her team have decided to focus on the internet of things. She has recommended acquiring a sensor company and an analytics company, with the intent of stitching them together to offer unique services based on the data generated by Partzelg's components.

That all sounds sensible, but let's see what happens when key leaders begin questioning Partzelg's commitment. Does the organization still care about A? Is it serious about making B happen? Will it make the tough calls in both cases?

Crises of Commitment

It's Friday afternoon, and George, unbelievably, is staring at two hours without any meetings on his schedule. "That's a relief," he thinks, because it gives him extra time to prepare for an important upcoming board meeting. He's planning to ask the board for formal approval for $500 million to back Bernadette's two acquisitions. The business case for each is solid, and his pre-meetings with key board members have all gone well. "No harm in further sharpening the material," he thinks. And it is refreshing to actually do real work.

He's knee deep in facts and figures when a sharp knock on his table breaks his concentration. Partzelg moved to an open floor plan six months ago in an effort to boost collaboration, and people are still figuring out how to do formerly simple things like alerting people when you want their attention. A knock on the door used to be so easy.

George looks up to see Andy hovering over him. "How long have you been there?"

"About five minutes," Andy says. "You look really absorbed, so I hate to bother you, but we need to talk."

"Sure—what's up?"

"Well, we've got a problem," Andy says. "The rumor mill says that Carla is going to leave to work at a software-as-a-service supply chain startup called SAASUP."

George groans. Carla is a vital cog in his core business. She manages supplier relations and does it extremely well. Partzelg hasn't announced the precise details about its new leasing model, but it will require tighter integration with suppliers, and this means Carla's responsibilities will increase.

"And, not to make your Friday worse," Andy continues, "but SAASUP called me too, and as much as I love working here, I have to admit I'm thinking about it. They have huge growth prospects and some blue chip investors, and, well, honestly, I'm just not sure how much juice is left in our component business. You've been so focused on these acquisitions, it's made me wonder if my team and I really matter for our future at all."

George puts down his presentation and turns his full attention to Andy.

"Thanks for telling me before you've made your decision," George says. "I admit I've been distracted pushing these acquisitions forward. They're important for our future. But what you and your team are doing is just as important, if not more so, Andy."

Andy still looks skeptical.

"Without a strong and healthy core business, we don't have any data to analyze or any services to offer," George adds. He rubs his eyes. "And remember, we provide the components that keep the world running. We're not some stupid startup trying to spin stories and siphon profits to chase a valuation. We do real things that matter for real customers."

"I know," Andy says.

George leans forward. "We can't deliver against our mission without you guys! If that business isn't running well, I know the board and shareholders will hammer us over performance, and we won't have the space to go and move full speed ahead with these new opportunities."

It's easy for leaders driving transformations to overindex their time on the B side of the equation. And it's equally easy for the people in the historical core business to wonder whether they have a future. Leaders must go out of their way to reassure the people in transformation A of the critical role it plays in dual transformation.

It shouldn't be hard. After all, transformation A produces cash to invest in transformation B. If transformation A is managed appropriately, those cash flows can be significant. The historical core also houses the critical capabilities that enable transformation B to pick unfair fights against competitors.

As dual transformation begins, it's easy for leaders to spend all their time talking about the future and about the new directions the company is taking. These changes are undoubtedly exciting, and, as discussed later, painting that picture is critical. But you need to make sure to clearly communicate how important the work of transformation A is to enable long-term success. Otherwise, the people in the core business will feel like second-class citizens. Some will naturally choose to abandon what they perceive to be a business in irreversible decline; others will clamor to join the team doing the "cool" work of transformation B, even if their capabilities and skills are best suited for the core business. Losing your best talent at a time when you need it most can accelerate a downward spiral.

It's also important that the transformation A team do more than fund B. Employees must believe there is a viable path forward for A that is compelling in and of itself, and, most important, that it is going to work. No one wants to preside over a sinking ship.

Two weeks later, George is taking advantage of a short break between wall-to-wall meetings to catch up on email. The subject of one from Bernadette catches his eyes: "need to talk."

George opens WhatsApp and sends Bernadette an immediate message, asking if he can come over this afternoon, and then sends a message to his assistant asking to clear his afternoon schedule. Bernadette works in an office about forty-five minutes away from headquarters, and George knows she is the last person to cry wolf.

Four hours later, he pulls into the overpriced parking lot next to the office housing Bernadette and her team. As he walks into the office, he is struck, as he has been before, by the contrast between this urban office—with its hip, exposed industrial fixtures, bright colors, and polished concrete floors—and the more traditional suburban office he calls home. Is that someone going by on a hoverboard? "Better not tell HR about that," he thinks.

He finds Bernadette finishing an afternoon standup meeting with some of her key lieutenants. The two of them go and grab a coffee from one of the ubiquitous machines and start to chat.

"Let me cut to the chase," she says. "My team is wondering whether we're really serious about these acquisitions. Sure, we've talked about being bold and moving in new directions. And we did execute those small deals to bring in Fred and his team. But the big stuff is moving so slowly."

George pauses for a minute before responding. It's true the board asked for further analysis on the bigger of the two acquisitions, but from his point of view Bernadette's team has been moving incredibly fast, especially compared with business as usual in the core.

Bernadette takes advantage of the pause to jump in. "Fred said he has seen this before—the incumbent that announces something bold, but then doesn't really have the stomach to follow through. They get excited, hire a bunch of people, but never pull the trigger on the big deal. Two years later, no surprise, the business isn't growing as fast as anyone thought and the plug gets pulled."

George nods. "I understand where Fred is coming from," he says. "And the reason we bought his company was really to get him. He's seen it from both sides. He has firsthand experience at big companies doing what we're trying to do, and he's built a real startup that was, let's face it, pretty small but doing interesting things. So I empathize."

He takes a sip of coffee and looks closely at Bernadette. "But at the same time, I'm not sure he has the full picture. Does he know the board has authorized a billion dollars in spending over the next four years? Or that you have approval to make ten more hires? Or that we're about to launch a venture capital fund to get an early look at other bolt-on acquisitions?"

"How would he know any of those things?" Bernadette says, her voice rising a notch. "This is the first I'm hearing about them!"

"That's my fault," George responds quickly. "We're ready to do what it takes to make this happen. Maybe I should start spending a day a week out here without my schedule packed with meetings. I need to have more casual conversations with the team to show them how committed we are to making this work."

While George had been spending a lot of his time on transformation B, he hadn't clearly highlighted the resource commitments to his team. The difficulty of large companies driving disruptive growth is well documented, so the leader needs to make sure to inspire the team that's driving new growth. Remember, a big company, almost by definition, cannot innovate faster than the market. And hitting speed bumps can be very frustrating. But a big company can innovate better than the market, if it can find ways to fuse unique capabilities with entrepreneurial moxie.

In the early days, transformation B is likely to be small, giving plenty of fodder for the skeptics—and there will be many of them. Further, every successful innovation effort has its fumbles and false starts. The leader needs to be the light of optimism through those dark times, and, through continued support and allocation of resources, demonstrate an unwavering commitment to driving the organization in new directions.

That said, in many cases the moment when leaders have to pay the most attention to transformation B is when it seems to be hitting its stride. In around 2012, Deseret Media hit a key inflection point. The decline of the old core slowed, innovation efforts close to the core accelerated, and newer efforts began to mature to the point that the overall business began to grow. It hadn't yet returned to the level it was when the story started, but it was moving in the right direction. Coauthor and then Deseret Media CEO Clark Gilbert believed this was a fragile time in this overall transformation journey, because it would have been easy to declare premature victory and stunt the growth of transformation B. "If I had left Deseret then," Gilbert said. "They probably would have sucked B back into A, and killed it." The organization would have remained stable for the next few years, but lacking a robust growth engine it would have been susceptible to the next wave of industry disruption. Gilbert made clear during this period that he was going to fight, and fight hard, for what still was the underdog in the corporate portfolio.

Gilbert believes this is a perpetual fight for a leader driving dual transformation. He uses the metaphor of treating an artery that is blocked by plaque ("occluded"), slowing the flow of blood to the heart. "You do your balloon angioplasty to open the artery," Gilbert says, "but the plaque comes back in what is called restenosis. You work really hard to protect and nurture transformation B, but the restenosis rate is really high. You'd better be putting in strong stents [mesh scaffolds that hold open the walls of the artery], ideally stents coated in drugs that ward off the plaque, and constantly checking to see if you need to intervene again. As a leader, the job just never ends."

Crises of Conflict

The second category of crises is of conflict. It's not surprising that one source of conflict is between A and B. What might be more surprising in some cases is that the biggest cause of conflict can actually be between the leader and some of his key stakeholders.

———————

Another few months pass at Partzelg. Both acquisitions have received board approval, and the market is beginning to take notice of the company's efforts to drive new growth. George has delivered on his commitment, both to reassure the historical core of its critical role in the future and to spend the time to inspire the emerging growth engine. After the acquisitions, he, Andy, and Bernadette start having weekly meetings to help coordinate across the capabilities link. Halfway through the third weekly meeting, it becomes clear that there is a key issue to resolve.

"Andy, you have to tell IT that they've got to respond to Frank's requests more quickly," Bernadette says. "We need to offer our customers solutions that seamlessly integrate with our current products, or else our entire value proposition is out the window. And if we can't implement that quickly, we're going to miss huge opportunities."

"I totally get it," Andy says. "And don't worry, it's high on our list." He pauses and then continues. "But what you never seem to understand is, we have to take care of this one big customer, or we might lose them to one of these new guys out of Indonesia. If we lose this customer we're going to fall short of our target for the quarter. And if we fall short of our target for the quarter, that might affect your funding." Andy looks at his hands folded in front of him. "After all, we're the ones that produce *real* cash flows—you just use them. Next quarter I promise, IT for you guys will be our first priority."

"Come on!" Bernadette says. "That's what you said six weeks ago when we put the request in. We've made the case that this integration gives us unique advantages in the market, but if I can never get access to IT, it's an empty promise. I don't think you see the big picture on this, Andy. You're still stuck in the old model!"

While they talk, George reflects on the discussion. He knows both Bernadette and Andy are making valid points. Delivering against current customer needs is indeed vital to hitting the near-term targets. And integration is potentially a real competitive advantage for the new businesses. He feels as if he's being forced to answer the question any parent dreads from his children: which of us do you love more?

"OK, OK," George says. "You both make good points. But I'm going to have to side with Bernadette here. What our customer is asking for is borderline unreasonable anyway. We give them so much already, I'll be shocked if they really defect. And if they do, we can scrap to hit our numbers. This is our only chance to get the new stuff right." He turns to Andy. "Tell IT to put Frank's request at the top of their list."

Both Bernadette and Andy had legitimate perspectives. Had George not been in the room and made the personal call to rule in favor of Partzelg's new growth business, there's little doubt that the gravitational pull of the core business would have overwhelmed the new. The capabilities link cannot be delegated down the organization. As painful as it can be, the leader must be ready to stand in and actively arbitrate, with a bias toward the new, even while not making people in the legacy core business feel abandoned.

Any company's core business casts a powerful shadow. Most of a company's top leaders have graduated from it. Even if it isn't growing the way it once was, at the beginning of a dual transformation it will provide the vast majority of revenues, and potentially profits. Early wins for transformation B will be nice but won't materially move the overall organizational needle. A smart legacy manager will make a comment like, "One point of share in our core provides more benefit than all this risky new stuff." The core systems will naturally privilege today over tomorrow.

For Deseret Media, allowing the web team to have editorial control over the placement of stories on the online sites was a powerful signal of the importance the leadership team placed on transformation B. For generations, the most critical moment for many newspapers was the afternoon meeting when editors would run down stories and the top brass would determine what would go above the fold on the front page. When Gilbert made it clear that, even though the traditional editorial team was free to provide input, it would be his digital team that shaped web content, it signaled that transformation B would get leadership attention disproportionate to its current revenue and profit production.

As with many elements in this book, leaders need to strike a careful balance. Selectively privileging the new doesn't require disparaging the old. Both businesses should be valued and respected. After all, to repeat an important message, the core business is providing the cash flow to invest in growth and the enabling capabilities to help transformation B succeed.

———————

Fall turns to winter. George ends up being wrong; Partzelg loses that core customer to the Indonesian competitor and hasn't been able to find other business to close the gap. It isn't going to be a disaster of a year, in part because Bernadette and her team are overdelivering against their targets. But it looks as if revenues and earnings will come in at the low end of analyst expectations. The services business is getting early traction, garnering market buzz, and winning a couple of early customers, but despite overperforming, it still is less than 10 percent of the company's revenues.

As snow flies outside the window of the conference room, George meets with Rob, one of Partzelg's independent directors.

"So, how do you think everything is going?" Rob asks. The question sounds innocent. Rob was probably the loudest advocate on the board when George first laid out his strategy. George expected that outcome; Rob had been specifically selected by the nominations committee because he sat on the board of a large software company, giving him vital experience in the new business Partzelg hoped to create.

George describes the important milestones his team has hit and transparently explains the areas where they've fallen short. "All in all," he says, "I think we should be pleased with where we are. We have a ton of work to do, but I think we'll start to see some real results next year, and 2020, boy, that is looking like it could be magical."

The corners of Rob's mouth turn down. George knows him well enough to know it means that what's coming next is going to be . . . not good.

"Look, George," Rob starts, shifting in his seat. "The board supports you and this transformation program. We really do. We've backed some big bets and spent some real money. But." He pauses. "We need to see faster results. You promised us a stronger core and a vibrant growth engine. Now I hear we're losing customers, and it will be another year before our new business is material. This isn't what we were promised. Maybe we should consider slowing down some of Bernadette's work to make sure we don't take our eye off the core."

George considers how to respond. The results are actually almost exactly what he promised the board. He told them there would be some short-term pain, and some quarters, or even years, that would fall short of expectations. And Bernadette is doing a great job, delivering against every target put in front of her. It just takes time to build new businesses. Further, he told the board from the beginning that the real measures to watch weren't arbitrary numbers in a given month or quarter, but more strategic and operational milestones. If anything, the company is making progress faster than George expected.

"Rob, believe me, there's no one more concerned about the pace of progress than me," he says now. "And there's no one driving the team harder than me. Andy is focused like a laser beam on his transformation effort, and he's doing a great job. There are going to be these blips along the way. But let's step back and look at the bigger picture and see where we're going."

———————

Rob could easily have been a key investor, a union leader, or even another member of George's executive team. The day-to-day of dual transformation can be painful, and there can be steps sideways and backward along the way. The leader needs to keep pulling back and up to describe the overall vision and direction, needs to have confidence in the path, and needs to make sure that there are legitimate milestones that demonstrate progress. And transformation B must deliver results, or else it fans the flames of critics chanting, "Stick to our knitting."

There is a particular moment when these conversations are most acute. That is, as it was for Partzelg, when the data and the story are in conflict. It's instructive to look back at figure 1-3, detailing the combined operating profit of the *Deseret News* and Deseret Digital from 2010 to 2015. Gilbert's crucible moment was in 2012. In the first two years of Gilbert's tenure, he put in place many of the pieces of the dual transformation: streamlining the core print staff, building Deseret Connect to get content from stringers, creating a digital growth team, and launching a range of community-focused offerings.

But the ship didn't right immediately. In those early days, even though Gilbert was convinced the strategy would work, profits continued to slide. Transformation B was growing, and the decline of the core was slowing, but overall profits were still down from the previous high. That led to natural questions, even from people who strongly supported the team's efforts.

Not every situation will look like this—after all, Gilbert came in more than a decade after the disruptive seeds were sown in the industry—but the impact from executing a dual transformation strategy will inevitably lag investing in it. During this period, leadership needs to maintain faith that it is going in the right direction and give the strategy time to flourish.

Unfortunately, faith is a scarce commodity among most executives, particularly those who must withstand the withering glares of analysts and investors. Indeed, CEOs of publicly traded companies need to gird themselves for tough conversations with shareholders.

Chapter 5 details how, in the midst of record profits, Aetna CEO Mark Bertolini made his courageous decision to radically reconfigure the health benefits company. Some of the analysts—those at banks that provided research reports and recommendations to people who were considering investing in the stock—rebelled. As Bertolini recalls, "I walked into a room of analysts and I said, 'You either think of me as stupid or that I'm lying to you, neither of which makes me want to spend more time with you.' I have had shareholders who have said to me, 'Why don't you double your dividends?' Well, I want to invest in the company. So I said that one of my largest shareholders should get the hell out of my stock."

Bertolini followed a deliberate strategy to find investors who understood the nature of disruption and the depth of the struggle to lead a dual transformation. At the same time, Bertolini believed it was critical that his new growth businesses develop sustainable business models.

> Creating new business models is a leadership challenge. In order to create those new businesses in any organization, I don't care how old it is, you have to start to look at what is going to be the operating model that's going to make that new business commercially viable and sustainable for the long run. That's a leadership issue. If a leader can't make that call and force that issue, if they're concerned about resistance from their staff or their team or the organization and they don't want to get in the way of that, they don't want to fight that battle then they should sell their company and get out of business.

Crises of Identity

The final category of crises is crises of identity. Remember, transformation involves changing the fundamental form or substance of an organization. How do you describe the difference between who you are and who you will be? How do you describe the connective tissue between who you have become and who you were? Before the journey even begins, how can you communicate both the need and the potential impact in the absence of perfect data?

Crises of identity can be subtle, but it's critical to anticipate and overcome them. Let's crash Partzelg's summer party to learn more.

This year, George's events team is making the summer party a family-oriented event. They've taken over one of the local theme parks for the afternoon. Kids have been whirling around on rides and adults have looked on fondly, with a few taking the plunge as well. It's a laid-back day, and everyone is clearly enjoying this well-deserved break in the middle of a year when everyone has worked hard to push the transformation agenda along.

It's time for the evening barbeque, and, to George's amazement, his thirteen-year-old daughter, Catie, has lifted her head out of her smart phone long enough to join in a conversation with him and a couple of his longer-serving colleagues. She listens intently, and George feels a swell of pride as she asks smart questions that show good listening skills and an instinct for business.

"So Dad," Catie asks after the conversation ends. "What exactly does your company do?"

"You know what we do," George replies. "We make stuff that goes in planes and cars."

"I thought that," Catie replies. "But Sam and Allison didn't mention that stuff once. And I've been talking to other people about what they do, and, well, no one is talking about *stuff*. Sally over there talked about the cool app she was working on. It actually even sounded kind of interesting. Ed was talking about how he was working on a deal with Amazon. That's really different than selling stuff."

George smiles. "First of all, I can't believe you've actually been talking to people about work!" he says. "But it's true. You're right. We've always been a *stuff* company. But we've been changing. I guess the way we describe things hasn't really caught up with it."

Helping your teenage daughter understand a party conversation might seem a low priority for most CEOs, but Catie's confusion illustrates what can be one of the most hidden crises of the transformation journey. An organization's dominant gene is its legacy, its core business—what we've been calling A. Even when B has grown to the point that it is clearly on track to become the dominant producer of revenue and profits, that dominant gene exerts significant influence.

If you don't have a smart plan to communicate and cement the change, the great sucking sounds of yesterday can subtly but importantly pull an organization back to what it was trying to get away from. Although the case study of Partzelg has George as its protagonist and the case examples in this book have had senior leaders in starring roles, superheroes don't scale. If you ultimately want your business to continue to act in materially different ways, you need to drive the change deep into underlying systems and structures. It starts with communicating clearly that the essence of the company has changed. Remember the transformation blurb from chapter 6. George needed to be able to say—in language that made sense to his organization—that Partzelg was a *stuff* company, but it was well on its way to becoming a *solutions* company.

A crisis of identity can sneak up on you, because even seemingly slow-moving industries can change quickly. Consider BYU-Idaho, where Gilbert became president in 2015. Recall that the school grew out of Ricks College in 2000 to become a teaching-oriented companion to its sister institution, BYU in Provo, Utah. But just as BYU-Idaho's annual campus enrollment figures approached those of its sister institution, BYU-Idaho's online program enrollments surged past classroom enrollments. This means that now more than 50 percent of the university's sixty thousand students will never come to campus, and by 2020 nearly 75 percent of students will be online only (see figure 8-1). After less than two decades of existence, the university clearly needs to consider its emerging identity as an online university.

As the summer party draws to a close, George finds himself on the edge of a dwindling crowd, sipping a drink and watching a beautiful summer sunset. Among the gentle din of people enjoying each other's company, his mind drifts back to the board meeting where he received approval to move forward with his plan.

The outcome certainly wasn't preordained. He had spoken to each board member before the discussion and knew that the board was equally divided between advocates, sceptics, and those squarely on

FIGURE 8-1

Enrollment by year at two universities

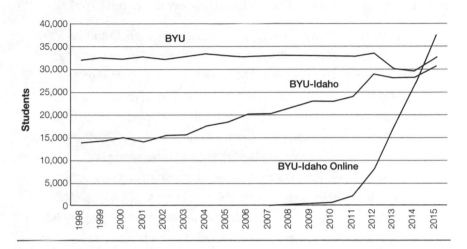

the fence. George had done his homework and had assembled a 120-page PowerPoint document detailing industry trends and sophisticated models showing (in his mind) the clear advantage of bold action now versus watching and waiting. But because the trends were (at the time) still emerging and the models were, well, models, it was easy for the sceptics to dismiss them.

Strangely, the insight for how to change the conversation had come when he was reading a book to his young son Horace. The book was called *Tiddler*, by Julia Donaldson and Axel Scheffler, the duo behind modern children's classics like *The Gruffalo* and *Room on the Broom*. The book describes a little fish named Tiddler, who habitually shows up to class late and spins elaborate fantasies explaining his tardiness. Then, one day, he finds himself lost. How does he get home? It turns out Tiddler's stories have spread throughout the sea, so he simply follows the chain of storytellers back home. "I was lost, I was scared, but a story led me home again," Tiddler says.

A story.

That's what George was missing. The numbers were there, but because of the uncertainty behind them, he couldn't win the day with a number-based approach. The numbers had to inform the story, of course. But there had to be a compelling story at the center of his strategy.

At last the day arrived for the pivotal board meeting. George stood up and asked the board members to close their eyes. When a few stared at him blankly, he insisted they close their eyes. Then he spoke.

I want you to imagine a meeting in this room ten years from now. After the usual chit-chat about the progress of Chelsea Clinton's political career, you're ready to get down to business. The first item on the agenda is to review last year's performance. The CFO—let's call her Abbi—reports how, for the first time, profits from outside the United States make up more than two-thirds of our overall profits. And the big driver of surging overseas profitability is an end-to-end set of data-driven services that have only gotten stronger as the company has scaled.

"It's all working in perfect harmony," Abbi says. "Our legacy business continues to gently decline, but we've remained a category leader, and our products serve as a key entryway for our solutions sales team. Those solutions have gotten so strong that we've been able to sell them as a service to manufacturers in completely disconnected industries."

Everyone around the table nods.

Abbi continues. "The stock market looks at us, not as an industrial company, but as a high-growth technology company. And they should. Because we are. We should be thankful, again, that the previous generation of leaders had the foresight to send us on this journey." There is a smattering of applause as the white-haired trio sitting together smile and recline their heads.

We have our challenges, of course. In only two years, a white-hot startup from Singapore's surging entrepreneurial ecosystem has now become the number two player in the services market, with a radical new business model. And, after years of sluggish underperformance, our two biggest rivals have merged, putting price pressures on the core market.

But there's no doubt that the Partzelg of the future is better positioned to handle these kinds of challenges, and it's because of what happened over the past decade. It's a different company, but it can now do an even more effective job of delivering against its mission of making transportation safer and more efficient.

Now, long after that board meeting, enjoying a last glimpse of the summer sunset, George feels a glow of satisfaction, remembering. He told a compelling story, showing the board members where Partzelg could get to, and the story bought him time in those early days when results were still slow in coming. It was the same story, after all, that convinced Bernadette to move from a fast-track position in the core to working on an uncertain growth business.

It was, indeed, a story that got George home again. And, speaking of going home, George rises from his reverie and calls to his family. "Come on, guys! Time to go home."

Preparing for the Crises of Dual Transformation

By following the guidance described in this book, you should have a robust strategy and a compelling story for what you're doing and why you're doing it. The theories on which the guidance is built, particularly the disruptive innovation theory, helps make compelling predictions in the absence of complete data. You also should have underlying metrics that serve as early proof points of success. For Gilbert, that was the growth of his new businesses. Even though they were small, highlighting double-digit growth rates helped reaffirm that the media organization collectively was moving in the right direction.

Chapter 9 will conclude *Dual Transformation* by sharing words of advice from senior leaders tied to key milestones in the transformation journey. But first, we offer two general pieces of advice to help you prepare for the predictable crises of dual transformation. First, keep repeating the mantra, "A does A, B does B." And second, ground your efforts in a motivating purpose.

The Mantra: A Does A, B Does B

Generally, one of the biggest challenges for leaders driving dual transformation is to simultaneously celebrate the executive doing the hard work of transformation A and the one overseeing transformation B, and to keep them focused on doing their jobs. One of Gilbert's responsibilities was to stop well-intentioned intervention in digital by his print team, and vice versa. His job was to stomp on the camel's nose based on the proverb, "If the camel gets his nose in the tent, his body will soon follow."

Transformation A should largely be separate from transformation B, except for the careful management of the capabilities link by select leaders. This isn't a democratic decision, and there is no point in having the A and B organizations constantly arguing about the future. As Gilbert notes,

> You're never going to fully win the argument until you are way down the road. You waste huge amounts of organizational energy on this type of perpetual debate. That creates two problems. First, it creates a lot of energy in the organization around the conflict and not the solution. Second, the concern about the other group often keeps you from finding more productive solutions in areas of distinctive strength.
>
> If I made mistakes, it was in spending too much energy explaining to A how important B is, and why we're going to spend so much time there. Efforts are much better spent having a clear, motivating, and distinctive role for A, and then just simply carving out separate resources, energy, and attention for B. One of the things I had to learn, both at Deseret and as a university president, was that I needed to have a clear role, purpose, mission, and strategy for A, and it needed to be so compelling that frankly they didn't want to get distracted or spend a lot of time on B. Meanwhile I still needed to provide the focus, autonomy, and energy to the new B organization so that it could be successful and get the resources it needed.
>
> From a leadership standpoint it puts a lot of responsibility on the chief executive: if you're excited about B, you want to talk about it in every setting you're in, but you always need to reinforce the importance of A, so that the A organization can hear that and be motivated by that and not get distracted.

"A does A, B does B." The leader's job is to spot and manage the points of interconnection. The quip earlier that *superheroes don't scale* doesn't just refer to senior leaders. Every superhero has his or her vulnerability (Superman and Kryptonite, for example). That's why superstar performers in A often struggle in B, and vice versa. Of course, we've met people that indeed have the mental flexibility and diverse capabilities to play enabling roles in both transformations A and B. For example, at BYU-Idaho there are a handful of teachers who can teach in the classroom and online equally effectively. However, failing to build systems around the new organization creates dependency on a small number of individuals, which doesn't scale and creates conditions for failure when working with other faculty. "A does A, B does B." If everyone does everything, no one will do anything well.

A Motivating Purpose

In 1960, marketing legend Ted Levitt provided his seminal contribution to *Harvard Business Review*: "Marketing Myopia." The article castigated companies for losing sight of the essence of their business, setting themselves up for challenges from competitors and ultimately for obsolescence. To avoid that, Levitt exhorted leaders to ask themselves the seemingly obvious question, "What business are you really in?" Posing that question continues to be a powerful way to catalyze important strategic conversations.

Why does your company exist? Peter Drucker famously said that the point of a business is to create a customer. Almost every organization starts with humanity coursing through its veins. A group has come together to solve a particular problem for a particular person. If it solves that problem for enough people, the organization earns the right to grow and expand. Leaders are emotionally intimate with early customers or stakeholders. They know their names. They might know them so well that they become lifelong friends.

Levitt pointed out, however, that over time companies come to define themselves not by what they do for customers but by the products they sell or the categories in which they compete. Back in the 1950s, for instance, the railroad companies defined themselves as *railroad* companies. But had they looked at themselves from the point of view of their customers, they would have seen that they were really in the transportation, logistics, and communications business. In that way, the railroad executives would have better understood the challenge, and the opportunities, represented by the planes that flew over their heads and the telephone and telegraph wires that ran alongside their tracks.

Things have gotten worse, because now if you ask most companies why they exist, it isn't even to sell a particular product or service, much less to serve any customers. No, it is to maximize shareholder value.

As Harvard Business School professor Clayton Christensen likes to note, the primary job of many managers is to "source, assemble, and ship numbers." And short-term numbers at that. Worshipping at what Christensen calls the "church of finance" hollows out a company's competitive advantage; it loses the capacity to invest in innovation, and that drives the perpetual reinvention necessary in the world of temporary competitive advantage.

In 2010, Christensen was asked to speak to the HBS graduating class. Word had spread about his "last class" lecture. HBS is famous for its case-based teaching method. Students read a twenty-page description of a situation, and then the professor facilitates a discussion that draws out general lessons about management. In the last class of a semester, however, many professors end by telling stories about their own lives and beliefs.

Christensen—who at the time had survived cancer, a heart attack, a stroke, and thirty years of type 1 diabetes—described how he used the models he taught students to guide his personal decisions. In the 2010 *Harvard Business Review* article summarizing the speech, Christensen described the importance of having a purpose for your life. "Over the years I've watched the fates of my HBS classmates from 1979 unfold; I've seen more and more of them come to reunions unhappy, divorced, and alienated from their children," Christensen wrote. "I can guarantee you that not a single one of them graduated with the deliberate strategy of getting divorced and raising children who would become estranged from them."

The root problem from Christensen's perspective was that "they didn't keep the purpose of their lives front and center as they decided how to spend their time, talents, and energy." A steady stream of incremental decisions without a clear focus on purpose too often led to unanticipated outcomes.

A New Era

One of the world's great innovations was the limited liability company, with which an organization became in fact treated like an individual that is separate and distinct from its investors and operators. This innovation allowed organizations and investors to take new risks and develop new models. Yet something has perverted the corporation.

For example, a 2011 article in *Psychology Today* notes that corporations display attributes of psychotic individuals.

Over the past few years, a number of critics have suggested that the era of shareholder value maximization needs to come to an end. Top business thinkers such as Christensen as well as Roger Martin, former dean of the Rotman School at the University of Toronto, and HBS legend Michael Porter have argued that shareholder value has been exposed as a flawed paradigm. Even Michael Jensen, an academic and consultant—whose seminal 1976 article (with William Meckling) helped kick off both the focus on shareholder value as the measure of top executives' success and the incentive of extensive stock grants (which was intended to encourage them to act like owners)—now rues the unanticipated impact of some of his contributions. And no less than Jack Welch—credited with ushering in the shareholder era with a speech in 1981 at the Pierre Hotel in New York proclaiming that General Electric (where Welch served as chairman and CEO from 1981 to 2001) would increase its focus on maximizing returns for its investors—said in 2009 that optimizing a business for shareholder returns is the "dumbest idea in the world."

A leadership imperative in dual transformation is to unite the leadership of both A and B around a galvanizing purpose that serves as a light during dark times. Gilbert found that the mission statement at Deseret Media—"Trusted voices of light and truth reaching hundreds of millions of people worldwide"—served as a critical aid during the organization's journey. Focusing on strengthening families and preserving faith helped unify the company, clarify the criticality of transformation A, and provide a guide to both big strategic decisions and day-to-day decisions. Aetna similarly focused on improving and expanding access to health care. Note too how George, Partzelg's CEO, repeatedly came back to his organization's purpose of facilitating transportation. Grounding your efforts in this kind of shared mission gives reasons for the A organization and the B organization to cheer for the success of the other. Defining and reinforcing a shared sense of mission become central functions for senior leaders driving a dual transformation.

Behind many great organizations is a clear and compelling purpose to create value for customers. Johnson & Johnson takes its credo so seriously that it is etched inches deep in granite in its headquarters in

New Brunswick, New Jersey, and appears in every J&J office around the world. The credo puts the needs of the people it serves—doctors, nurses, patients, mothers and fathers—first; employees, second; the communities it serves, third; and its stockholders, last. As it notes, "When we operate according to these principles, the stockholders should realize a fair return."

We are willing to bet that you can identify many organizations by their statement of purpose:

- Be the Earth's most customer-centric company, where customers can find and discover anything they might want to buy online

- Give people the power to share and make the world more open and connected

- Work to proactively pursue long-term high-impact benefits as well as assertively optimize diverse technology

- To accelerate the advent of sustainable transport by bringing compelling mass market electric cars to market as soon as possible

- Organize the world's information and make it universally accessible and useful

The first is Amazon, the second Facebook, the fourth Tesla, and the fifth Google. The third is a trick; it is a random collection of words from a website that spits out random mission statements (clearly the reason the internet was created).

A Prison with a Purpose

An example of an organization that used purpose to accelerate its transformation comes from Singapore. The organization had a strange problem: its customers were coming back too frequently, and that was decreasing employee motivation. What kind of a business doesn't like repeat customers?

A prison.

In 1998 the government-run Singapore Prison Service (SPS) was on the brink of a crisis. Prisons were crowded, and SPS found it difficult to attract and retain staff. In 1999, director of prisons Chua Chin Kiat led a yearlong exercise to land on a new statement of purpose: "We aspire to be captains in the lives of offenders committed to our custody. We will be instrumental in steering them towards being responsible citizens with the help of their families and the community. We will thus build a secure and exemplary prison system."

Over the next decade, recidivism shrank from 44 percent to 28 percent, and SPS now is one of the world's most efficient systems.

Changing the status quo is hard work. If you're attempting to motivate people by urging them to protect the dividend or increase return on invested capital from 13.2 to 13.6 percent, you can expect your efforts to struggle.

Dual transformation should be based on a motivating human purpose. You need to find ways to move your organization beyond the mindless management of numbers to the creation of customer and employee value, organized around a clarifying and motivating purpose. In the end, your shareholders, the real ones—the ones who care about long-term performance—will thank you for it.

CHAPTER SUMMARY

Dual transformation in the face of disruptive change is the hardest challenge a leadership team will ever encounter. Twists and turns and fumbles and failures are inevitable. Leaders need to be prepared for three categories of crises.

1. *Crises of commitment.* Transformation A needs to be reassured, and B needs to be inspired.

2. *Crises of conflict.* The leader needs to arbitrate between A and B with a bias toward B, and to deflect criticism from key stakeholders.

3. *Crises of identity.* The leader needs to capture and share the essence of the reason for and the results of the transformation.

You prepare for these crises by repeating the "A does A, B does B" mantra and grounding efforts in a motivating purpose.

9. Postcards from the Dual Transformation Journey

Dual Transformation contains no easy answers. Leaders driving dual transformation need to reposition their core business in the face of market disruptions, an action that can entail significant cost cutting. They must in parallel create a powerful, disruptive growth business that isn't fully distinct from the core but is connected by a carefully stocked and actively managed capabilities link. Success requires leaders to demonstrate the courage to choose before the data is clear, the clarity to focus on the highest-potential opportunities, the curiosity to explore in the face of uncertainty, and the conviction to persevere in the face of predictable crises. And, as the Xerox example in chapter 1 shows, the reward for success is that you get the chance to do it all over again as the next gale of creative destruction starts to blow.

We've aspired to build your confidence that dual transformation is possible by presenting here a diverse set of case studies, and to arm you with a set of tools to assist you as you follow your own dual transformation journey. The word *journey* is purposeful. Look at the length of the stories in this book. It took four years after commercial introduction for streaming video to constitute more than half of Netflix's revenues. Gilbert spent six years driving dual transformation at the *Deseret News*. It took seven years at Adobe for digital marketing to become one-third as big as its traditional businesses. Steve Jobs returned as CEO of Apple in 1998. It took more than a decade before the full impact of his work was felt. Xerox's dual transformation took place over fifteen years. And in none of these cases could leaders shake their fists, proclaim victory, and ride off into the sunset.

Transforming a company is indeed a journey, one that is both unpredictable and perpetual. It requires patience, discipline, and constant attention. Don't expect that you'll speed through your journey in a business quarter. Rather, you need to come up with a rough view of how you will balance activities over a three-year period. The appendix to this book contains a simple template that lists almost twenty milestones that you could think about staging through your journey (along with several other tools and discussion guides to help you implement the ideas in this book).

Viewing dual transformation as a journey is another way to maintain conviction when challenges arise. That the crises described in chapter 8 will arise is predictable, but exactly when is not knowable in advance. A multiyear view allows you to take any single event in stride and react appropriately.

In this concluding chapter, we share postcards from the journey, with leaders like you sharing the lessons they learned at critical moments along the way, grouped by the three categories of crises described in chapter 8. Let's first meet the protagonists from this chapter and then go through fourteen specific moments.

Leader Profiles

This chapter shares firsthand quotations from leaders at six organizations. Aetna, Arizona State University, Manila Water, and Singtel are featured in other parts of the book; Ford and Settlement Music School appear here only. Following are the leaders, with their organizations in alphabetical order.

Aetna: Mark Bertolini, CEO and Chairman

Mark Bertolini became CEO of Aetna in November 2010, and the chairman of the board in April 2011. He joined Aetna in 2003 after spending time at large insurers (Cigna and New York Life) as well as upstarts (SelectCare). His passion for health care reform traces to deep personal involvement when his son was diagnosed with a rare form of cancer in 2001. Bertolini's passion for alternative medicine springs from a devastating ski accident he suffered in 2004, when he broke his neck in four places; he eschewed traditional pain killers and embraced acupuncture, yoga, and meditation.

Since 2010, Bertolini and his leadership team have been working to transform Aetna from a company that sells health insurance policies to businesses, to one that sells insurance to consumers (transformation A), and IT solutions to providers (transformation B). Aetna has made big bets, ranging from the $500 million acquisition of Medicity to a huge attempted acquisition of Humana (the outcome of this attempt is unknown as of this writing). Bertolini's quotations come from a series of discussions we had with him in 2014 and 2015.

Arizona State University: Michael Crow, President

Michael Crow became president of Arizona State University (ASU) in July 2002. The son of a navy sailor, Crow had a long career in academia before assuming his role at ASU, with previous roles as the executive vice provost of Columbia University, where he helped develop Columbia's online education strategy, and professor at the University of Kentucky and at Iowa State University. Since joining ASU, Crow has focused on creating what he calls the "new American university," with a commitment to research excellence in a select number of fields; digitally enhanced, accessible teaching on ASU's campus; and the creation of a powerful online platform to bring education to broader populations.

"We have taken the classic university structure and highly modernized it by changing the culture of the faculty, the culture of the students, and the design of institution," Crow said. "That has resulted in dramatic changes in performance along every dimension you can imagine." In a September 2016 interview with coauthor Scott Anthony, Crow described ASU's transformation as one from a "rigid, bureaucratic, public-agency modeled public university" to a "high-speed, adaptive, public enterprise university."

Ford Motor Company: Mark Fields

Mark Fields became president and CEO of Ford Motor Company in July 2014. A graduate of the Harvard Business School, he joined Ford in 1989 and served as the head of Mazda Motor Corporation, then a Ford subsidiary, from 1998 to 2000. Fields became the business unit chief of Ford's Americas operations in 2005, leading the effort to develop a plan called The Way Forward, which helped Ford successfully navigate the 2007–2008 global financial crisis without needing to seek government bailouts. Soon after taking the CEO role, Fields launched an ambitious effort to streamline and reconfigure Ford's core automotive business (transformation A) and to aggressively create new mobility service businesses (transformation B) as part of an overall effort to shift the company from being an automotive company to an automotive and mobility company. His quotations are from an interview with coauthor Mark Johnson in August 2016.

Manila Water: Gerry Ablaza, CEO and President, and Ferdz dela Cruz, COO for Manila Water Operations

Gerry Ablaza joined the board of directors of Manila Water in 2009 and became its president and CEO in 2010. He previously spent a decade as CEO of Globe Telecom, a sister company in the portfolio of the Ayala Group. Ferdz dela Cruz worked with Ablaza at Globe before joining Manila Water in 2011.

Ablaza and dela Cruz arrived at a critical moment in Manila Water's history. The company had solved the problem it sought to address in its 1997 formation: providing basic potable water to six million consumers in the eastern portion of Manila. The duo launched a dual transformation effort, with the aspiration of doubling net income. Transformation A involved fundamentally restructuring Manila Water's operations in existing markets and developing a new water-as-a-service model that would allow Manila Water to expand to new geographies; transformation B involved building a portfolio of new service offerings.

The remarks from Ablaza and dela Cruz are from an August 2016 interview with coauthor Scott Anthony, where both executives agreed that Manila Water was roughly halfway along its transformation journey. "We are like a baby that has just started to stand up and walk," Ablaza said. "We are learning new skills and trying to develop new competencies to learn how to walk, and then how to run."

Settlement Music School: Helen Eaton, Executive Director

In 2010, Helen Eaton became executive director of the Settlement Music School, a not-for-profit organization that provides music education in the Philadelphia area. An accomplished musician who trained at The Juilliard School, Eaton soon set out to transform the more than one-hundred-year-old organization, whose six branches typically provided about ten thousand classes to five thousand students each week.

Transformation A involved going beyond Settlement's traditional target of children and youth to developing innovative offerings for adults. Offerings such as Adult Rock Band—where a group of adults, initially strangers, would come together weekly and get instruction from an expert—were aimed to reposition Settlement facilities into places that provided adults a sense of connection and community. Transformation B involved working with other local providers to bring equitable access to music instruction for all children in the Philadelphia area. Eaton's efforts won Settlement a range of prestigious grants and have the potential to drive a lasting impact in the local area and beyond.

Singtel: Chua Sock Koong, Group Chief Executive Officer

Chua Sock Koong became Group CEO of the Singtel Group in 2007. Singtel is Southeast Asia's largest telecommunications company, with more than 600 million subscribers. In its 2016 fiscal year, fully owned operations in Singapore and Australia contributed close to S$17 billion in revenues and S$5 billion in EBITDA (equivalent to roughly US$12.2 billion and US$3.6 billion, respectively), and substantial investment in regional operators in markets such as the Philippines (Globe Telecom), Thailand (AIS), India and Africa (Bharti Airtel), and Indonesia (Telkmosel) contributed another S$2.8 billion (US$2 billion) in pre-tax profits.

Chua (following eastern convention her family name appears first; Sock Koong is her given name) joined Singtel in 1989 as treasurer. She then served in various key capacities, most notably as the CFO before assuming the Group CEO role. Starting in 2010, Chua and her leadership team chartered a dual transformation strategy where they would shift the core business from voice to data and create new digital businesses that extended Singtel into markets such as advertising and cybersecurity. Her quotes are from an October 2016 interview with Anthony.

Crises of Commitment

Does your historical core have a future? Are you serious about investing in new growth? What will you do when a hyped new growth effort stumbles? Here's how our leaders describe making the commitment to transform, handling setbacks, and leveraging the advantages of incumbency.

On Committing to Transformation

Fields (Ford): "When we have affected new strategies as a company it has always been when our back was up against the wall. Now, the business is on a firm foundation. There is no burning platform. Yet, we have an incredible amount of change going on in our industry. We have a number of new nontraditional competitors interested in automotive, as well as established competitors doing new things. There's a real sense that we have to deal with this. We have the opportunity to be proactive to secure our future, as opposed to reactive to secure our future."

Crow (ASU): "It has been easier than I thought [it would be] to convince the faculty that they needed to become part of a student-centered culture. People were ready for that. I think it has also been easier to find a way to break down departments and disciplines. Yes, there were people against it, but not enough to stop it. The creativity and the design power of the faculty has been greater than I thought, if not remarkable."

Bertolini (Aetna): "I don't think transformation begins and ends. I think it's a continuous process. I think every organization I've ever been a part of has been in constant transformation. Everybody has the same problem. We need to look to ourselves as leaders to make that happen. The tools are there, the ideas are there, the theory is there, but I think in the end analysis, we have to personally have the courage to take it out and make it happen."

On the Critical Role of Transformation A

Chua (Singtel): "For us, the transformation A is actually even more important, because we have to get our core right to earn the right to do transformation B. I speak from the perspective of a listed company that has shareholders who expect yield and growth. People seem to have the impression that transforming the core is less dramatic than building a new business. That's a misperception. If you look back far enough in Singtel's history, our core was once telex and telegram. Then IDD [international direct dialing] became the main revenue and profit contributor. Today, our business is all about data, mobile data, and fixed data. That's all around the transformation of the core. Without that transformation, we risked becoming irrelevant. In fact, there were some telcos whose livelihood was entirely dependent on IDD. They never transformed themselves and now they've just disappeared."

On Challenges, Setbacks, and Stumbles

Fields (Ford): "It would be easy to say that we have a harder job because we have this whole new element of the business that we never had before. But that's not how we view it. Our predecessors forty years ago had their own issues and their own crises. We try not to think about that too much, because if you do, you can rapidly find yourself in the abyss of paralysis. It's more like, 'It's hard. The world is big. Okay, we're at an inflection point. Let's figure it out.'"

Dela Cruz (Manila Water): "It is not easy. My advice to other leaders is, the further you get from the core, the more you need to be resilient and support the team that is still in the trenches learning. We were way off on our assumptions. To use the Mike Tyson analogy, we were punched hard in the face. We have to keep reminding ourselves that it is a process, because we get impatient. You have to trust the process."

Eaton (Settlement Music): "Transformation is a roller coaster ride. You have moments of great highs and lows, moments where you are certain about what you are doing, and moments where you question deeply. It is never easy. If it were easy, everyone would be doing it. We have had a host of successes and some failures along the way. We have developed systems to evaluate those successes and failures, and learn from them. We understand our audiences better, because we are asking the right questions and responding thoughtfully. This has all led to the organization's capability of doing even greater and more impactful work, and so we become more ambitious, and the journey continues."

Chua (Singtel): "Getting into the digital business was a lot more difficult than we expected. The cultural norms such as the pace of change and what motivates people in a company like ours and in startups are very, very different. These are some aspects that we are still trying to address in order to better attract and retain digital talent because we need this talent not just for our digital business, but also for all our businesses going forward. We're trying to change how Singtel is perceived and also our compensation policies. For example, when we made acquisitions like Amobee and Trustwave in the United States, we created long-term incentive schemes based on Amobee and Trustwave's own performance rather than Singtel Group LTI [long-term incentive] plans. This was quite a big departure for us. We like the Singtel Group LTI plans because we want Amobee and Trustwave employees to buy into Group objectives. But we recognize that the motivation and connection may not be as strong for them as compared to the rest of our staff."

On Leveraging Scale Capabilities

Crow (ASU): "The most significant asset we have is the faculty, and we share that widely. We also share our library, which is far more than a library. We have millions of books and tens of thousands of journals and millions of digital assets, all of which is completely searchable. It is nothing like Google. This is reviewed, certified, published material that is digitally searchable and usable. In essence, we have made the entire set of faculty products available through our enhanced technology platform. This new conceptualization of a library helps to bridge the gap between faculty research outputs and students on campus, students on online platforms, and students on emerging platforms."

Chua (Singtel): "We have always believed that any new investment we make must provide a strategic difference and a competitive advantage compared to any company that wants to get into that new business. If all we bring is money, there are lots of companies that probably have cheaper cost of funds, and there won't be a sustainable differentiation that would generate superior outcomes. That's why when we were identifying new businesses to go into, we made sure that they were businesses that leverage on our telco assets and customer relationships. An example is cyber security. At Singtel, we monitor and secure traffic flows and have trusted relationships with our customers so it very naturally led to the business of protecting networks and services from cyber threats."

On the Positive Spillover Effects of Driving Dual Transformation

Ablaza (Manila Water): "Our transformation communicated to the organization that we are embracing innovation and change. This opens up two innovation tracks. One is in the core, where we find innovative ways to improve things that we do there, such as turning waste to energy or creating cost-neutral plants. Telling our people that we are looking to do new things gives them permission to innovate where they are today."

Dela Cruz (Manila Water): "We have a lot of good young engineers that run boring plants. We can give them new excitement by having them work across our two entities."

Crises of Conflict

Whom do you back in the battle between today and tomorrow? Who gets dibs on scarce resources? What happens when key stakeholders complain that progress is too slow? Here's how leaders selectively separated A and B, managed tensions between the two, stared down stakeholders, and used results to quiet critics.

On the Importance and Limitations of Separate Disciplines

Bertolini (Aetna): "Setting out to transform an organization, as we have learned at Aetna, requires a different approach than what we do to drive excellence in our core businesses. For the core, we typically have a version of 'the truth' that is expressed in numbers and spreadsheets, and we manage our business against the variance of those numbers. This makes sense within a well-understood business, but it suboptimizes our ability to innovate. For the more forward-looking businesses, we know that whatever numbers we come up with will likely turn out to be wrong; so what is most important are the ideas those numbers represent, and the assumptions behind them. When you look at the full range of assumptions, then, you have a sense of the risks inherent in that direction, and you can have a discussion about what you need to believe to take those risks."

Dela Cruz (Manila Water): "Leaders need to wear two hats. One is for the core business, and the other is for a new venture. The visual of the two hats helps us make sure we are clear what conversation we are having and wear the right hat. Our CFO served as one of the best symbols to the organization on this point. I think we are fortunate that Chito [Manila Water's CFO] in prior roles was exposed to ventures. Organizationally the CFO is such a strong symbol of how much risk an organization is willing to take. Some companies have problems because the CFO blocks everything. For us, the CFO is a strong symbol of embracing dual tracks."

Chua (Singtel): "Traditionally, for a mobile business case, you know what your cost drivers and revenue drivers are and monitor them. For new businesses, it is still necessary to do a business case and track the drivers. But these drivers are different as they relate more to customer usage. If the customer numbers are way out from what was in your business case, you know that you're never going to achieve the business case. So, you still need to determine the milestones and targets, but you'll probably be tracking different indicators and at a different frequency than you would in the traditional businesses."

Fields (Ford): "When you have separate teams, some of the things coming from the new role can threaten the established role. You ultimately have to make choices on capital allocation, and so it becomes a skins-versus-shirts exercise. Our approach is to think about these things at the same time, which, ultimately, allows you to get more buy-in for the hard choices you need to make. It also develops a team. It also develops the team. The other way we've dealt with this is we've spent a lot of time with the management team talking about how we are not going from an old business to a new business—we are building a bigger business. Our core business and the emerging opportunities are interconnected. In mobility services, you have to have a car or a truck, and it's got to be world class. These things are part and parcel."

On Using Results to Quiet Critics

Crow (ASU): "We operate an institution within a set of institutions that are not interested in change. For example, we want to introduce new technologies into teaching and learning paradigms. There are all sorts of people out there that say what they were really concerned with was whether using keyboard on iPads was diminishing of the learning process, because you think more slowly when you use a pencil. Learning needs to be a slow process, but ultimately it needs to be something that is done in the context of access to massive amounts of information and data, and massive amounts of knowledge, and massive amounts of access to other people being available to almost everyone. What we have decided to do is to outperform everyone and take Cicero's adage to heart: we criticize by what we create. We have decided to create a student body truly representative of our population at scale, run [the university] in ways contrary of a lot of normal logic, and simply outperform everyone else."

   Bertolini (Aetna): "To have the right to move towards transformation, you have to deliver performance in your core businesses. This is like 'jacks or better to open' in draw poker; unless you meet a certain threshold, you can't play. You meet your commitments, and, as you get results, you earn the right to broaden the vision. At that point, it's critical to take everyone through the logic behind how you made the transformation choice, how observing the fault lines creates the case for change. It's also important to emphasize that the broad outlines of the required changes are clear, but that the strategy will likely evolve over time. So you highlight the markers to look out for what will indicate whether we're on track or if another change is required."

On Breaking Free of Constraints

Crow (ASU): "What I would have done differently is to break out of the constraining model more quickly. I'd build a network outside of the university more quickly. I'd make that network local and national and global more quickly. Do not allow the institution to chase others. We are not here to be the next UCLA, the next Minnesota, or Ohio State. We are not here to be measured against the previous attainment by some other institution. Ford is not measured by whether or not its cars are the same as Maserati's. We have a silly business in education where people are ranking schools, not against what they did or the value they added, but, if you are measured against highly exclusive institutions you are measured by how well you do at becoming highly exclusive."

Chua (Singtel): "The most important thing is to be open to new ideas. If you are very successful in what you have been doing, it is sometimes even more difficult to want to change. In our case, if we were not open to new ideas, such as going overseas or creating new digital businesses, we'd be a lot smaller than we are today. Could you imagine Singtel being in the advertising business five years ago? Probably not. Well, we're now in the digital advertising business. The fact is we can't allow our past success to limit what we will do in the future. As a leader, I have learned personally to be more open to ideas. There are times when I hear a new idea, and my instinct is to say, "No forget it, it's crazy." I try to refrain from saying no, look at things from the other party's perspective and think about why the person believes this idea would work. After a while, I sometimes begin to see that this actually could make sense. I think I've become better at this."

On the Importance of Senior Support

Ablaza (Manila Water): "The Zobel brothers [Jaime Augusto Zobel de Ayala and Fernando Zobel de Ayala, the CEO and COO of the Ayala Group] have taken an active interest in the work. They visited one of our Healthy Family plants personally. That sends a very strong signal. It gets blasted in our online gazettes and publications, and showcases that there is support at the highest level of the company."

Crises of Identity

Who are you? Whom do you hope to become? What does it mean when the answer to those two questions is meaningfully different? Many of the challenges in dual transformation are existential in nature. Here's what leaders have to say about alignment, communication, and the power of purpose.

On Aligning Leadership and the Board

Fields (Ford): "Making decisions and choices is hard. Not just where to play, but even more important, where not to play. When you decide where not to play, there are implications for the business. Previously, we've always had that burning platform where we had to make really hard decisions to close plants, eliminate product lines, and say goodbye to people. It's harder now, because the business is on a firmer foundation, but the strategic choices are just as important."

Bertolini (Aetna): "Your top leaders have to be aligned around the long-term vision and the assumptions about the future that underpin it. But you also have to change the nature of the dialogue with them, away from one about certainty and predictability, and towards one about assumptions, managing risks, and 'what you have to believe' for a certain course of action to be the best one. This is a significant shift for even the most successful leaders, and some might not be able to make it. You can't expect everyone to evolve at the same pace, but you have to see progress; for me this means being 'realistically expectant' and 'patiently tolerant of progress.'"

Ablaza (Manila Water): "I was surprised by how easily the leadership team embraced this type of innovation, and I think a lot of credit goes to the idea that you have to create separate governance practices. We were able to find a structure where we are not trying to use old tools to answer new problems."

Chua (Singtel): "The board plays a part in setting strategy for the business. So it's easier for our board of directors to understand the threats of disruption and better appreciate the exciting opportunities out there that we bring to their attention having seen it themselves. That's why we took the board to Silicon Valley, Israel, and more recently to India. We recently increased our exposure to India, and we wanted them to feel the buzz in the market place to really appreciate it."

On Clarifying and Communicating Focus

Bertolini (Aetna): "Changes are rarely going to happen as fast as you think they will. When they don't, doubt can start to creep in with your stakeholders. This is why it's so important to frame the vision as resting on a foundation of clear assumptions about the future. People can debate the assumptions, but once you agree on them, the logic behind the vision solidifies, and people recognize the danger of not changing."

Fields (Ford): "We've always had five-year business plans, and that has been our strategy. This is the first time we're taking a future-back view of what the world is going to look like fifteen years from now, and then putting together a strategy that allows us to have the maximum chance of success in that world that we see. We're answering questions about where to play and how to win, who we are and who we are not, what we do well, what we do better than others, and where do we need to improve. I've been very pleased with how the team has really opened up their minds to think about this in a very expansive way—without biases or preconceived notions. The spirit of the discussions has been very thought provoking. The senior team knows we're going to really focus. Some vehicle platforms will make it, and some won't. In emerging markets we're going to pick our shots, and some will work out and some won't. That clarity is refreshing for the organization."

On Motivating through Purpose and Mission

Fields (Ford): "Most of our senior leadership team have spent their entire careers here at Ford. On the one hand, you can get very hardened in how you think about things. On the other hand, we all think in terms of the legacy we want to leave for the next generation. We're part of the Ford family. It's not just a job. We're standing on the shoulders of the people before us, and we want to pay it forward for the next generation.

That's part of the pride of a 113-year-old company. It's going to be messy. We're working new muscles. It's important to acknowledge people's fears or concerns, and make sure people feel like they are part of the process—a participatory process, although it may not always be a democratic one. This can't be about us coming in and saying, 'Here is the strategy.' It's like that old saying: 'If you want to build a ship, you don't teach the team to go out to the forest, cut the trees, saw them, bring the planks back, and nail them together. You teach them the love of the sea.' The process here is how do we teach ourselves—and our entire organization—the love for where we want to take Ford and then organize the extraordinary efforts we'll ask them to do to get us there."

Crow (ASU): "We had to change the culture of the faculty. First, you basically say to the faculty, in all seriousness and with a sound intellectual and behavioral argument, 'We are not here for you. We are here for the students.' If you stick with that message, it has a huge impact on people's behaviors. And second, we also say that you are no longer required to stay within the rigid, conservative design of academia. You are no longer bound to the bonds of structures of other institutions. What do you wish we could be doing on life sciences? What do you wish we could be doing on other complicated topics? Moving from faculty centric to student centric, and making faculty free agents that could design their own intellectual agenda, turned out to have huge impact."

On Communicating to Employees and Other Stakeholders

Bertolini (Aetna): "It's easy to underestimate the amount of communication that is needed. You have to be tireless about it, consistent and persistent, and keep battering the core messages home week after week. Your leaders have to as well, and they have to tailor the message so it has the appropriate level of fidelity relevant to each part of the organization. A person working in a call center might need a different set of messages to understand how he docks in to the big picture than a line manager, and so on. Communication is an ongoing challenge, but I try to make it easier by creating a company culture consistent with our vision, including being approachable and available to everyone who works here."

Crow (ASU): "Communications is a big deal in changing any culture. Culture trumps strategy every day of the week. The German army had fantastic strategies, all of which were defeated because their culture was fundamentally weak to the core. We have been able to constantly give the message that we are here to measure ourselves against the success of our students. You have to constantly project those messages, or you can't change the culture."

Eaton (Settlement Music): "From the beginning, I decided on a three-pronged approach to change management. The first is that I would have the highest level of transparency with our staff, teaching artists, and board members even when it meant telling them something that they did not want to hear. The second is that I would also take the necessary time to seek input on the most critical decisions. And the third is that I would personally take responsibility when something did not go well. This approach has led to tremendous support of the changes, and even when people have not been fully behind the changes, they have accepted them for the good of Settlement."

On the Challenges and Opportunities of Transformation

Fields (Ford): "Transformation is uncomfortable and exciting at the same time. If this is big enough to make a difference for the company, it should be extraordinarily exciting, but at the same time scare us. It's like when we redesign [an] F-150 or redesign the Mustang. You hold these two things in your head where you feel incredible pride and excitement because you're working on this icon, but gosh, you don't want to be the team that screws it up. It's the tension that comes from holding two conflicting thoughts in the mind at the same time. We get to help set the rudder for Ford Motor Company going forward, but at the same time we're responsible for 200,000 employees and their families and communities. That drives us to make sure we make the right decisions for the future."

Chua (Singtel): "We've set five-year milestones and targets for our transformation journey and we track our progress towards our five-year goal on a yearly basis. Transformation is a continuous journey and you need to set milestones and targets so that you know how you're doing. You also have to constantly calibrate against the external environment and decide if the goals that you have set are sufficiently ambitious or realistic. Sometimes when you set the targets, you may look at them and think you are not going to get there. But when you break it down into smaller parts, it may be easier to achieve than you think."

Eaton (Settlement Music): "Our transformation has been both complex and inspiring. Complex because we have needed to honor a hundred-plus-year-old institution—Settlement Music School—and its heritage that is deeply embedded in our community, work with and keep very close to us a great number of teaching artists, staff, and board members who have dedicated decades of service to Settlement, and at the same time acknowledge that our field of work is changing and the business model needs continual analysis and renewal. It has been inspiring because, despite all of these challenges, our community has come together to stay true to the founding mission and at the same time embrace change for the betterment of the school."

Crow (ASU): "Students are a huge source of inspiration. We have a university representative of the totality of society, and the aspirations of their dreams are no different than yours or mine. I am deeply and personally inspired by helping them to reach those dreams. I have little doubt of the outcome of our collective future because of the nature of the people we have gathered at the university. It is truly inspiring."

Afterword: Who's Next?

This book begins with cautionary stories from the silver halide film, newspaper, and mobile phone industries. In each case, disruption started when the market leaders seemed to be at the very top of their games. Change didn't happen overnight, but when the full force of the disruption became clear, industry leaders were almost powerless to respond. As the pace and scale of change accelerate, these stories will become increasingly frequent. As we put the finishing touches on this book in late 2016, a natural question, then, is, Who's next? What industries are facing early signs of disruptive change?

Disruptions are often likened to earthquakes. Is it an accurate comparison? Because of sophisticated equipment and detailed scientific understanding, we're never completely surprised by earthquakes. After all, we have a good understanding of fault lines, and we know that certain areas are more susceptible to them. And there is always at least some signal before a big quake hits. But generally we have precious little time to react to major earthquake events. Fortunately, although the aftershocks don't help recovery, they're always significantly smaller than the event itself.

Disruption has some parallels with earthquakes, with one big difference. As with earthquakes, the fundamental fault lines that make an industry susceptible to disruptive change are readily visible. However, in contrast to earthquakes, the disruptive event itself isn't the problem; the problem is the aftershocks. Despite hype about so-called big bang disruptions, initial disruptive developments are almost by definition small and isolated in impact. Market leaders don't really lose their position overnight, because it takes time for new companies to form, perfect their solution, and spread it globally. The shock waves that disruption unleashes, however, reverberate and grow until they reach a point where they can topple even the seemingly safest market leaders.

The forces of disruption affect every industry. For example, mining looks to be an industry that is safe from disruption. But movie mogul James Cameron has backed a startup that plans to harvest precious metals from asteroids. Crazy? Maybe. Worth watching? Definitely. That said, we're pretty sure Rio Tinto and other mining giants won't be threatened by asteroid-derived metals in the next few years.

Which industries warrant the closest attention? Our consulting team used an advanced version of the simple questions described in chapter 5 to analyze dozens of industries. We coupled those findings with a survey of members of our community and Harvard Business School graduates who took a course created by Clayton Christensen that features the disruptive model at its core.

Informed by that work, the text that follows details five industries where we see the potential for substantial change in the next few years: consumer banking, shipping, medical devices, automobile manufacturing, and professional services. Make sure to check out dualtransformation.com, where we'll share our latest views on these and other industries.

Consumer Banking

Historically, data showed that people were more likely to change their spouses than their bank accounts. In modern terms bank accounts are highly "sticky," as routines harden and automatic deposit and payment mechanisms reinforce the relationship.

Now, however, the cornerstone of many local towns risks being ripped apart by a range of seemingly disruptive developments. Peer-to-peer payments such as PayPal, now almost twenty years old, have started to change the conception of what banking looks like. The rise of the smart phone and the increasing ubiquity of always-on high-speed networks mean that a generation is used to swiping, tapping, waving, or just leaving a car (in the case of Uber) to consummate a payment. Distributed ledger solutions, such as ones that use a technology called blockchain as their backbones, create decentralized transaction registers that are impervious to fraud or manipulation, albeit with legitimate questions about scalability and usability. In the future, will people need to have a central repository that holds their savings, or will what we conceive of as banks increasingly be companies such as Starbucks (whose prepaid cards held more than $1 billion in assets as of mid-2016), Apple, Samsung, and more?

Emerging disruptors in Asia show that telecommunications companies as well as technology upstarts also serve as credible threats. For example, in 2004 Globe Telecom of the Philippines launched GCash, a branchless way for subscribers to manage remittances from family members living overseas. That's a beautiful foothold market in a country where more than 10 million of its 110 million citizens live outside the country. Over the next decade Globe quietly built a base of more than a million users and increasingly expanded from cash transfers to e-commerce payments, a vital service in a country where fewer than 10 percent of the people own a credit card. As of the writing of this book, almost ten thousand local merchants in the Philippines accept GCash, with Globe increasingly looking set to join the phenomenal success story of Safaricom's M-PESA offering in Kenya.

In China, e-commerce giant Alibaba launched its online payment platform, Alipay, alongside its e-commerce marketplace, Taobao, in 2003. Like Globe, Alibaba took advantage of the fact that at the time there were only three million credit cards in circulation. Although consumers with bank accounts could pay via bank transfer, many were worried that sellers would not hold up their end of the deal after receiving payments. Alipay introduced an escrow model that takes funds from the buyer's bank account but releases them to the supplier only after the buyer confirms order delivery, giving Chinese consumers the peace of mind they needed to start shopping online and driving e-commerce adoption against the backdrop of weak consumer protection laws. Alipay also targeted small and medium enterprises as merchants on Alibaba's e-commerce websites and provided them a wallet where they could easily store the money they received from payments.

Alipay faces fierce competition from another internet company: Tencent. That company used its popular WeChat messaging service to become the payment mechanism of choice for hundreds of millions of Chinese consumers and businesses. In India, Alibaba backed a payment technology startup company called Paytm, whose digital wallets and related solutions promise to bring similar solutions to hundreds of millions of unbanked consumers in India.

As always, disruption presents threats as well as opportunities to incumbents. Market leaders sit on treasure troves of data about the spending patterns of consumers and businesses. Historically, businesses look to banks to finance operations and growth. But what if they were to use the data embedded in payment flows to provide additional value-added services to help businesses realize their full potential? Could they emerge as competitors to—dare we say it—consultants that help clients with these issues?

Shipping

The shipping industry seems to be one of the least innovative in the world. After all, what does it involve beyond putting stuff in a container and putting that container on a ship? Of course, as obvious as it seems now, the idea of the container itself—a standard-sized, stackable box that is plug-and-play compatible with any ship and relatively easy to transport—was an industry-changing notion that allowed companies to make ships bigger and ports more efficient. Large container ships can carry almost twenty thousand containers, in industry parlance *twenty-foot equivalent units* (TEUs).

Modern ports can turn ships around in a single day, compared with their languishing on docks for weeks at a time in the past. Bigger doesn't always mean better, however, and the industry slumped significantly in 2016, dragged down by overcapacity.

More ominously, three broad disruptive trends—additive manufacturing (or 3-D printing), drone-based delivery, and smart, connected devices—promise to change the face of the industry. As the name describes, additive manufacturing involves building things from materials up rather than traditional manufacturing, which involves cutting, molding, and piecing things together. Traditional manufacturing works best at massive scale; additive manufacturing can be done effectively at very small scales.

As of 2016, additive manufacturing is used primarily by hobbyists or commercially for customized parts. But it is simultaneously getting better and cheaper. As manufacturing decentralizes, additive manufacturing clearly has the potential to have a huge impact on companies whose entire business model rests on moving something from point A to point B.

So, too, could unmanned aircraft, known colloquially as drones. Drones started, as many new technologies do, in the military. As prices have dropped, use by hobbyists has exploded. Companies—most notably Amazon (in the United States) and Alibaba (in China)—have begun to experiment with drone-based delivery. Imagine a world with localized microproduction delivered by armies of drones. What happens to shipping giants then?

Smart, connected devices, on the other hand, present interesting growth opportunities for shipping companies. The customer's fundamental job to be done is to confidently move something from point A to point B. The ability to precisely know where things are at any moment creates opportunities both to streamline current operations and to develop new services. The question will be whether industry leaders seize this opportunity or cede it to component manufacturers, telecommunications service providers, or upstarts.

Medical Devices

Chapter 3 describes how the essence of disruption in health care involves moving from centralized to decentralized locations, or moving from expert to self-provided care or both. Emerging technologies present the clear possibility for a radical reconfiguration of many pieces of the health care ecosystem. As semiconductor manufacturers relentlessly follow the Moore's Law improvement trajectory, computing devices are getting smaller and drawing less power. That has facilitated the rise of so-called wearable technology, ranging from special-purpose wristbands (like the simple Fitbit, which tracks wearers' footsteps) to more sophisticated devices such as smart watches by Apple and Samsung, or eyewear with advanced technologies like Google's Glass effort. Not all these efforts will succeed, of course (with Glass being a noted flop, to date at least), but computing will increasingly disappear into accessories, fabrics, and, in the foreseeable future, our skin.

These trends also have allowed companies that sell medical devices to make them increasingly smart and sophisticated, enabling monitoring and diagnosis without requiring visits to a hospital. Further, genetic understanding is similarly advancing rapidly, enabling increasingly accurate diagnosis and precise prescriptions. Companies like IBM are betting heavily on technology's ability to make sense of the explosion of data that is emerging, through its Watson diagnostic platform.

It isn't hard to see how these trends could drive a huge disruption in health care. Instead of an industry focused on treatment, there will be booming businesses related to monitoring and prevention. The devices that enable this, such as smart watches and sensors, will surely grow, but history suggests that the people who figure out integrated business models to enable collection, processing, and behavioral nudges will be massive value creators.

Some companies in the broad health care ecosystem are making early moves to take advantage of these disruptive trends. For example, in the early 2000s Nestlé made the strategic decision to shift from being a food company to being more of a health and nutrition company. In July 2016 its Institute for Health Sciences announced a partnership with Samsung to "to better understand the voice of the body and empower millions of people to live well and be well." Perhaps food and consumer electronics companies will emerge as medical device giants, providing wellness and prevention, not in hospitals but in day-to-day behaviors.

Automobile Manufacturing

Knowing the demographics of most business book readers, we imagine that for you, one of the most meaningful events in life was the day you were old enough to get a piece of laminated plastic that allowed you to drive a car. Freedom! There's a reason many songs in the 1950s and 1960s were about cars. Heavy investment in a world-class road infrastructure. Cheap gas. Affordable cars. If you combine them, as The Mamas and the Papas sang in 1966, you could "go where you wanna go."

The world changes, always. Now consumers summon Uber or Lyft from their smart phones to get from point A to point B. Instead of owning a car, they can participate in a fractional ownership program like Zipcar (purchased by Avis Budget Group for $500 million in 2013). Then in 2005, Sebastian Thrun, coinventor of Google Street View, led a team whose robotic car won a $2 million prize from the US Department of Defense. Over the next decade Google invested to further develop the technology behind self-driving cars and to change local regulations to welcome autonomous cars. In 2014 it introduced a new car with no wheels and no pedals. In August 2016, Singapore's first autonomous taxi debuted on the roads of a cluster of buildings with far-out names like Fusionopolis. Scenes in movies with legions of driverless cars—such as *I, Robot* and *Minority Report*—increasingly seem less like science fiction and more like a preview of the next decade. And, of course, that's to say nothing of the rise of electric vehicles.

The rise of self-driving cars will have systemwide effects. Here are examples.

- Parking consumes significant, and pricey, real estate in urban areas. What happens when we no longer need to worry about parking?

- Companies like GEICO and Progressive make almost all of their money providing insurance to drivers. What happens when cars don't crash?

- Some governments trace a significant amount of their revenues to fines paid by speeding drivers. What happens when cars don't speed?

The automotive world will surely be dramatically different over the next two decades. Automotive companies will need to deal with the reality that their core business is likely to contract, and they need to make sure they reconstruct their business model appropriately. And they need to think about the new opportunities that will emerge as cars and computers increasingly converge, in terms of products as well as new business models.

Professional Services

After founding Netscape and Opsware, in 2009 Marc Andreessen cofounded a venture capital firm with entrepreneur Ben Horowitz (who was also part of the founding team at Opsware) called Andreessen Horowitz. In a few years the firm became one of the most influential in Silicon Valley, investing in companies like Twitter, Airbnb, Jawbone, Oculus VR, and many more. In a piece in the *Wall Street Journal* in 2011, Andreessen summarized one of his key investment theses with a phrase that rings true to entrepreneurs and executives of companies under disruptive assault: "Software is eating the world."

The first paragraph of a widely shared article in 2015 on Tech-Crunch summed up the powerful pull of software-based platforms: "Uber, the world's largest taxi company, owns no vehicles. Facebook, the world's most popular media owner, creates no content. Alibaba, the most valuable retailer, has no inventory. And Airbnb, the world's largest accommodation provider, owns no real estate. Something interesting is happening."

Historically, providers of high-end professional services, such as lawyers, investment advisors, and, yes, management consultants, seemed impervious to disruption. Yet four trends promise to have a significant impact on professional services.

1. *Democratized knowledge.* Coauthor Scott Anthony remembers that, when he started his first consulting job at McKinsey & Company in 1996, leadership talked about how the consultancy's centralized library was a source of competitive advantage, because it was stocked with difficult-to-find, expensive reports. With that kind of knowledge dispersed throughout the world, it's hard to compete based on knowing more than clients.

2. *Platforms.* Have a tough business problem that requires a few hours of careful attention? If you go to hourlynerd.com you can, yes, rent a nerd for a short period. To do whatever you want, within reason, of course.

3. *Software-based solutions.* A significant amount of work that lawyers do is complex, requiring expert knowledge and

seasoned judgment. But the dirty secret of many law firms is that much of the work is done by low-paid paralegals. These kinds of solutions can easily be automated, or served by a lower cost business model such as LegalZoom. That company, which was founded in 2001, offers basic legal service at very affordable rates.

4. *Artificial intelligence.* A provocative report by Oxford University in 2013 found that almost 50 percent of jobs in the United States could be automated in the next fifty years. Those jobs aren't only mundane manufacturing jobs; the rapid improvement in computers' cognitive capabilities means that tasks such as providing investment advice, determining key strategic issues for a company, or developing a company's tax strategy, could also be automated away.

These trends help explain why the professional services industry has seen significant consolidation over the past decade, as companies 'seek to gain the scale required to lower operating costs. Companies are also experimenting with hybrid solutions. By analogy, computers can now reliably beat even the best chess masters, but a chess master paired with a computer proves impossible to beat, at least thus far. Imagine an Innosight consultant augmented with Watson's processing power. A scary thought.

The Innovator's Choice

Table AF-1 summarizes the industries we've profiled here, highlighting the underlying disruptive trends and the new growth opportunities we expect to see over the next few years.

This chapter isn't meant to be a death sentence for traditional market leaders in these industries. Far from it. Remember, disruption grows markets, even as it transforms business models. Leaders who catch the disruptive changes early and respond appropriately will have the ability to thrive in the years to come. Those who don't, well, Darwin has a way of taking care of them.

TABLE AF-1

Disruption by industry

Industry	Disruptive trends	New competitors	Growth opportunities
Consumer banking	Peer-to-peer lending and payments, blockchain	Telecommunications companies (e.g., Globe), technology giants	Data-driven advisory support for businesses
Shipping	3-D printing; drone delivery; smart, connected devices	Amazon	Real-time tracking, new inventory management services
Medical devices	Smart, connected devices; customized medicines	Apple, IBM, Nestlé	Wellness and prevention
Automotive	Driverless cars, integration of cars and commerce	Uber, Apple, Google	Transport and logistics services and solutions
Professional services	Democratized knowledge, platforms, software, artificial intelligence	Hourlynerd, LegalZoom	Software-enabled, AI-enhanced services

Appendix: Dual Transformation Toolkit

This appendix presents a set of checklists, discussion guides, and simple analytical models that help you apply key concepts in the book. Electronic versions of these can be accessed at dualtransformation.com. The pages that follow detail the following:

1. Leadership discussion questions to help start conversations around key concepts in *Dual Transformation*

2. Future-back strategy dialogue guide to help you gain alignment around your dual transformation strategy

3. Three-year transformation map to help you plan key milestones in your transformation

4. Early warning signs assessment to gauge the risk of disruptive change to your business

5. Growth gap assessment to determine the gap between your aspirations and your reality

6. Transformation A blueprint to identify key business model changes as you reposition your core

7. Goals and boundaries capture form to guide discussions about what is on and off the table

8. Transformation B strategic opportunity area identification guide to zero in on the highest-potential areas for new growth

9. Capability assessment guide to shape how you manage existing capabilities that could provide competitive advantage

10. *First Mile* risk-reduction toolkit to identify and address the biggest uncertainties behind an idea in a resource-efficient way

11. Corporate curiosity checklist to identify leverage points to encourage the habit of day-to-day curiosity

1. Leadership Discussion Questions

If you are looking to start a conversation with your leadership team about the concepts in *Dual Transformation*, consider the following questions.

1. Which disruptive trends have the potential to change our competitive landscape?

2. What is the new way we will compete in today's core? What old metrics are no longer relevant? Which new ones are?

3. What are the most exciting growth opportunities that are now options for us?

4. Who will be our new competitors? What unique capabilities will allow us to win?

5. How will we sharpen current capabilities and build new ones?

6. If we successfully execute, who will we become? What will be different? What will be the same?

7. What organizational changes will maximize our chances of success? What things, if we don't change, will inhibit success?

2. Future-Back Strategic Dialogue Guide

Developing a future-back strategy should be an inclusive process, grounded in a series of dialogues involving top management and key stakeholders. Each dialogue should be at least four hours in length, with at least half the time set aside for strategic discussion (versus receiving and clarifying information). Ideally, all data should be provided and read before the meeting. The following table describes four key dialogues, highlighting required input and expected output from each discussion.

Future-back strategic dialogue guide

Dialogue	Input	Seek to align on . . .
Align on the future environment	• Trend analysis • Internal interviews • Competitive research • Future customer analysis	• Priority trends • Future competitors • Future customers
Define the company's future state	• Capabilities assessment • Current business headroom and adjacency potential • Goals and boundaries	• Future targets • New growth requirements • Where-to-play choices • How-to-win options
Identify specific strategic imperatives	• Growth gap analysis • Future core business model • Potential strategic opportunity areas	• Priority gaps • Required future capabilities • Transformation A and B strategic imperatives
Detail the path forward	• Walk back from desired future state • Assessment of current culture and systems	• Near-term strategic initiatives • Governance and structure • Implementation road map

3. Three-Year Transformation Map

Not every transformation will occur in the same way, but our experience is that it takes three years to show meaningful progress. Use the following table to place milestones in the appropriate six-month increment for your effort.

Three-year transformation map

Sample milestones	1–6 months	13–18 months	25–30 months
Strategy/program • Change imperative defined • Future state target determined • Growth gap assessment calculated • Alignment around future-back strategy • Creation of stakeholder engagement plan • Implementation of governance mechanism	*Strategy/Program* • • •	*Strategy/Program* • • •	*Strategy/Program* • • •
Transformation A • Postdisruption job to be done identified • Future business model blueprinted • Plan formulated • Plan executed	*Transformation A* • • •	*Transformation A* • • •	*Transformation A* • • •
	Transformation B • • •	*Transformation B* • • •	*Transformation B* • • •
	Capabilities Link • • •	*Capabilities Link* • • •	*Capabilities Link* • • •

Sample milestones	7–12 months	19–24 months	31–36 months
Transformation B • Strategic opportunity areas identified • New growth unit formed • Pilots executed • First dollar of revenues earned • Plan to plug capabilities gap created • Plan to plug capabilities gap executed • Transformation B >20% of total enterprise	*Strategy/Program* • • •	*Strategy/Program* • • •	*Strategy/Program* • • •
	Transformation A • • •	*Transformation A* • • •	*Transformation A* • • •
	Transformation B • • •	*Transformation B* • • •	*Transformation B* • • •
Capabilities link • Strategic capabilities identified • Link management approach determined • Capabilities link activated	*Capabilities Link* • •	*Capabilities Link* • •	*Capabilities Link* • •

4. Early Warning Signs Assessment

How worried should you be about looming disruptive threats? Use the table below to gauge the seven early warning signs of disruptive change.

Assessing early warning signs of disruptive change

Stage	Sign	Low risk	Moderate risk	High risk
Stage 1: Circumstances	*Customer loyalty*	Stable or increasing	Slow decline	Rapid decline
	Venture investment	Little or none	Substantial seed and early-stage activity	Substantial growth-stage activity
Stage 2: Catalysts	*Policy changes*	Little or none	Under consideration or discussion	In the process of being implemented
	Industry entrant activity	Little or none	Growth at the low end or fringe of the market	Entering or present in the mainstream
	Customer habit shift	Habits are stable	Change at the fringes	Change in the mainstream
Stage 3: Impact	*Business model innovation*	Entrants optimizing existing models	Entrants experimenting with different models	Entrants successfully executing different models
	Profit margins	Stable or increasing	Slow decline or increasing due to cost management	Rapid decline

5. Growth Gap Assessment

Complete the following steps to assess the gap between today's business and your future aspirations.

1. *Set a target.* Pick a year far enough in the future that people feel safe discussing what will need to have happened by then, but not so far that uncertainty about technological or market developments renders a discussion meaningless. Determine target revenues, profits, cash flows, or enterprise value in that year.

2. *Estimate the potential of current operations.* Assess how much room you have to further expand within existing markets and edge into adjacent ones. Make sure to take account of underlying competitive forces that likely make future business more competitive than now.

3. *Estimate the potential of existing new growth investments.* Make a list of current new growth investments. Estimate the financial potential and required investment for each one. Risk-adjust the list by multiplying the potential with its probability of success. Use historical analysis or industry benchmarks to ground that probability.

4. *Calculate your growth gap.* Add the results from steps 2 and 3 and compare them to step 1.

6. Transformation A Business Model Blueprint

Seizing the White Space, by coauthor Mark Johnson, provides a detailed view of how to describe and innovate a business model. Use the following table to map out the key elements of your current business model and the critical changes involved in transformation A.

Transformation A business model blueprint

	Area	Today	Tomorrow
How you create value	What job are you doing for customers?		
	What specifically are you selling or providing?		
	How (or where) does the customer get it?		
	How does the customer pay for it?		
	What support does the customer receive?		
How you deliver value	How do you produce it?		
	How do you distribute it?		
	How do you support it?		
	Who are your key suppliers and partners?		
How you capture value	How do you make money?		
	What are your key variable costs?		
	What are your key fixed costs?		
	What are your key investments?		

7. Goals and Boundaries Summary Form

Use this table to determine which strategic options are on the table (desirable), which are possible in the right circumstances (discussable), and which are clearly off the table (out of bounds). Make sure there is at least one out of bounds choice for each row.

Goals and boundaries summary

Element	Desirable	Discussable	Out of bounds
Target customer type (e.g., consumer, business, government)	• • •	• • •	• • •
Distribution channel (e.g., direct, online)	• • •	• • •	• • •
Steady-state revenues (actual amount)	• • •	• • •	• • •
Steady-state margins (% of revenues)	• • •	• • •	• • •
Type of offering (e.g., product, service)	• • •	• • •	• • •
Target geography	• • •	• • •	• • •
Brand name or approach	• • •	• • •	• • •
Revenue model (e.g., licensing, leasing, transaction fees)	• • •	• • •	• • •
Suppliers and partners	• • •	• • •	• • •
Tactics (e.g., test markets, M&A, partnerships)	• • •	• • •	• • •
Allowable investment (in total)	• • •	• • •	• • •
Other	• • •	• • •	• • •
Other	• • •	• • •	• • •

8. Transformation B Strategic Opportunity Area Identification Guide

What will be your most promising growth opportunities? Form a small team, give them ninety days, and ask them to do the following.

1. *Blitz the market.* Conduct twenty to thirty in-depth interviews in or around the periphery of the market, including fringe users, futurists, and startup companies.

2. *Analyze trends.* Look at patent filings, venture capital investment, demographic shifts, and regulatory changes.

3. *Align on goals and boundaries.* Have senior leadership clarify what they will consider under the right conditions, and what they will not do under any circumstance.

4. *Brainstorm.* Your goal is to develop fifty or more opportunity areas.

5. *Synthesize.* Detail five to ten high-potential opportunity areas.

Now describe and analyze each short-listed opportunity area using the following template.

Assessing transformation B strategic opportunity areas

Key question	Proposed answer	Assessment score from 1 (highly disagree) to 5 (highly agree)	
What problem will you address (job to be done)?		The problem is important and unsatisfied.	
Who struggles most acutely with this problem today?		A large number of people face this problem.	
How do you propose addressing the problem?		The solution is achievable without requiring miracles.	
Why is now the right time for us to pursue this?		The area fits our capabilities and underlying trends.	
		Total Score	

Clearly, higher scores are better than lower ones, and scores above 15 generally suggest high-potential opportunity areas. The most critical question, from our view, is the first one. If you aren't targeting an important problem, the rest of the answers are somewhat irrelevant.

9. Capability Assessment Guide

Succeeding with dual transformation means strategically selecting capabilities that can provide a competitive advantage for transformation B and carefully managing the capabilities link between the core and the new growth engine to ward off the innovator's dilemma. Use the following steps to maximize your chances of success.

Step 1: Identify Your Unique Capabilities

Use the following questions to determine any existing capabilities that could be the source of a competitive advantage.

- What are your current capabilities? Consider what you have (e.g., brands, assets, talent, IP) and how you do what you do (e.g., process know-how, talent management).

- Who are the natural competitors for your transformation B opportunities? What capabilities would make them envious?

- What emerging startups are competing in the space? What capabilities do you have that they wish they had?

Determine no more than five capabilities that could give you advantages in transformation B.

Step 2: Determine Your Link Management Approach

For each capability, use the next table to determine the approach you will follow to manage the link between the core and your new growth effort.

Managing your capability links

Enabling capability	Link management approach	Responsible leaders
	❏ Transfer pricing ❏ Exchange team ❏ Formal rules ❏ _____	
	❏ Transfer pricing ❏ Exchange team ❏ Formal rules ❏ _____	
	❏ Transfer pricing ❏ Exchange team ❏ Formal rules ❏ _____	
	❏ Transfer pricing ❏ Exchange team ❏ Formal rules ❏ _____	
	❏ Transfer pricing ❏ Exchange team ❏ Formal rules ❏ _____	

Step 3: Identify How to Fill Capability Gaps

Odds are that you don't have all the capabilities you need to succeed with transformation B. Ask the following questions to determine how to plug critical gaps.

- What other capabilities are required for success?
- Who has these capabilities?
- How can you obtain them (e.g., license, acquire)?
- How can you build a repeatable skill to source and onboard new capabilities?

10. *The First Mile* Risk-Reduction Toolkit

The First Mile, by coauthor Scott Anthony, provides a step-by-step guide to address the uncertainty in any new idea. As you progress with populating a strategic opportunity area, follow the process shown next. Remember the acronym DEFT: document, evaluate, focus, and test:

1. **Document** your proposed strategy with a high degree of rigor. You don't need to produce a PhD-length thesis, but make sure

you have comprehensively thought about and detailed what you hope to do.

2. **Evaluate** your idea both quantitatively and qualitatively. Keep returning to three key questions:

   - Is there a need?

   - Can we deliver?

   - Is it worth it?

3. **Focus** on the areas of greatest uncertainty. Use the next table to roughly gauge where you know the least (definitions of each level of uncertainty are available online at www.dualtransformation.com).

First mile certainty table

Question	Low ⟶		Degree of certainty		⟶ High	
Is there a need?	Said	Shown	Used	Purchased	Repeated	Advocated
Can you deliver?	Dreamed	Drawn	Prototyped	Piloted	Delivered	Scaled
Is it worth it?	Envelope model	Transaction model	Business model	Unit economics validated	Line of sight to profitability	Sustainable profitable business

4. **Test** rigorously and adapt quickly. Design and execute experiments to learn more. Remember the following best practices of disciplined experimentation.

   - Keep the team small and focused on a handful of critical uncertainties at any given time.

   - Be disciplined by making sure every experiment has HOPE (hypothesis, objectives, prediction, and execution plan to measure and check predictions).

   - Cultivate a bias toward action, and seek to learn as close to the market as possible.

   - Prioritize flexibility, even if it means spending a bit more in the near term.

11. Corporate Curiosity Assessment

How curious is your organization? Use the table to assess your "corporate curiosity quotient." Consider interventions to improve identified weaknesses.

Assessing your curiosity quotient

Cultural element	Poor fit	Average fit	Clear fit
Customer intimacy	No customer knowledge	Analytical understanding of customers	Intimate, empathetic understanding of customers
External orientation	Heavily internal perspective	Occasionally bring in outside speakers and seek outside stimuli	Regularly bring in outside speakers and seek outside stimuli
Idea sourcing	No mechanisms to source ideas externally	Ideas sourced from customers, employees, or suppliers	Ideas sourced from customers, employees, and suppliers
Team diversity	Lacks team diversity	Diversity along one dimension (industry, education, etc.)	Diversity along multiple dimensions (industry, education, etc.)
Cross-company interaction	Largely operate in silos	Regular interaction between functions or geographies	Regular interaction between functions and geographies
Openness to experimentation	No means to design and run experiments	Experiments run with approval from top leaders	Experiments part of day-to-day operations
Idea sharing	Ideas shared only when they are "perfect"	Ideas shared when they are well documented	Rough (but well thought out) ideas are shared to get fast feedback
Failure tolerance	Failure carries heavy stigma	No penalties for the "right kind" of failure	Learning from failure celebrated equally with commercial success
Number of answers			
Weighting	× 1	× 3	× 5
Total score			

Total	
8–14	Hostile to curiosity
15–22	Pockets of curiosity
23–29	Foundations of curiosity
30+	Culture of curiosity

Notes

Chapter 1

Steve Sasson "that's cute" quote: Claudia H. Deutsch, "At Kodak, Some Old Things Are New Again," *New York Times*, May 2, 2008.

Decline in newspaper advertising revenue: Henry Blodget, "And Now Let Us Gasp in Astonishment at What Just Happened to the Newspaper Business," *Business Insider*, September 15, 2012, http://www.businessinsider .com/newspaper-advertising-collapse-2012-9.

Jim Balsillie interview: CBC, *The Hour*, April 1, 2008, https://www .youtube.com/watch?v=wQRcEObmSRM.

Schumpeter quotes: Joseph R. Schumpeter, *Capitalism, Socialism, and Democracy* (New York: Harper & Brothers, 1942).

Forecast of six billion mobile phones: Ingrid Lunden, "6.1B Smartphone Users Globally by 2020, Overtaking Basic Fixed Phone Subscriptions," TechCrunch.com, June 2, 2015, http://techcrunch.com/2015/06/02/6-1b-smartphone-users-globally-by-2020-overtaking-basic-fixed-phone-subscriptions/.

Xerox's split into two companies: Nathan Bomey, "Xerox Names Spinoff Conduent," *USA TODAY*, June 16, 2016, http://www.usatoday.com/story/money/2016/06/16/xerox-conduent/85977386/.

Janssen's dual transformation: "Thinking Differently about Healthcare," www.janssen.com, http://www.janssen.com/research-and-development/thinking-differently-about-healthcare-disease-interception-accelerator; Arlene Weintraub, "Johnson & Johnson Pegs Its Long-Term Future on Prevention," *Forbes*, May 20, 2015, http://www.forbes.com/sites/arleneweintraub/2015/05/20/jj-pegs-its-long-term-growth-potential-on-prevention; Johan Verbeeck, "The Story of J&J Innovation: Proximity as a Priority," February 8, 2016, European PharmaRela8 Summit; William N. Hait quotes are from an interview with Innosight, conducted August 11, 2016.

Chapter 2

Mark Garrett and Kevin Lynch quotes: Sunil Gupta and Lauren Barley, "Reinventing Adobe," Case 9-514-066 (Boston: Harvard Business School, 2015). More details on Adobe can be found at Richard Waters, "Monday Interview: Shantanu Narayen, Adobe CEO," *Financial Times*, February 22, 2015, and "Adobe Super Subs, Adobe's Bold Embrace of the Computing Cloud Should Inspire Others," *Economist*, March 22, 2014.

Adobe revenue numbers: Adobe financial filings, various years, http://www.adobe.com/investor-relations.html, accessed August 15, 2016.

Blockbuster passes on buying Netflix for $50 million: Celena Chong, "Blockbuster's CEO once passed up a chance to buy Netflix for only $50 million," *Business Insider*, July 17, 2015, http://www.businessinsider.com/blockbuster-ceo-passed-up-chance-to-buy-netflix-for-50-million-2015-7. See also James Surowiecki, "Content and Its Discontents," *New Yorker*, October 20, 2014.

2015 Netflix DVD subscriber numbers: Emily Steel, "Netflix Refines Its DVD Business, Even as Streaming Unit Booms," *New York Times*, July 26, 2015.

Concept of job to be done: Clayton M. Christensen, Taddy Hall, Karen Dillon, and David S. Duncan, *Competing Against Luck* (New York: HarperCollins, 2016); Clayton M. Christensen, Taddy Hall, Karen Dillon, and David S. Duncan, "Know Your Customers' 'Jobs to Be Done,'" *Harvard Business Review*, September 2016.

Peter Drucker quote: Peter F. Drucker, *Managing for Results* (London: William Heinemann Ltd., 1964), p. 87–88.

Importance of new metrics for transformation A: Scott Anthony, "What Do You Really Mean by Business Transformation?" *Harvard Business Review Online*, February 29, 2016, https://hbr.org/2016/02/what-do-you-really-mean-by-business-transformation.

Chapter 3

Decline in US mail volume: United States Postal Service, "Postal Facts 2015," https://about.usps.com/who-we-are/postal-facts/postalfacts2015.pdf.

Wilson Tan quote: "A Surgical Approach to Orchestra: How SingPost Is Bracing Itself for Change," Knowledge@SMU (Singapore: Singapore Management University, 2010), http://ink.library.smu.edu.sg/cgi/viewcontent.cgi?article=1250&context=ksmu.

Baier quote: Reddi Kotha and Havovi Joshi, "Singapore Post: Transforming Mail Services in the Internet Age," SMU-13-0016 (Singapore: Singapore Management University, 2013), p. 5.

Alibaba's investment in SingPost: "SingTel Hits Unexpected Jackpot with Alibaba-SingPost Deal," *Singapore Business Review*, June 13, 2014.

Singapore Postal Services Statistics: Infocomm Development Authority of Singapore, http://www.ida.gov.sg/Policies-and-Regulations/Industry-and-Licensees/Standards-and-Quality-of-Service/Quality-of-Service/Postal-Services, accessed July 2, 2016.

Simon Israel's commitment to transformation and transparency: Speech at the 24th SingPost Annual General meeting, July 14, 2016, http://infopub.sgx.com/FileOpen/Chairman%20Speech.ashx? App=Announcement&FileID=412793.

Creation of Amazon Web Services: Charles O'Reilly and Michael Tushman, *Lead and Disrupt: How to Solve the Innovator's Dilemma* (Stanford, CA: Stanford University Press, 2016); Brad Stone, *The Everything Store: Jeff Bezos and the Age of Amazon* (New York: Little, Brown and Company, 2013).

AWS market share: "AWS, Google, Microsoft and IBM Pull Away from Pack in Race for Cloud Market Share," *Business Cloud News*, April, 29, 2016, www.businesscloudnews.com/2016/04/29/aws-google-microsoft-and-ibm-pull-away-from-pack-in-race-for-cloud-market-share/.

Jeff Bezos quote: Scott Anthony, "Constant Transformation Is the New Normal," *Harvard Business Review Online*, October 27, 2009, https://hbr.org/2009/10/constant-change-is-the-new-nor/.

Campus amenities arms race: Scott Carlson, "What's the Payoff for the 'Country Club' College?" *Chronicle of Higher Education*, January 28, 2013, http://chronicle.com/blogs/buildings/whats-the-payoff-for-the-country-club-college.

Christensen's prediction that 50 percent of universities would fail: Mark Suster, "In 15 Years from Now Half of US Universities May Be in Bankruptcy. My Surprise Discussion with @ClayChristensen," *Both Sides*, March 3, 2013, https://bothsidesofthetable.com/in-15-years-from-now-half-of-us-universities-may-be-in-bankruptcy-my-surprise-discussion-with-979f93bd6874.

Details about Arizona State, Southern New Hampshire University, and BYU-Idaho: Michael Crow and Clark G. Gilbert, "Dual Transformation in Higher Education," unpublished working draft.

Michael Crow quotes: Interview with authors, September 29, 2016.

Growth in EdPlus students: Data provided by Arizona State University.

Walgreens: Innosight, "A Roadmap for the Future Helps the Pharmacy Giant Widen Its Health Care Mission," http://www.innosight.com/impact-stories/walgreens-case-study.cfm.

Sources of nonconsumption: Scott D. Anthony, Mark W. Johnson, Joseph V. Sinfield, and Elizabeth J. Altman, *The Innovator's Guide to Growth: Putting Disruptive Innovation to Work* (Boston: Harvard Business School Press, 2008).

Xerox's transformation B strategy: Clark Gilbert, Matthew Eyring, and Richard N. Foster, "Two Routes to Resilience," *Harvard Business Review*, December 2012.

ChoiceMed example: Scott D. Anthony, *The First Mile: A Launch Manual for Getting Great Ideas into the Market* (Boston: Harvard Business Review Press, 2014).

Percent of disruptions launched by large companies: Scott Anthony, "Can Established Companies Disrupt?" *Harvard Business Review Online*, December 10, 2008, https://hbr.org/2008/12/can-established-companies-disr.

The discipline of testing: Anthony, *The First Mile*; Steven Gary Blank and Bob Dorf, *The Startup Owner's Manual: The Step-by-Step Guide for Building a Great Company* (Pescadero, CA: K&S Ranch, 2012); Rita Gunther McGrath and Ian C. MacMillan, *Discovery-Driven Growth: A Breakthrough Process to Reduce Risk and Seize Opportunity* (Boston: Harvard Business Press, 2009); Eric Ries, *The Lean Startup: How Today's Entrepreneurs Use Continuous Innovation to Create Radically Successful Businesses* (New York: Crown Business, 2011).

Chapter 4

Paul Graham quote: Startupquote.com, http://startupquote.com/post/10855215114.

Medtronic and Plunify case examples: Scott D. Anthony, "The New Corporate Garage," *Harvard Business Review*, September 2012.

Gilbert's salesforce decision: Scott D. Antony, "What the Media Industry Can Teach Us About Digital Business Models," *Harvard Business Review Online*, June 23, 2015.

Rumelt on the Boeing Planner: Richard P. Rumelt, *Good Strategy/Bad Strategy: The Difference and Why It Matters* (New York: Crown Business, 2011). Emphasis in original.

Pandesic case study: Clayton M. Christensen and Michael E. Raynor, *The Innovator's Solution: Creating and Sustaining Successful Growth* (Boston: Harvard Business School Press, 2003), chapter 7.

Identifying unique capabilities: Scott D. Anthony, "Three Questions to Jump Start Your Company's Growth," *Harvard Business Review Online*, October 4, 2012, https://hbr.org/2012/10/three-questions-to-jumpstart-your-company. See also C. K. Prahalad and Gary Hamel, "The Core Competence of the Corporation," *Harvard Business Review*, May–June 1990.

Keys to successfully implementing portfolio management systems: Scott D. Anthony and David S. Duncan, *Building a Growth Factory* (Boston: Harvard Business Review Press, 2012).

Ursula Burns, "I had to make a call": Clark Gilbert, Matthew Eyring, and Richard N. Foster, "Two Routes to Resilience," *Harvard Business Review*, December 2012.

Chapter 5

Elop's speech: Charles Arthur, "Nokia's Chief Executive to Staff: 'We Are Standing on a Burning Platform,'" *Guardian*, February 9, 2011, https://www.theguardian.com/technology/blog/2011/feb/09/nokia-burning-platform-memo-elop.

Steve Jobs's view on the Rokr: Jim Dalrymple, "Steve Jobs Discusses Music Labels, iPods and Intel Macs," *PCWorld*, September 20, 2005, http://www.macworld.com/article/1047053/jobsparis.html.

Hastings, "even I overestimated the pace of change": Innosight 2008 CEO event, Boston, MA Excerpts from his interview are available at http://www.innosight.com/innovation-resources/loader.cfm?csModule=security/getfile&pageid=2523.

Hastings, "I slid into arrogance": Edward Moyer, "Netflix CEO: 'I Slid into Arrogance,'" CNET, September 18, 2011. See also Lauren Effron, "Netflix CEO Reed Hastings Says Company Has 'Sincere Regret' over Handling of Service Changes," *ABC News*, September 26, 2011, http://abcnews.go.com/Business/netflix-ceo-reed-hastings-company-sincere-regretcustomers/story?id=14608865.

Turner's five thrusts: Anthony and Duncan, *Building a Growth Factory*; and Innosight, "Outpacing Disruption by Reimagining the Future," http://www.innosight.com/impact-stories/turner-case-study.cfm.

Five ways Aetna is transforming: Mark Bertolini, David Duncan, and Andrew Waldeck, "Knowing When to Reinvent," *Harvard Business Review*, December 2015.

Bertolini on creating a "stark reality": Innosight 2015 CEO event, Lexington, MA, August 6, 2015.

Ronn on experiments: Scott D. Anthony, *The Little Black Book of Innovation: How It Works, How to Do It* (Boston: Harvard Business Review Press, 2012).

Assessing the cost of inaction: Clayton M. Christensen, Stephen P. Kaufman, and Willy C. Shih, "Innovation Killers: How Financial Tools Destroy Your Capacity to Do New Things," *Harvard Business Review*, January 2008.

Number of GMAT takers: Sherri London, "Fewer People Are Taking the GMAT, Says Study," *Business Administration Information*, February 10, 2015, http://www.businessadministrationinformation.com/news/fewer-people-are-taking-the-gmat-says-study.

Venture investment in education: Frank Catalano, "Can You Count to $2 Billion? Education Technology Investment Hits New Record," *GeekWire*, January 25, 2015, http://www.geekwire.com/2015/can-count-2-billion-education-technology-investment-hits-new-record/.

Harvard Business School capital campaign: Julia E. Debenedictis, "HBS Campaign Reaches $925 Million of $1 Billion Goal," *Harvard*

Crimson, March 3, 2016, http://www.thecrimson.com/article/2016/3/3/business-school-nears-goal/.

Chapter 6

Kennedy quote: "May 25, 1961: JFK's Moon Shot Speech to Congress," SPACE.com, May 25, 2011, http://www.space.com/11772-president-kennedy-historic-speech-moon-space.html.

Definition of moonshot: encyclopedia.com, http://www.encyclopedia.com/doc/1O999-moonshot.html.

Rumelt on the moonshot: Rumelt, *Good Strategy/Bad Strategy*.

Mao, snakes out of the lairs: Gilbert King, "The Silence That Preceded China's Great Leap into Famine," Smithsonian.com, September 26, 2012, http://www.smithsonianmag.com/history/the-silence-that-preceded-chinas-great-leap-into-famine-51898077/.

Manila Water case: Scott D. Anthony, David S. Duncan, and Pontus M.A. Siren, "Build an Innovation Engine in 90 Days," *Harvard Business Review*, December 2014.

Ablaza and dela Cruz quotes: Interview with Scott D. Anthony, August 16, 2016.

Percent of venture-backed startups that fail to return capital to investors: Deborah Gage, "The Venture Capital Secret: 3 Out of 4 Start-Ups Fail," *Wall Street Journal*, September 19, 2012, http://online.wsj.com/article/SB10000872396390443720204578004980476429190.html.

Andy Hill quote: Interview with Innosight, Boca Raton, FL, February, 2013.

David Bohm quotation: David Bohm, *On Dialogue* (New York: Routledge, 1996), p. 8.

F. Scott Fitzgerald quotation: F. Scott Fitzgerald, "The Crack-Up," *Esquire*, February 1936, http://www.esquire.com/features/the-crack-up.

Chapter 7

Bukit Panjang fire: Irene Tham, "SingTel Fined a Record $6m for Bukit Panjang Exchange Fire, OpenNet and CityNet Also Fined," *Straits Times*, May 6, 2014.

Odeo story: Biz Stone, "Twitter's Cofounder on Creating Opportunities," *Harvard Business Review*, June 2015, https://hbr.org/2015/06/twitters-cofounder-on-creating-opportunities.

Pfizer creates Viagra: Mark Hoffnagle, "The Road to Sildenafil: A History of Artificial Erections," *ScienceBlogs*, October 15, 2007, http://scienceblogs.com/denialism/2007/10/15/the-road-to-sildenafil-a-histo/.

Martin on sommeliers: 2015 Innosight CEO event, Lexington, MA, August 6, 2015.

The difference between corporate planners and venture capitalists: Scott Anthony, "How Corporate Investors Can Improve Their Odds," *Harvard Business Review Online*, May 27, 2014, https://hbr.org/2014/03/how-corporate-investors-can-improve-their-odds/.

Ablaza on separate governance: Innosight, "A New Innovation System Helps a Water Utility Flow into New Markets," https://www.innosight.com/client_impact_story/manila-water/.

Simon Israel's view on the size of Singtel's commitment to acquisitions: Interview with Scott Anthony, Singapore Institute of Directors 2015 Conference, Singapore, September 16, 2015.

Singtel CEO Chua Sock Koong's view on the importance of local visits: Interview with authors, October 21, 2016.

Size of Learning Fiesta: *Singtel Sustainability Report 2015*, Section 7.3: Training and Education, http://info.singtel.com/sustainabilityreport2015/trainingAndEducation.html.

Edgar Schein on company culture: Edgar H. Schein, *Organizational Culture and Leadership, 4th Edition* (San Francisco: Jossey-Bass, 2010).

Adobe Kickbox program: David Burkus, "Inside Adobe's Innovation Kit," *Harvard Business Review Online*, February 23, 2015, https://hbr.org/2015/02/inside-adobes-innovation-kit.

Tata Sons' Dare To Try program: "Tata InnoVista 2015 Celebrates 10 Years of Innovation," Tata.com, May 2015.

Singtel CEO Chua reports being pleased with Singtel's progress: Amit Roy Choudhury, "Tapping High-Performing Markets," *Business Times*, August 29, 2016.

Marc Benioff on Drew Houston: Victoria Barret, "Marc Benioff, Mister Disruptor," *Forbes*, July 20, 2011, http://www.forbes.com/sites/victoriabarret/2011/07/20/marc-benioff-mister-disrupter/.

Dave Gledhill on learning to code: Scott Anthony, "Leading a Digital Transformation? Learn to Code," *Harvard Business Review Online*, September 2, 2015, https://hbr.org/2015/09/leading-a-digital-transformation-learn-to-code.

Alan Mulally story: Rita Gunther McGrath, *The End of Competitive Advantage: How to Keep Your Strategy Moving as Fast as Your Business* (Boston: Harvard Business Review Press, 2013).

Chapter 8

Bertolini's "get the hell out of my stock" and perspectives on creating new businesses: Innosight CEO Summit, Lexington, MA, August 6, 2015.

The importance of purpose: Portions of this section previously appeared in Scott Anthony, "How Will You Measure Your Company's Life?" *Harvard*

Business Review Online, June 27, 2012, https://hbr
.org/2012/07/how-will-you-measure-your-companys-life; and Scott
Anthony, "In 2014, Resolve to Make Your Business Human Again,"
Harvard Business Review Online, January 13, 2014, https://hbr.org/2014/01/
in-2014-resolve-to-make-your-business-human-again/.

Ted Levitt's seminal contribution to *Harvard Business Review*: Theodore
Levitt, "Marketing Myopia," *Harvard Business Review*, July–August 1960.

Christensen's view on purpose: Clayton M. Christensen, "How Will You
Measure Your Life?" *Harvard Business Review*, July–August 2010. Clayton
M. Christensen and Derek van Bever, "The Capitalist's Dilemma," *Harvard
Business Review*, June 2014.

Article noting the psychosis of corporations: David Niose, "Why
Corporations Are Psychotic," *Psychology Today*, March 16, 2011, http://
www.psychologytoday.com/blog/our-humanity-naturally/201103/
why-corporations-are-psychotic.

Jack Welch's "dumbest idea in the world": Francesco Guerrera, "Welch
Condemns Share Price Focus," *Financial Times*, March 12, 2009.

J&J credo: Johnson & Johnson, "Our Credo," http://www.jnj.com/sites/
default/files/pdf/jnj_ourcredo_english_us_8.5x11_cmyk.pdf.

Singapore Prison Service discovery of purpose: Leona Leong, "The Story of
Singapore Prison Service: From Custodians of Prisoners to Captains of Life,"
Singapore Civil Service College, April 2010, https://www.cscollege.gov.sg/
Knowledge/Pages/The-Story-of-Singapore-Prison-Service-From-Custodians-
of-Prisoners-to-Captains-of-Life.aspx.

Afterword

Balance on Starbucks prepaid cards: Andrew Meola, "Starbucks' Loyalty
Program Now Holds More Money Than Some Banks," *Business Insider*, June
13,2016,http://www.businessinsider.com/starbucks-loyalty-program-now-holds-
more-money-than-some-banks-2016-6.

History of Alipay: Jenny Chung, Annabel Tio, and Scott D. Anthony,
"Disruption Ahead: Financial Services in Asia, an Innosight Industry Briefing,"
Innosight, March 2015, http://www.innosight.com/innovation-resources/
strategy-innovation/disruption-ahead-financial-services-in-asia.cfm.

Moore's Law improvement trajectory: The theory, based on an observation
by Intel cofounder Gordon Moore in 1965, that the number of transistors on
a chip were doubling regularly, holds that computing power doubles every
eighteen months. See Investopedia, "Moore's Law," http://www.investopedia
.com/terms/m/mooreslaw.asp.

Nestlé and Samsung partnership: Samsung, "Samsung and Nestlé Collaborate on the Internet of Things and Nutrition to Advance Digital Health," Samsung.com, July 28, 2016, https://news.samsung.com/global/samsung-and-nestle-collaborate-on-the-internet-of-things-and-nutrition-to-advance-digital-health.

TechCrunch on platforms: Tom Goodwin, "The Battle Is for the Customer Interface," TechCrunch.com, March 3, 2015, https://techcrunch.com/2015/03/03/in-the-age-of-disintermediation-the-battle-is-all-for-the-customer-interface/.

Oxford research on job automation: Aviva Hope Rutkin, "Report Suggests Nearly Half of U.S. Jobs Are Vulnerable to Computerization," *Technology Review*, September 12, 2013, https://www.technologyreview.com/s/519241/report-suggests-nearly-half-of-us-jobs-are-vulnerable-to-computerization/.

Index

Acknowledgments

From the team

The central idea in *Dual Transformation*—that leaders need to simultaneously reposition today's business while creating tomorrow's—has been core to each of our professional careers since 2000. In fact, if you looked at slides from the executive training sessions two of us (Clark and Mark) ran in 2001, you would see a version of the "two circle" chart that we have adapted to summarize the dual transformation framework. Fleshing that framework out required the firsthand experience we have had over the subsequent fifteen years as corporate leaders, board members, and strategic advisers, and assistance from a multitude of clients, colleagues, and thought partners.

Before each of us offers our individual thanks, we want to acknowledge a range of individuals who helped to shape *Dual Transformation*. First, we would like to thank former colleagues Richard Foster and Matt Eyring. They were coauthors, with Clark, on the 2012 *Harvard Business Review* article that introduced the term "dual transformation," and we all owe a substantial debt to Dick's career-long quest to help executives confront the challenges of creative destruction. More broadly, we are grateful for the leadership roles both Dick and Matt played during their time at Innosight. We are equally grateful for the support, friendship, and spirit of partnership from Innosight cofounder and Harvard Business School Professor Clayton Christensen. His seminal work on disruptive innovation continues to have an outsized influence on our own thinking, as does the thought leadership of our friends Vijay Govindarajan, Roger Martin, and Rita McGrath. A number of Innosight colleagues helped with key portions of this book, most notably Jenny Chung, Asher Devang, Dave Duncan, Christian Kruse, Rahul Nair, Cathy Olofson, Evan Schwartz, Josh Suskewicz, Elliot Tan, Annabel Tio, Coenraad de Vos van Steenwijk, and Andy Waldeck.

We are extremely thankful for the tremendous support we received from the team at Harvard Business Review Press. Tim Sullivan has been a thought partner during the book's development process, providing critical guidance at key inflection points. Jennifer Waring did an expert job shepherding the manuscript through production. Betsy Hardinger did an amazingly thorough job reviewing the manuscript, deftly tightening language and keeping all of us honest. Julie Devoll and her team helped to crystallize key messages and drive book-related marketing. And Isaac Tobin designed the beautiful book you hold in your hands (if you are viewing it on a device, at least look at the physical copy; it is a beauty).

Finally, the three of us have, collectively, been connected to Innosight for forty-four years: Mark since its inception in 2000, Clark since 2001, and Scott since 2003. We can't say enough about colleagues past and present who have shaped our thinking and helped to make Innosight the truly great firm it is today. It's become a cliché to say that when you love what you do, you don't work a day in your life, but we certainly feel that way about Innosight. The Innosight team is whip smart, passionate about the work, and dedicated to client impact. That such a talented group chooses to spend its time with us never ceases to amaze us. Thanks, team.

—Scott, Clark, and Mark

From Scott

If it takes a village to raise a child, it takes a city to create a book. Of course, *Dual Transformation* would not have happened without my coauthors. Clark's dogged determination to demonstrate that institutions can turn disruption into opportunity and Mark's persistent efforts to reframe the way leaders approach strategy through uncertainty were essential inputs into the book. I am forever grateful for the unending support and advice both have given me, both personally and professionally.

By the time this book hits the shelf, my family will have celebrated our seventh anniversary in Singapore. It continues to feel like a grand adventure. I'm thankful for all of the friends that have helped to keep it interesting, like Fidah Alsagoff, Bill Chang, Paul Cobban, Rachel Eng, Nick Evans, Kuen Loon Ho, Parag Khanna, Koh Boon Hwee, Tony May, Bernard Nee, Dilhan Pillay, Guillaume Sachet, Shaun Seow, Tan Ka Huat, Teo Ming Kian, Kwee Eng Thien, SC Tien, Ernest Wong, Zia Zaman, and many others. I'm also thankful that my friends at Manila Water, notably Gerry Ablaza, Ferdz dela Cruz, and Boogz Baffrey, and at Singtel, namely Tony May and Chua Sock Koong, were gracious enough to share their inspiring stories with broader audiences.

Speaking of my family, the process of creating *Dual Transformation* coincided with moments of both sadness and joy. Early in the writing process, in August 2015, my mother, Bonnie Anthony, passed away after a too-short battle with pancreatic cancer. She left behind a devoted husband and my four siblings. It hasn't been smooth sailing for us, but I have great faith that time, as they say, will heal all wounds. The biggest moment of joy came in early September 2016, when my wife, Joanne, and I welcomed our fourth child, Teddy, into the world. Joanne approached our new arrival as she approaches everything: mixing fierce determination, selfless compassion, and get-it-done practicality. She is my idol, and I try valiantly, if in my own flawed way, to emulate those characteristics as we work together to raise our children. Charlie, Holly, and Harry continue to come into their own, with Charlie as the loquacious baseball freak, Holly as the lithe, sharp-as-a-tack ballerina, and Harry as our lovable, insatiably curious goofball. The best part about traveling for work is always the same: coming home. I never know exactly what will happen when I open the door to unit 22-02, but I know it will be spectacular.

—Scott
Singapore Airlines, Seat 22D
Somewhere over the Bay of Bengal

From Clark

I am grateful for my collaborators on this book project and for the Innosight team, who have constantly pushed my thinking and provided thought leadership on innovation and organizational change. I'm also grateful for the remarkable innovators I have worked with in pursuing these ideas in practice. Special thanks to the *Deseret News* and Deseret Digital Media leadership team, who showed an industry not only the power of creating a culture of change, but the impact of finding meaning and purpose in the content and publications they created. Special thanks also to the members of the Brigham Young University-Idaho and Pathway organization, who continually inspired me with their student focus and their ability to step outside traditional models of education to find a better way. Finally, to my wife, Christine, and to my family, who keep me grounded and continually refocus me on the things that matter most, thank you all.

—Clark Gilbert
Rexburg, ID

From Mark

I am very grateful for the collaboration with Scott and Clark and for their dedication to making this book a reality. The long journey from concept to writing a book would not be possible without their deep commitment from the very beginning. Scott's envisioning of the book and his prolific ability to shape, simplify, and crystallize ideas has led to taking a somewhat complicated management topic and translating it into what I believe is a very accessible book. Clark's leadership in the real-world development and application of the Dual Transformation concept in the media and education sectors has made this book a reality. I am also grateful to all my clients, but my colleagues at Ford and Johnson & Johnson, in particular, were especially willing to provide valuable insight about how Dual Transformation can work effectively in a large corporation. I'd like to thank Mark Fields, CEO of Ford, and Bill Hait, head of R&D at J&J's Janssen Pharmaceuticals, for their willingness to share experiences in their own Dual Transformation journeys. I am also appreciative of my other colleagues at

Innosight, who have contributed immeasurably to the Dual Transformation approach in many important ways. My deepest gratitude goes to my wife, Jane, and to my family. They are always so supportive and understanding of my work. They bring the greatest joy to my life.

—Mark Johnson
Belmont, MA

About the Authors

Scott D. Anthony is the Managing Partner of Innosight, an elected role he has held since 2012. Based in Innosight's Singapore office since 2010, he also leads the firm's Asian consulting operations and its venture-capital investment activities. *Dual Transformation* will be the seventh book Scott has authored or coauthored. His previous work includes *The First Mile* (2014), *The Little Black Book of Innovation* (2011), and *Seeing What's Next* (2004, with Harvard professor and Innosight cofounder Clayton Christensen). Scott is on the board of directors of MediaCorp, a diversified media company based in Singapore, and he chairs the investment committee for IDEAS Ventures, a venture investment fund Innosight runs in conjunction with the Singapore government. He is a prolific contributor to *Harvard Business Review* and in 2015 was named a "Light Bulb Thinker" by Thinkers50. He is a member of the Silicon Valley Guild, a collection of thirty international thought leaders and bestselling authors who write about the ideas and trends shaping business and society. Scott earned a BA in economics, summa cum laude, from Dartmouth College and an MBA with high distinction from Harvard Business School, where he was a Baker Scholar. He lives in Singapore with his wife, Joanne, and their four children. His Twitter feed is @ScottDAnthony.

Clark G. Gilbert became the sixteenth president of Brigham Young University-Idaho in April 2015. BYU-Idaho is one of the most rapidly growing universities in America, serving nearly seventy thousand campus and online students in 2016, with a focus on providing broad access to high quality, affordable education. Prior to BYU-Idaho, Clark served as CEO of Deseret News Publishing Company and Deseret

Digital Media, a media group that has been repeatedly recognized for its innovation and digital growth. Clark was previously an associate academic vice president at BYU-Idaho. In that role he helped launch the school's online learning initiative and Pathway program, a global educational on-ramp with 450 locations around the world. Before coming to BYU-Idaho, Clark was a professor of entrepreneurial management at Harvard Business School. He is the author or coauthor of several articles on innovation and entrepreneurship in *Harvard Business Review* and *MIT Sloan Management Review* and the coauthor (with Joseph L. Bower) of *From Resource Allocation to Strategy* (2005). He has served as an adviser to Innosight since 2001. He graduated from Brigham Young University, earned a master's degree from Stanford University, and a doctoral degree in business administration from Harvard Business School. Gilbert's faith and his family are the organizing priorities in his life. He and his wife, Christine, are the parents of eight children. His Twitter feed is @ClarkGilbert.

Mark W. Johnson is a cofounder and Senior Partner of Innosight, a strategy consulting firm focused on advising corporations on creating new growth and managing transformation. He cofounded Innosight in 2000 with Harvard Business School professor Clayton M. Christensen. He has consulted to the Global 1000 and startup companies in a wide range of industries—including health care, aerospace/defense, enterprise IT, energy, automotive, and consumer packaged goods—and has advised Singapore's government on innovation and entrepreneurship. His previous work includes *Seizing the White Space: Business Model Innovation for Growth and Renewal* (2010), and a number of *Harvard Business Review* articles, including the McKinsey Award–winning article, "Reinventing Your Business Model," and "New Business Models in Emerging Markets." He has also published articles in the *MIT Sloan Management Review*, *BusinessWeek*, *Advertising Age*, and *National Defense*. Mark earned an MBA from Harvard Business School, a master's degree in civil engineering and engineering mechanics from Columbia University, and a bachelor's degree with distinction in aerospace engineering from the United States Naval Academy. He and his wife, Jane Clayson Johnson, are the parents of five children.